THE EXORCIST & L

also in the Classic Screenplays series

The Apartment
Billy Wilder and I. A. L. Diamond

Bonnie and Clyde
David Newman and Robert Benton

Peeping Tom
Leo Marks

Sweet Smell of Success
Clifford Odets and Ernest Lehman

THE EXORCIST
&
LEGION

William Peter Blatty

faber and faber

First published in 1998
by Faber and Faber Limited
3 Queen Square London WC1N 3AU

Photoset by Parker Typesetting Service, Leicester
Printed in England by Clays Ltd, St Ives plc

A CIP record for this book
is available from the British Library

ISBN 0-571-20015-X

2 4 6 8 10 9 7 5 3 1

CONTENTS

INTRODUCTION

> 'I have dreams of a red rose, and then of falling down a long flight of steps . . .'
>
> Patient X, *Legion*

'David Lynch's good twin', is how *People* magazine once described William Peter Blatty, the leading exponent of contemporary theological thrillers, and a writer whose Oscar-winning work has been both hailed as 'deeply spiritual' by the *Catholic News* and condemned as satanic by the Reverend Billy Graham. Having made a name for himself in the sixties as a writer of comic novels and screenplays (he penned the Inspector Clouseau romp *A Shot in the Dark* and his prose was compared favorably with that of satirist S. J. Perelman), Blatty achieved international fame through more serious works such as *The Exorcist, The Ninth Configuration* and *Legion* which used popular fiction formats to address weighty philosophical issues surrounding the nature of good and evil, blending the surreal dreaminess of outlandish fantasy with the solid conviction of magical truths revealed.

Blatty's own obsession with 'magic', or more precisely with 'evidence of transcendence', has its roots in a youthful terror of death, and a desire to subdue the waking dream of obliteration which the author attributes to beleaguered mother Chris MacNeil in *The Exorcist*, but which is in fact entirely autobiographical. This blurring of the line between fact and fiction is a recurrent feature of Blatty's work; both *The Exorcist* and *Legion* were inspired by well-documented events, and both use extensive research to fuel their elaborate flights of fantasy. Even Blatty's most recent comic novel, *Demons Five, Exorcists Nothing,* has its roots in reality, using real-life incidental characters such as Florence Mahoney (who owned the Georgetown house which Blatty and director William Friedkin inadvertently made infamous) to produce a fictional reflection on the filming of *The Exorcist* and *The Exorcist III*.

Just as real events float in and out of Blatty's fiction, so ideas, phrases and characters cross-pollinate from book to screenplay to film, making all of Blatty's best work read like chapters in an ongoing debate. A casual, seemingly irrelevant exchange about lemon drops between the two priests, Father Dyer and Father Karras, dropped from the film of *The Exorcist*, resurfaces in *Legion* as a conversation between Father Dyer and Lieutenant Kinderman, subtly suggesting that the spirit of the deceased Karras now lives on in the unusual friendship between these two men. When the astronaut Cutshaw demands to know how God can allow innocent creatures to suffer in *The Ninth Configuration*, he must wait for Kinderman to suggest an answer at Karras' graveside in the final moments of *Legion* – and when that answer is itself excized from the recut movie of *Legion* that became *The Exorcist III,* it reappears in the mouth of the resurrected Father Karras in an epilogue to *The Exorcist* written twenty-five years after the movie was first completed.

While Patient X's dream of Karras' death in *Legion/Exorcist III* echoes the priest's guilty nightmare about his mother in *The Exorcist*, so Karras' dream reappears identically in Blatty's non-fiction work *I'll Tell Them I Remember You* as the author's own haunted vision of *his* dead mother. And throughout all of these works, the characters come back to a single rhetorical question posed variously by Colonel Kane, Father Dyer, Sprightly God and ultimately Blatty himself, namely: If all the evil in the world makes you believe in the devil, then how do you account for all the good?

For William Peter Blatty, the tangible evidence of a 'force of evil' is itself ironically a reaffirmation of the existence of divinity – evil is always the crucible of good, and the devil cannot but do God's bidding. Although he has been wrongly perceived as a purveyor of horror fiction, Blatty's novels and screenplays can more accurately be characterised as evangelical entertainment in which shocks provide the emotional charge while the intellect edges towards an acceptance of faith. This is the paradox that lies at the heart of both *The Exorcist* and *Legion* – the strange realization that die-hard sceptics Father Karras and Lieutenant Kinderman both ultimately long for manifestations of the supernatural because they would provide evidence that the world is more than just 'a homicide victim' in which 'our children suffer and our loved ones die.'

This is the key to understanding *The Exorcist* (both novel and film), whose positive message has often been overshadowed by its misleadingly terrifying reputation. In Blatty's story, an avowedly atheist actress, Chris MacNeil, turns to two Jesuit priests to free her daughter from what she has come to believe is demonic possession. While investigating the case, Father Karras comes face to face with undeniably paranormal phenomena which force him to address his own lack of faith, and which ultimately facilitate his salvation.

Although fictional, Blatty's narrative has its roots in real-life events reported in the *Washington Post* on 20 August 1949 under the eye-catching headline 'PRIEST FREES MT. RAINIER BOY REPORTED HELD IN DEVIL'S GRIP'. According to Bill Brinkley's front page story, a fourteen-year-old boy from a suburb of Maryland had become beset by poltergeist and severe behavioral disorders which had only desisted following a lengthy series of exorcisms. The boy's symptoms allegedly included uncontrollable rages and the mouthing of religious and sexual obscenities; a hideous transformation of voice and features; and the appearance on his skin of 'dermal brandings', bold red welts that seemed to form numbers, letters and on one occasion 'the image of a bat-like devil'. During the three-month period of the 'infestation', many observers also witnessed telekinetic phenomena, including the unassisted moving of a bedstand and a heavy armchair, and the levitation of a hospital nightstand.

As a freshman at the Jesuit-run Georgetown University, Blatty had taken a particular interest in this story, which seemed to him to present 'tangible evidence of transcendence'. Years later, he attempted to put together a non-fiction account of the case with the co-operation of the exorcist Father William Bowdern, but was refused permission by the Bishop of St Louis who had laid down strict instructions forbidding any publicity. Instead, Blatty wrote a fictional novel inspired by the Mount Rainier exorcism, but also drawing on other reported cases of possession, such as that involving a forty-year-old woman in Earling, Iowa, in 1928. Other sources included Frank Sheed's respected tome *Satan*, Traugott Oesterreich's *Possession* and Aldous Huxley's *The Devils of Loudun*, as well as Carl Jung's essay 'On the Psychology and Pathology of So-Called Occult Phenomena', which grippingly describes the case of a fifteen-year-old girl who manifested three different personalities, one of whom spoke a High German dialect unknown to the girl herself.

In all of these sources, claims of 'demonic possession' are consistently balanced against more scientific solutions which describe even apparently supernatural phenomena such as telekinesis in the more down-to-earth terms of psychosomatic disorders. Whatever his own beliefs, Blatty was aware that as early as 1583, the Synod of Rheims was warning potential exorcists that 'lunatics often declare themselves to be possessed and tormented by the devil; and these people are nonetheless more in need of a doctor than an exorcist'. Thus, in fashioning his fictional tale of Regan MacNeil, the twelve-year-old child whose apparent demonic possession offers 'evidence of transcendence' to the priest of faltering faith, he retained throughout the possibility that her disorder may be hysterical rather than supernatural. This was an element which would prove particularly important to agnostic director William Friedkin when the time came to bring Blatty's startling tale to the screen.

Sold to Warner Bros as a movie while the novel was still at galley stage, Blatty's first screenplay for *The Exorcist* (published in *William Peter Blatty on The Exorcist from Novel to Film*) was, frankly, unfilmable. Utilizing an array of stylistic quirks including flashbacks, freeze-frames and lurid montages, this script was immediately rejected by Friedkin whom Blatty had personally selected as the only man capable of bringing his novel to the screen. An Oscar-winning director, and an extremely accomplished script editor, Friedkin objected to the narrative complexity of Blatty's first-draft screenplay, and stingingly informed the author that he wouldn't use it because it was 'unfaithful to the novel'. Rather than working on a series of ad hoc revisions, Friedkin simply insisted that they start again from scratch, and presented Blatty with a marked-up copy of his own novel with scenes for inclusion in the film clearly delineated by the director. It was from this that Blatty fashioned the revised shooting script of *The Exorcist,* which is published here for the first time, offering a fascinating insight into the movie that Blatty and Friedkin set out to make when filming began on 14 August 1972.

Missing the distracting subplots which Blatty had initially transposed wholesale from his novel, this revised screenplay nevertheless included key scenes which the author felt were crucial to understanding the message of *The Exorcist.* During the lengthy filming process, further changes were made to this screenplay by Blatty at Friedkin's request, sometimes to increase the verbal obscenities of the demon's attacks from which Blatty had initially shied, elsewhere to tone down any clear explanations of the events depicted, which the director always insisted the audience should interpret for themselves.

But while those alterations made during shooting were jointly agreed upon by the writer and director, other more significant changes happened during the editing of *The Exorcist* when Friedkin autonomously sliced scenes whose omission Blatty sorely mourned. These included an early scene of Regan (Linda Blair) exhibiting a melancholy preoccupation with death during a birthday outing; a conversation between Chris (Ellen Burstyn) and Doctor Klein (Barton Heyman) which built up a more gradual onset of Regan's disorder and set the scene for her later use of verbal obscenities; and a sentimental, upbeat epilogue in which Father Dyer (Father William O'Malley) and Lieutenant Kinderman (Lee J. Cobb) strike up an unlikely friendship by the site of Father Karras' final sacrificial fall.

Most significantly, Friedkin also snipped an exchange between Father Merrin (Max von Sydow) and Father Karras (Jason Miller) during a lull in the exorcism in which the ageing priest explicitly verbalizes the *reason* for Regan's possession – that the demon's target is not the little girl, but 'us', the observers, for whom Regan's suffering is intended as a cause for despair. As Friedkin has subsequently said; 'To me, the whole movie is about what they're talking about so *why are they talking about it?*' Blatty disagreed, but his protestations were in vain. By the time *The Exorcist* opened on Boxing Day 1973, it was about fifteen minutes shorter than the director's first fine cut which Blatty had enthusiastically endorsed, but which Friedkin subsequently opted to streamline into a two-hour roller-coaster ride.

Despite (or possibly *because of*) the cuts which Friedkin imposed, *The Exorcist* became one the biggest-grossing movies of its day, garnering ten Academy Award nominations, dividing critics and audiences who seemed in equal measure elated and appalled by the movie, and sparking an international wave of interest in the subject of demonic possession and the mysteries of the supernatural. A sequel seemed inevitable, but Blatty declared no interest in revisiting the crowd-pleasing shocks of *The Exorcist*, preferring instead to develop a screen adaptation of his 1966 satirical novel *Twinkle Twinkle 'Killer' Kane* – later republished as *The Ninth Configuration* – in which an apparently deranged astronaut challenges his psychiatrist to prove the existence of God in a world palpably filled with pain and suffering. If Warner were willing to finance a movie based upon that novel, only then would Blatty agree to address the issue of an *Exorcist* sequel, about which he would only say that such a work would *not* involve Regan MacNeil. As Father Merrin had stated in that crucial exchange which Friedkin had cut from *The Exorcist,* the target of the demon's attacks was never the little girl, but everyone else who was witness to her suffering. If the story of *The Exorcist* were to be continued, it would center on those disparate onlookers whose lives had been touched by the shocking events in Georgetown, in particular on Lieutenant Kinderman (the character around whose distinctive mental quirks the novel of *The Exorcist* had first started to crystallize) and Father Dyer, with whom the detective had developed a 'beautiful friendship'.

Although Warner were enticed by the idea of Kinderman investigating the deaths of Father Merrin and Father Karras in a sequel (much opportunity to use unseen out-takes from the original film), the death of Lee J. Cobb in 1976 left any such proposal without a name star from *The Exorcist*. Nor did they much care for the '*Killer' Kane* project, on which both Blatty and Friedkin had actually collaborated briefly back in 1969, but which was now deemed uncommercial. Instead, playwright William Goodhart and screenwriter Rospo Pallenberg were commissioned by John Calley and John Boorman to pen a sequel which rounded up Linda Blair, Kitty Winn (Chris MacNeil's secretary, Sharon, from the original *Exorcist*) and Max von Sydow, and sent Richard Burton flying to Africa on the back of a locust. Despite umpteen on-set rewrites and extensive post-release recuts which produced two entirely different versions of *Exorcist II: The Heretic*, Warner's eagerly awaited sequel was rejected by audiences and critics. Blatty, in the meantime, signed a deal elsewhere to write and direct *'Killer' Kane* as *The Ninth Configuration*, a long-standing cult favorite which beat *Raging Bull*, *The Elephant Man* and *Ordinary People* to the coveted Golden Globe award for Best Writing.

Still, the desire to return to the magical streets of Georgetown haunted Blatty, as did an eerie occurrence about which technical advisor Father John J. Nicola had told the writer during a lull in filming of *The Exorcist*. According to Father Nicola, a resident psychiatrist at St Elizabeth's Hospital in Baltimore had recounted being in the disturbed ward when an anonymous man in a business suit casually passed through. Suddenly pandemonium broke loose, with the patients screaming, shouting obscenities, banging on their bedsteads and howling in anguish until the man left the room, at which point calm returned. Shocked by the outburst, the psychiatrist pursued the visitor who turned out to be a priest, out of uniform, but carrying communion in his top pocket. Just as the possessed Regan had instantly identified Karras as a priest in civilian garb in *The Exorcist*, so Father Nicola suggested that perhaps the inmates had made a metaphysical connection with their plain-clothed visitor.

Blatty was already intrigued by the juxtaposition of medicine and demonology, particularly since a key element of the 1949 case was that two exorcisms had been performed on the boy within the confines of hospitals, first at Georgetown University Hospital in Washington, and later at the Alexian Brothers Hospital in St Louis, Missouri. While researching *The Exorcist*, Blatty had also heard that the chief psychologist at Mendocino State Mental Hospital, Dr Wilson Van Deusen, believed that many patients in his disturbed ward were 'possessed' and indeed occasionally practised therapeutic exorcism. This, of course, flew in the face of the more respected Freudian notion that those symptoms which had been historically interpreted as 'demonic possession' should now more properly be interpreted as the natural articulation of hysteria, or the physical eruptions of the unconscious mind. Although largely unconvinced by Van Deusen's conclusions, and well aware that the curative power of such exorcisms could be entirely autosuggestive, Blatty was nonetheless struck by the dramatic potential offered by the doctor's unusual diagnosis.

Sometime later, Blatty's interest would equally be piqued by news of an experiment conducted by a group of Edinburgh neurologists who had allegedly used magnetic tape to record the ethereal 'voices' of patients who were either in coma, catatonic or had injuries which prevented them from speaking. These experiments were inspired by the work of Latvian psychologist Dr Konstantin Raudive whose controversial 1969 book *The Inaudible Becomes Audible* (published in Britain as *Breakthrough* in 1971) claimed to document the recording of discarnate voices in a manner first explored in 1959 by Friedrich Jürgenson. Jürgenson was later created a Knight Commander of the Order of St Gregory the Great by Pope Paul VI, and the work which Raudive continued was cited by Father Pistone, Superior of the Society of St Paul, as providing 'confirmation (if such confirmation were necessary) that there *is* life after death'. However bizarre the thought of grown men stoically listening to amplified static in search of the voices of the dead may now seem, within certain sections of the Catholic Church these experiments *were* briefly viewed as first contact with the great hereafter, and as such they were a source of both fascination and inspiration for Blatty.

From all these disparate elements, a viable sequel to *The Exorcist* finally emerged, a supernatural thriller in which the spirit of a dead serial killer (*not* a demon) invades the bodies of catatonic hosts in a Georgetown Hospital, using them to revisit his past crimes. Investigating the string of murders, which bear the mark of the long-deceased Gemini Killer, is Lieutenant Kinderman, the world-weary sceptic whose investigation of the death of director Burke Dennings in *The Exorcist* led him to the strange disturbances in the MacNeil home, and who is now forced to confront the *possibility* of a supernatural solution to these grisly murders in *Legion*.

Although Friedkin now disavows any involvement with an *Exorcist* sequel, negotiations between Friedkin, Blatty and producer Jerry Weintraub regarding *Legion* did apparently take place in the early eighties. But when Friedkin got cold feet, Blatty instead developed his screenplay into a novel which brought clustered fragments of *all* his psychic explorations – from Raudive's tapes to an ex-Jesuit's theory of angelic evolution and Blatty's own waking dreams of death into an elaborate cosmic murder mystery which became a successful best-seller. This novel then provided the basis for a rewritten screenplay which would be known variously over the years as *Legion*, *The Exorcist: The Next*

Chapter, The Exorcist:1990 and *The Exorcist III: Legion*, and which Morgan Creek signed up to produce in 1989 with Blatty directing under the working title *The Exorcist: 15 Years After.*

In Blatty's screenplay, reproduced here for the first time, special effects were notably absent. With the exception of one creepy incident involving the semi-catatonic Mrs Clelia (who takes her name from a psychic experiment recounted in the novel of *The Exorcist* and whose radio is plagued by the Raudivian voices of 'dead people talking'), the pyrotechnics are entirely verbal, with the mysterious Patient X – whose body strangely resembles that of the deceased Father Karras – taunting Detective Kinderman to overcome his 'unbelief' and accept the unthinkable possibility that he is Lazarus, returned from the dead. As the solidity of the material world gradually melts away, Kinderman comes to accept that 'matter is really a kind of illusion'.

What happened next was perhaps predictable. Dividing his time between location work in Georgetown and interior shoots in Wilmington, North Carolina, Blatty directed a quirkily low-key *Exorcist* sequel centring on the edgy interplay between George C. Scott's ever rational Lieutenant Kinderman and Brad Dourif's otherworldly Patient X. In Blatty's original cut, it was the performances that provided the fireworks, with *The Ninth Configuration*'s Scott Wilson, Ed Flanders and George DiCenzo offering colorful support, while exotic cameos from the likes of Samuel L. Jackson and Patrick Ewing enlivened the hallucinatory visions of this world and the next. And then the demons descended . . .

Following a cursory preview screening with producers Morgan Creek who demanded to know 'what the hell this has to do with *The Exorcist?*', costly reshoots were ordered, replacing Brad Dourif with *Exorcist* star Jason Miller, and pulling in theatrical legend Nicol Williamson to perform a spectacular exorcism which clearly had no place in Blatty's *Legion* narrative. Contractually unable to disagree, Blatty struggled to retain his original vision with limited success, overseeing an effects-laden finale which was duly plastered on to the recut film which was now retitled simply (and misleadingly) *The Exorcist III.* In only one respect did Morgan Creek's demands benefit Blatty's original: impressed by Brad Dourif's performance, but forced to accept the recasting of Jason

Miller, Blatty struck upon the idea of using *both* actors to portray the schizophrenic nature of Patient X, subtly blending the appearances of Father Karras and the Gemini Killer James Venamun into one chameleonic character.

Whether a mainstream audience would have accepted *Legion* in its original format remains unknown, even with Blatty's rewritten climax – which *was* shot – in which Kinderman actually executes Patient X in his cell. The version of the script which is published here represents the movie as Blatty wanted it, a version of which only tantalizing fragments remain in the released movie *The Exorcist III.* Meanwhile, the legendary 'missing scenes' from *The Exorcist*, for whose inclusion Blatty has always argued so passionately, have recently resurfaced in the Warner vaults, providing the opportunity for their restoration *if* William Friedkin felt such a move to be valid. For the moment, these two screenplays present Blatty's vision of the magical Georgetown saga in as complete a form as possible. Read the scripts, and judge for yourself.

Mark Kermode, 1998

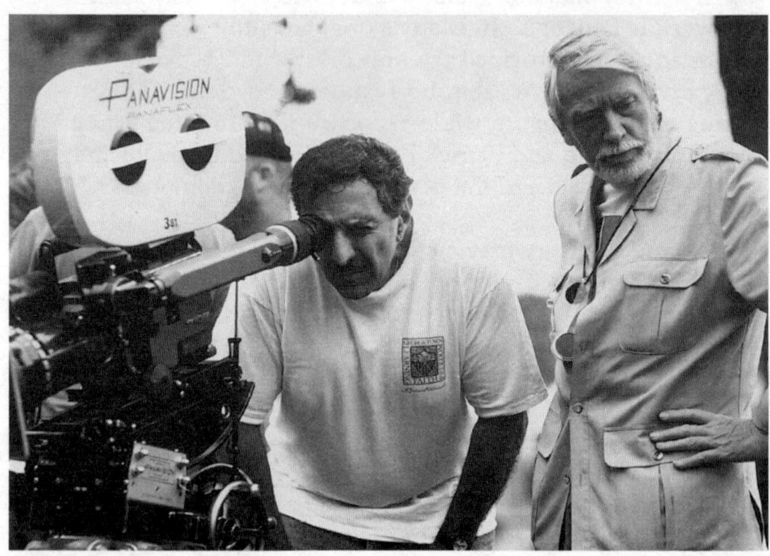

William Peter Blatty behind the camera, with cinematographer Gerry Fisher on the set of *The Exorcist III.*

William Peter Blatty (right) with William Friedkin during the shoot of *The Exorcist.*

The Exorcist

FADE IN:

Warner logo followed by minimal opening titles done in black lettering on white background. We then lose the final title, retaining the white background which quickly gives way to:

Full shot. Broiling noon sun.

EXT. EXCAVATION SITE. NINEVEH. DAWN

An Old Man in khakis works at section of mound with excavating pick. (In background there may be two Kurdish Assistants carefully packing the day's finds.) The Old Man now makes a find. He extracts it gingerly from the mound, begins to dust it off, then reacts with dismay upon recognizing a green stone amulet in the figure of the demon Pazuzu.

Close shot. Perspiration pouring down Old Man's brow.

Close shot. Old Man's hands. Trembling, they reach across a rude wooden table and cup themselves around a steaming glass of hot tea, as if for warmth.

Close shot. Old Man's face. The eyes staring off, haunted, as if by some chilling premonition – and some frightening remembrance.

EXT. LONG SHOT. ROADSIDE. CHAYKHANA. ERBIL AREA. DAY

SUPERIMPOSE: NORTHERN IRAQ

The chaykhana (teahouse) is set among poppied, green hills and athwart a ragged, rock-strewn bolt of road. In the background, the beautiful mound city of Erbil floats upward, scraping the clouds. The Kurdish Proprietor is seen leaning in the chaykhana doorway. He watches the only other character visible, the Old Man, who sits at an outdoor table, inexplicably cold beneath the fiery sun. Abstractedly, he sips at his tea. Nearby, parked off the road, an ancient jeep. LOSE SUPER. *The Proprietor shuffles out, stands beside the Old Man, speaks to him in Kurdish indistinctly. The Old Man appears not to hear at first, then comes to, looks up at Kurd, shakes head mutely, and reaches into the shirt pocket, removing coins to pay for his tea.*

Close shot. Coins slipped on to table.

Close shot. Ignition key in jeep. The Old Man's hand reaches into frame, starts engine. The jeep takes off, disappearing down the road. The Kurd comes into frame, and we end CLOSE *on him as he watches the jeep. Mirrored in his face are sadness, love, respect.*

INT. ROOM IN MOSUL. CURATOR OF ANTIQUITIES' OFFICE. DAY

The camera is in motion, slowly panning the tagged finds of a recent archeological dig now spread out in neat rows on a long table. The camera stops finally at an Assyrian pendant as the Curator's hand reaches into frame, lifting the tag on the pendant so that the writing on it can be read by him. The only sound is the soft, regular ticking of an old-fashioned pendulum clock.

Close shot. Ledger containing entries of the finds. It is clearly headed (in the Curator's handwriting) 'Nineveh Excavation: Merrin'. On a fresh line of the entries, the Curator's hand now writes: 'Pendant, Assyrian; Palace of Assurbani –' Here, the hand breaks off.

Close shot. Arab Curator. He is seated at same table on which rest the finds and is looking up curiously from ledger at someone off-screen.

Close shot. Old Man. He is standing over another section of the same table. He is staring down at something on it off-screen.

Close shot. Amulet on table. Tagged – it is the Pazuzu amulet.

Close shot. Curator. His gaze is now on the amulet.

CURATOR

(*softly*)

Evil against evil.

Intercut. Old Man and Curator. The Old Man does not react, continuing to stare down at amulet, his expression haunted. After a beat:

Father?

We are on the Old Man now as, after several beats, the ticking of the clock abruptly ceases; and it is this sudden silence that, after a beat, unconsciously causes the Old Man to look up at the Curator, who is still staring at him. Still no response. Something is worrying the Curator, but he doesn't know what.

CURATOR
(*in Arabic*)
My heart has a wish: that you would not go, old friend.

OLD MAN
(*in Arabic*)
I have an errand.

On Curator and Old Man. They stand by an open door to the street; the Old Man is about to leave. The Curator has hold of the Old Man's hand in both of his. He is troubled, as if the Old Man's premonition has invaded him. The Old Man slowly looks up at the Curator, searching his face with great affection. Then, with a squeeze of his hand:

Goodbye.

EXT. CURATOR'S OFFICE. DAY

The Old Man exits, leaving frame as he steps into the gathering gloom of the streets of Mosul. The Curator watches him, great love in his expression as:

POV: The Old Man. Street outside Curator's office. The Old Man almost collides with a fast-moving droshky.

Close moving shot. Droshky's sole passenger. A corpulent, Old Arab Woman in black, her face a shadow behind the lace veil draped loosely over her like a shroud.

On Curator. His expression darkening at this.

EXT. LONG SHOT. MOSUL OUTSKIRTS. NINEVEH EXCAVATION. DUSK

The Old Man is slowly and warily walking amid the ruins of a former temple area.

Old Man's POV: An Arab Watchman approaches, rifle at the ready, but then stops and waves as he recognizes the Old Man.

Moving shot as the Old Man slowly resumes his walk with the manner of someone sifting vibrations. He is like one looking for something, yet is afraid that he will find it. At last, upon seeing something off-screen, he freezes.

POV: Full shot: statue of Demon Pazuzu in situ. *On Old Man. This is it. He lowers head, closing eyes against a dread confirmation of his premonition. A shadow of the statue lengthens and creeps on to the Old Man's face as, in the distance, we hear the dim yappings of savage dog packs.*

Angle on shadows quickening across the desert. Still the dogs, yelping and howling distantly. A breeze rises up, blowing dust and sand across the frame.

On Old Man. He slowly lifts his head, his gaze on the off-screen statue of Pazuzu. But in his expression now is acceptance and grim determination. The shadow on his face has grown longer and the breeze is whipping gently at his shirt.

Old Man's POV: statue of Pazuzu.

High down shot. Temple area. Statue. Old Man.

They stand motionless like two ancient enemies squared off in a massive arena.

Angle on setting sun. It sinks into darkness. The dog packs.

EXT. SUNRISE SHOT. WASHINGTON, DC.

The sound of savage dogs gives way to distant sounds of friendly neighborhood dogs, children's voices, a city waking up.

SERIES OF MOVING SHOTS. GEORGETOWN AREA. DAWN

Below us, the Potomac River; the Gothic spires and wooded walks of Georgetown University; a Priest or two walking, saying their Office; and then we are on Prospect Street, slowly approaching a house that sits beside a flight of steep, stone steps plunging precipitately down to 'M' Street below. An upstairs bedroom light is burning.

INT. CHRIS MACNEIL'S BEDROOM. DAWN

Chris is sitting up in bed. Her lips move silently as she studies lines from a film script. We hear light, off-screen rapping sounds; irregular, yet rhythmically clustered, like alien code tapped out by a dead man. Chris hears them, listens for a moment, then tries to ignore them, but she cannot concentrate. She irritably slams the script down and flounces out of bed. She exits into:

INT. MACNEIL HOUSE. SECOND-FLOOR HALL. DAWN

The rappings are louder. Chris listens for the source of the sound, locates it, throws open the door to Regan's bedroom.

INT. REGAN'S BEDROOM. CHRIS AT DOOR. DAWN

The rappings have ceased abruptly. Chris looks baffled.

POV: The room. Camera shifting to follow Chris's scrutiny. It is a typical child's bedroom. A large bay window with shutters overlooks the steps outside the house. Regan is asleep, her blankets kicked off and askew. Chris moves to the bedside. Heavy breathing, regular and deep. Chris considers, then abruptly notices goose pimples on her arms. She rubs at them, shivering as if at an icy coldness. She touches the nearby radiator. Hot. She looks at Regan, frowning in perplexity, for Regan's brow is wet with perspiration. Chris squints her eyes in consternation; looks back at her goose pimples. Now she hears sounds from above, like tiny claws scratching at the edge of a galaxy. She looks up at ceiling. The scrapings cease. Chris keeps staring a moment, then looks down. She leans over, adjusts Regan's pillow, then examines her features with warmth.

CHRIS
(*whisper*)
I sure do love you.

Car lights reflect on the ceiling of the darkened room.

INT. MACNEIL HOUSE. KITCHEN. CLOSE ON BACON FRYING. DAY

CHRIS
(*off-screen*)
Hi, Willie. Howya doin'?

Full shot. Kitchen. Chris and Willie.

Willie, a middle-aged housekeeper, is at the stove. Sleepy-eyed Chris, in bathrobe and carrying a script, is entering. Willie hastily puts down her fork, wiping hands on a dish towel as:

WILLIE
(*German accent*)
Oh, Mrs MacNeil! Good morning!

As Willie moves for the coffee pot, Chris is ahead of her.

CHRIS
Never mind, Willie, I'll get it.

She drops a pack of cigarettes and matches beside her cup and sits. Crusty-eyed, she picks up copy of the Washington Post *by plate and stares at it fuddled until she realizes it is upside down. She turns it right-side up. A man enters: Karl. Willie's husband. Very Teutonic. He is carrying a Sparklett's bottle to mount on cooler in exchange for the empty.*

KARL

Good morning, madam.

CHRIS

(*lights cigarette*)

Mornin'. Hey, Karl, we've got rats in the attic. Better get us some traps.

KARL

There are rats?

CHRIS

I just said that.

KARL

But the attic is clean.

CHRIS

Well, okay, we've got tidy rats.

KARL

No rats.

CHRIS

Karl, I heard them this *morning*!

KARL

Maybe plumbing. Maybe boards.

CHRIS

Maybe *rats*! Now will you buy the damn traps and quit arguing?

KARL

(*leaving quickly*)

Yes. I go now.

CHRIS

No, not *now*, Karl! The *stores* are all closed.

KARL

I will see.

CHRIS

Karl – !

Karl is gone. Chris and Willie exchange exasperated glances, and then we hear the front door open and close, off-screen. With a sigh, Willie turns back to the bacon, shaking her head.

WILLIE

They are closed.

EXT. CAMPUS OF GEORGETOWN UNIVERSITY. DAY

A film is being shot in front of the steps of Healy Building. The usual equipment, cast and crew are in evidence, as well as spectators made up of faculty and students. Chris, in jeans and sweatshirt, and indicating page in her script (titled 'Crash Course'), calls her director, elfin, British Burke Dennings. He has been drinking. Swigging from a paper cup, he looks over as:

CHRIS

(*argumentatively*)

Hey, Burke? Take a look at the damned thing, will ya?

DENNINGS

Oh, how marvelous! You *do* have a script, I see!

(*surgically shaves a narrow strip from the edge of the page of her script*)

Yes, how nice! I believe I'll just have a little munchie.

As they continue, Burke will nervously fiddle with the paper, then begin to chew on it. In the meantime:

CHRIS

Burke –

DENNINGS

Yes, I'm *terribly* glad that the star has a script. Now then, tell me, my baby: What is it? What's wrong?

CHRIS

(*indicating script*)

It just doesn't make sense.

DENNINGS

(*lying*)

Why, it's perfectly plain. You're a teacher at the college and you don't want the building torn down and –

CHRIS

Oh, well, Jesus, Burke. Thanks. I can read.

DENNINGS

Then what's wrong?

CHRIS

Why the hell should they tear down the building?

DENNINGS

Are you sending me up?

CHRIS

No, I'm asking 'What for?'

DENNINGS

Because it's *there*!

CHRIS

In the script?

DENNINGS

(*suppressing drunken giggle*)

On the *grounds*!

CHRIS

Well, it doesn't make sense. They wouldn't do that.

DENNINGS

They would!

CHRIS

No, they *wouldn't*!

DENNINGS

Shall we summon the writer? I believe he's in Paris!

CHRIS

Hiding?

DENNINGS

Fucking! Now then, shall we get on with it?

Chris stares momentarily, then sags on to Burke spurting laughter. Then she looks worriedly toward a priest (Damien Karras) off-screen among the spectators, afraid he's heard the obscenity. And now we cut to

Karras and see that he is smiling slightly but warmly. The angle then returns to Chris, Burke and the Assistant Director.

I said, 'Shall we get *on* with it?'

CHRIS

Huh? Yeah, okay, Burke. Let's go.

DENNINGS

(*to Assistant Director*)

All right, lights, love.

ASSISTANT DIRECTOR

Let's warm 'em!

DENNINGS

(*to Assistant Director*)

Now the extras should be . . .

And we hear the ad lib continuation off-screen a bit as the camera now follows Chris as she walks, head down, concentrating while the crew sets up. Then she looks over toward Karras. He's gone. She sees him walking slowly away toward the campus gates like a lone black cloud in search of the rain. Dennings comes to Chris.

Are you ready, ducks?

CHRIS

Do it.

DENNINGS

Roll the film.

ASSISTANT DIRECTOR

Okay, roll 'em.

TECHNICIAN

Speed.

DENNINGS

Action!

While Extras cheer and boo at her approach, Chris races up the Healy steps and seizes bullhorn from a Rebel Student Leader. There is pushing and shoving. Police are on the scene.

CHRIS

(*through bullhorn*)

Okay, now, hold it! Hold it a second!

(*as the commotion continues*)

Hey, give me a chance, will ya, huh? Just a minute?

We see now that various of the student factions are holding up signs and banners. Some read: 'KEEP CLASSES OPEN', 'FREE LOGIC!', 'SHUT DOWN!', 'CLOSE THE SCHOOL' *and* 'BURN IT!?' *Still other placards are* blank. *Many of the Students in one sector are affecting shrouds and death masks. As the commotion diminishes:*

Look, we're all concerned with human rights, but the kids who pay tuition have also got a right, the right to learn, and shutting those kids out of class solves nothing. It's answering one kind of tyranny with another, one kind of cruelty with another.

Commotion. At some point during the above speech, we will hear Chris off-screen while the camera goes to Dennings as the director turns a significant and imperious gaze to the Assistant Director, who dutifully pads over to him and proffers his open script like an aging altar boy proffers the missal to his priest at solemn Mass. Burke begins to slice off a fresh strip of page.

EXT. 'O' STREET. CAMPUS MAIN GATE. DAY

It has clouded over, threatening rain. Chris, wearing a raincoat, sends the limo driver home.

CHRIS

I feel like walking, Tommy. Thanks.

Tommy nods. Chris starts to walk home, thoughtful and weary. As she walks by Holy Trinity Auditorium, a Young Priest in nylon windbreaker passes her. Tense. He takes a right into an easement leading into a courtyard at the back of church. Chris pauses by the easement, watching him; curious. He heads for a white frame cottage from which an Older Priest emerges looking glum and nervous. He nods curtly toward the Young Priest, and with lowered eyes heads for a door to the back of the church. Again, the cottage door opens from within and Karras appears. He silently greets the Young Priest, putting his arm around his shoulder as he leads him inside, a gesture that is gentle and somehow parental. The door closes and they are gone. Chris is pensive, puzzled by the scene. A rumble of thunder. She looks up at the sky, tugging up raincoat collar.

EXT. MACNEIL HOUSE. DUSK

Chris enters.

INT. MACNEIL HOUSE. KITCHEN. DUSK

We open on Sharon Spencer, a pretty young blonde and Chris's secretary (and nurse to Regan) sitting at the breakfast table, typing. Stack of mail and messages. We hear the front door close; footsteps approaching. Chris enters, weary.

SHARON

(*continuing to type*)

Hi, Chris. How'd it go?

CHRIS

Oh, well, it was kind of like the Walt Disney version of the Ho Chi Minh story, but other than that it was really terrific.

Chris has come to the table, stands leafing through mail and messages. Sharon continues to type through:

Anything exciting?

SHARON

Do you want to have dinner next week at the White House?

CHRIS

Are you kidding?

SHARON

No, of course not; it's Thursday.

CHRIS

Big party?

SHARON

No, I gather it's just five or six people.

CHRIS

(*back to the table sifting mail and messages*)

No kidding? Where's Rags?

SHARON

Oh, she's down in the playroom.

CHRIS

What doin'?

SHARON

She's sculpting. She's making you a bird.

CHRIS

How'd the lesson go?

SHARON

(*frowning*)

Bad time with math again.

CHRIS

Oh? Gee, that's funny.

SHARON

I know. It's her favorite subject.

CHRIS

Oh, well, this 'new math'. Christ, I couldn't make change for the bus if –

She is interrupted by the bounding entrance of Regan, her eleven-year-old daughter. Freckles. Ponytails. Braces on teeth. Arms outstretched, she is racing for her mother.

REGAN

Hi, Mom!

She is in the scene now as Chris catches her in a bear-hug. Sharon resumes her typing.

CHRIS

Hiya, bearface!

Chris covers Regan with smacking kisses. Then, rocking her back and forth:

What'd ya do today? Anything exciting?

REGAN

Oh, stuff.

CHRIS

So, what *kind* of stuff?

REGAN

Oh, well, I studied, and I painted.

CHRIS

Wha'd ya paint?

REGAN

Oh, well, flowers. Ya know, daisies? An' – Oh! Mother! This *horse*!

(*excited; eyes widening*)

This man had a horse, ya know, down by the river? We were talking, see, Mom, and then along came this *horse*! He was *beautiful*! Oh, Mom, ya should've *seen* him, and the man let me *sit* on him! *Really*! I mean, practically a *minute*! It was a *gray* horse! Mother, can't we get a horse? I mean, *could* we?

CHRIS

We'll see, baby.

REGAN

Gee, Mom, I'm starving.

CHRIS

Run upstairs and get dressed and we'll go out for some pizza.

Regan races upstairs.

REGAN

Can I wear my new dress?

CHRIS

Honey, sure.

(*to Sharon*)

Got a date?

SHARON

Yes, I do.

CHRIS

You go on, then.

(*indicating mail*)

We can catch all this stuff in the morning.

Sharon rises, but Chris abruptly recollects something.

Oh, hey, wait. There's a letter got to go out tonight.

SHARON

(*reaching for dictation pad*)

Oh, okay.

Chris starts to dictate:

CHRIS

Dear Mr Gable . . .

Sharon reacts, amused; then Chris dictates in earnest: a letter to her agent. As she gets into it:

REGAN

(*off-screen*)

Moth-theeeeeerrrr! I can't find the dress.

CHRIS

Guess I'd better go find it for her.

SHARON

(*eyeing watch*)

Gee, it's time for me to meditate, Chris.

CHRIS

You really think that kind of stuff is going to do you any good?

SHARON

Well, it gives me peace of mind.

CHRIS

(*after a long beat*)

Right.

She turns away and starts to exit.

Correct. Terrific.

INT. MACNEIL HOUSE. SECOND-FLOOR HALLWAY. DUSK

Chris heads for Regan's bedroom and enters.

INT. REGAN'S BEDROOM. DUSK

The scene is odd: Regan is standing in the middle of the room, silently staring up at the ceiling, frowning.

CHRIS

What's doin'?

REGAN

Funny noises.

CHRIS

(*moving to the clothes closet and searching for dress*)

I know. We've got friends.

REGAN

Huh?

CHRIS

Squirrels, honey. Squirrels in the attic.

Regan looks unconvinced. She looks up at the ceiling again; then moves over to watch her mother's search for the dress which now ends in apparent failure.

REGAN

See, Mom? It's not there.

CHRIS

Yeah, I see. Maybe Willie picked it up with the cleaning.

REGAN

It's gone.

CHRIS

(*taking a dress off the rack*)

Yeah, well, put on the navy. It's pretty.

EXT. 'C & O' CANAL. DUSK

Karras and the Georgetown University President (Tom) are walking.

KARRAS

It's my mother. She's alone, Tom. I never should've left her. At least in New York I'd be close. I could see her.

TOM

I could see about a transfer.

KARRAS

I need reassignment. Get me out of this job, Tom; it's wrong. It's no good.

TOM

Are you kidding? You're the best that we've got.

They stop.

KARRAS

Am I really? It's more than psychiatry, Tom, and you know that. Some of their problems come down to vocation, to the meaning of their lives, and I just can't cut it, Tom. It's too much. I need out. I'm unfit.

After a pause.

I think I've lost my faith.

INT. BASEMENT PLAYROOM OF MACNEIL HOUSE. EARLY EVENING

Chris is coming down, calling to Regan.

CHRIS

Whatchya doin' down there?

REGAN

Come on down, Mom; I've got a surprise.

CHRIS

Oh, great.

Regan is standing by a games table in the basement-made-over-as-playroom, and hands her a sculpted clay 'worry bird' with a comically long painted nose. Chris oohs and ahhs.

REGAN

Do you like it?

CHRIS

Oh, honey, I do, I really do. Got a name for it?

REGAN

Uh-uh.

CHRIS

What's a good one?

REGAN

(*shrugging*)

I dunno.

CHRIS

(*pondering*)

Let me see, let me see. I don't know. Whaddya think? Whaddya think about 'Dumbbird'? Huh? Just 'Dumbbird'.

Regan is snickering, nodding; hand to mouth to hide the braces.

'Dumbbird' by a landslide! Super!

(*setting bird on table*)

Here, I'll leave it here to dry for a . . .

She has noticed an Ouija board and planchette on the table.

Hey, where'd you get the Ouija board?

REGAN

(*indicating*)

I found it.

CHRIS

Found it where?

REGAN

(*indicating*)

In that closet.

CHRIS

You been playin' with it?

REGAN

Yep.

CHRIS
(*surprised*)
You know how?

REGAN
(*moving to sit by board*)
Oh, well, sure. Here, I'll show you.

CHRIS
Well, I think you need *two* people, honey.

REGAN
No, ya don't, Mom. I do it all the time.

CHRIS
(*pulling up chair opposite*)
Oh, you do? Well, let's both play, Okay?

REGAN
Well – okay.

Regan has her fingertips positioned on the planchette, and as Chris reaches out to put hers there, the planchette makes a sudden, forceful move to the 'No' position on the board.

CHRIS
You don't want me to play?

REGAN
No, I *do*! Captain *Howdy* said 'No'.

CHRIS
Captain who?

REGAN
Captain Howdy.

CHRIS
Honey, who's Captain Howdy?

REGAN
Oh, ya know. I make questions and he does the answers.

CHRIS
That so?

REGAN

Oh, he's nice.

CHRIS

Oh, well, sure; he's terrific.

REGAN

Here, I'll show you.

Regan stares at the board, eyes drawn tight in concentration.

Captain Howdy, do you think my mom is pretty?

Seconds tick by. Nothing happening. Chris turns her head at an odd, off-screen creaking sound from the closet area. She holds the look for a moment, then looks back at the board. Another few beats of silence. Then:

Captain Howdy?

(*no response*)

Captain Howdy, that's *really* not very *polite*.

CHRIS

Honey, maybe he's sleeping.

REGAN

(*muttering*)

Let him sleep on his *own* time.

INT. REGAN'S BEDROOM. NIGHT

Regan in bed. Chris finishing tucking her in. Sits on bed.

CHRIS

Honey, Sunday's your birthday. Want to do somethin'?

REGAN

What?

CHRIS

Oh, well, *I* don't know. Somethin'. You want to go see the sights?

REGAN

Oh, *yeah*, Mom!

CHRIS

And tomorrow night a movie! How's that?

REGAN

(*a hug*)

Oh, I love you!

CHRIS

Oh, Rags, honey, I love you.

REGAN

You can bring Mr Dennings if you like.

CHRIS

Mr Dennings?

REGAN

Well, I mean, it's okay.

CHRIS

(*chuckling*)

No, it isn't okay. Honey, why would I want to bring Burke?

REGAN

Well, you like him.

CHRIS

Oh, well, sure I like him, honey. Don't you?

(*no response*)

Baby, what's going on?

REGAN

(*a sullen statement*)

You're going to marry him, Mommy, aren't you?

CHRIS

(*amused*)

Oh, my baby, of *course* not! What on earth are you *talking* about? Burke Dennings? Where'd you get that idea?

REGAN

But you like him.

CHRIS

I like pizzas but I wouldn't ever marry one! Honey, he's a friend, just a crazy old friend!

REGAN

You don't like him like Daddy?

CHRIS

Rags, I *love* your daddy. I'll *always* love your daddy. Mr Dennings comes by here a lot 'cause he's lonely, that's all, he's a friend.

REGAN

Well, I heard . . .

CHRIS

You heard what? Heard from who?

REGAN

I don't know. I just thought . . .

CHRIS

Well, it's silly, so forget it.

REGAN

Okay.

INT. MACNEIL HOUSE. STUDY. NIGHT

Stretched out on rug in front of the fire, Chris studying the script. Turns a page. Regan, half asleep, enters.

CHRIS

Hi, honey. What's wrong?

REGAN

There's these real funny noises, Mom. It's like knocking. I can't go to sleep.

CHRIS

(*struggling up*)

Oh, where the heck are those traps!

REGAN

Huh?

Chris takes her hand, leading her out of study.

CHRIS

Oh, nothing, hon. Come on. You can sleep in my bedroom and I'll see what it is.

INT. CHRIS'S BEDROOM. NIGHT

Chris is tucking Regan into her (Chris's) bed.

REGAN

Can I watch TV for a while till I sleep?

CHRIS

Where's your book?

REGAN

I can't find it. Can I watch?

CHRIS

(*turning on bedside TV*)

Sure, okay.

(*tunes volume control*)

Loud enough?

REGAN

Yes.

CHRIS

(*exiting; turning out light*)

Try to sleep.

EXT. MACNEIL HOUSE. NIGHT

Full shot: In an upper floor gabled window we see candlelight glow.

INT. MACNEIL HOUSE. NIGHT

Down shot: On Chris as she climbs narrow steps to attic with candle.

INT. ATTIC. AT DOOR. NIGHT

Door is pushed slowly open. Chris enters, tries the light switch. It doesn't work. She looks about the attic searching for something while slowly

advancing at the camera when the candle flame suddenly and astoundingly disengages from the candle and shoots up to the ceiling and is extinguished. Behind Chris, having come upstairs, looms Karl. Coming up silently behind Chris:

KARL

There is nothing.

On the 'Nothing', Chris leaps three feet out of her skin and emits a yelp of fright, spinning around and practically into Karl's arms. A hand to her fluttering heart:

CHRIS

Oh, good Jesus! Oh, Jesus H. *Christ*, Karl, don't *do* that!

KARL

Very sorry. But you see? No rats.

CHRIS

Yeah, no rats. Thanks a lot, Karl. Terrific.

KARL

(exiting)

Madam, maybe cat better.

CHRIS

What?

KARL

Maybe cat better – to catch rats.

He exits. Chris stares a moment, then releases a sigh of weariness and relief.

EXT. MACNEIL HOUSE. NIGHT

Bedroom light is turned off. All is peaceful.

EXT. MONTAGE. CHRIS AND REGAN SIGHTSEEING IN DC. MEMORIAL DRIVE AND LEE MANSION. DAY

Giving way to:

Chris and Regan at Tomb of Unknown Soldier.

They stare mutely. Regan has turned sad. After a few beats:

REGAN

Mom, why do people have to die?

Chris looks at her. She doesn't know how to answer. Finally:

CHRIS

(*tenderly*)

Honey, people get tired.

REGAN

Why does God let them?

CHRIS

(*frowning, a few beats*)

Who's been telling you about God, baby?

REGAN

Sharon.

CHRIS

Oh.

REGAN

Mom, why does God *let* us get tired?

CHRIS

(*after a beat*)

Well, after a while, God gets lonesome for us, Rags. He wants us back.

INT. CHRIS MACNEIL'S BEDROOM. NIGHT

Chris is pacing with the phone receiver to her ear, waiting, and in the meantime is talking to Sharon, who is seated on the edge of the bed, scribbling shorthand in a steno pad.

CHRIS

And get hold of that real estate agent and tell him we're staying till June. I want Rags to finish up the semester at school. And then –

(*half talk into phone*)

Yeah, yeah, I'm here. Yes, I'm waiting . . .

(*mouthpiece down, to Sharon*)
Good Christ, do you believe it?

INT. MACNEIL HOUSE. SECOND-FLOOR HALL. NIGHT

Despondent, Regan stands head down, hand on doorknob to her bedroom, listening to:

CHRIS
(*off-screen*)
Doesn't send a card or call his daughter on her birthday?

SHARON
(*off-screen*)
Well, the circuits might be busy.

CHRIS
(*off-screen*)
My ass, he just doesn't *give* a shit! He's just –

Regan sadly enters her room as:

(*off-screen; phone*)
Yes, goddammit, I'm *waiting*!

INT. CHRIS'S BEDROOM. NIGHT

CHRIS
(*pacing; muttering to herself*)
The whole fucking world is still waiting for the sunrise.

INT. CHRIS'S BEDROOM. DAWN

We are on Chris in bed as the phone rings. She answers. Wake-up call from the Assistant Director. Hangs up; gets out of bed; discovers Regan is in bed with her, half awake.

CHRIS
Well, what in the – !
(*amused*)
What are you doing *here?*

REGAN

My bed was shaking.

CHRIS

Oh, you nut.

(*kisses her and pulls up her covers*)

Go back to sleep.

EXT. HOUSE. NIGHT TO DAY TRANSITION

Follow Newspaper Boy on bike to Holy Trinity.

INT. HOLY TRINITY CHURCH AT REAR SIDE DOOR. DAWN

We hear key in door from the other side. The Pastor of Holy Trinity sluggishly enters, sets door stop to hold the door open, turns on the church lights, blows his nose into a handkerchief as he absently shuffles along; then genuflects at the altar railing. He says a silent prayer, and as he looks up and starts to bless himself he reacts with startlement and then shock as he sees before him:

POV: Statue of Blessed Virgin at side altar. It has been desecrated, painted over to suggest that the Virgin is a harlot. A slatternly, dissolute appearance. And glued to the appropriate spot is a sculpted clay phallus in erection.

INT. NEW YORK SUBWAY STATION. DAY

Silence, except for the low rumble of a distant train. Points of light stretch down the darkness of the tunnel like guides to hopelessness.

Angle on platform. Man. The station appears to be deserted. The Man stands close to the edge of the near platform. Black coat, hat and trousers. Powerfully built. He carries a valise resembling a doctor's medical bag, and stands with his back to us, head down, as if in dejection. Near him, a vending machine on a pillar.

Wide angle. Platform.

DERELICT

Faddah.

An old Derelict lies drunk, his back against the station wall.

Hey, Faddah! Couldja help an old altar boy, Faddah? I'm Cat'lic.

The Man looks up with dismay, disclosing the round Roman collar at the neck, and the face of Damien Karras, now filled with an even deeper pain than when we met him before. He shuts his eyes against this intrusion and clutches at his coat lapels, pulling them together as if to hide the collar. The train sound is up full now, and in another angle the train rushes across frame, blocking our view of Karras and the Derelict.

EXT. EAST 21ST STREET IN NEW YORK. DAY

High shot: Between 1st and 2nd Avenues. Karras walks despondently along the south side of the street, which is studded with decrepit tenement buildings. He pauses before one and with melancholy sees his past in the raggedly clothed, grim-covered, foul-mouthed urchins pitching pennies against the stoop. Karras looks up at front door. He starts up the steps.

INT. KARRAS'S MOTHER'S APARTMENT BUILDING. HALL. DAY

Karras. Cutting, we find the camera stationed by an apartment front door, trained on Karras mounting steps at the far end of the hall. He approaches and lightly raps. From within we hear faint sound of a radio tuned to a news station. Karras waits a moment, then digs out a key from his pants pocket, opens the door like an aching wound, and enters.

INT. TENEMENT APARTMENT. DAY

The radio is now more audible. We are in a railroad-flat kitchen. Tiny. Cracking plaster and peeling wallpaper. Unkempt. Sparse and ancient furnishings. In the kitchen, a small tub for bathing. Faded old newspapers spread on the uncarpeted floor. As Karras enters, he breathes in an aching sigh as his gaze brushes around at the painful reminders of his past. Then he glances to the right, from which we hear the sound of the radio. He puts down the valise and starts into the bedroom.

KARRAS

Mama?

No response. The camera follows him into a squalid living-room. Karras now sees his Mother, fully dressed, sleeping on a torn and grease-stained old sofa. On her right cheek, a prominent mole. *He observes her for a moment, sighs as he removes his raincoat.*

As he drapes it over a chair, his Mother awakens with a slight start, sees him, reacts with surprise and joy. Speaking with a thick Mediterranean accent:

MOTHER

Dimmy!

She hastily gets to her feet and throws her arms around Karras.

Oh, Dimmy, I so glad to see you!

INT. KARRAS'S MOTHER'S KITCHEN. DAY

We hear the radio still tuned to news. Karras and Mother sit at a tiny table in the kitchen. Karras sips at his coffee. His Mother drinks in his presence as:

MOTHER

Dimmy, you thin. You not eating.

(*rising*)

I fix for you.

KARRAS

No, Mom.

MOTHER

I fix.

CUT TO:

Karras and Mother at the table. Karras eating.

KARRAS

Really great, Mom! Just great!

MOTHER

You Uncle John come by to visit me.

KARRAS

(*pleased*)

Oh really, Ma? When?

MOTHER

Last month.

Karras looks saddened.

INT. MOTHER'S LIVING-ROOM. NIGHT

Mother (wearing holy medal) sits on the sofa, watching as Karras repairs a broken lamp. The room has been tidied up a little. In the scene we see a broom, a small plastic refuse container and a dilapidated carpet sweeper. Silence. Then:

MOTHER

Dimmy, you worry about something?

KARRAS

No, Mama.

MOTHER

You not happy. What's the matter, Dimmy?

KARRAS

Nothing, Mama. Really. I'm fine.

A pause. Then:

MOTHER

(*off-screen*)

I wish you was marry Mary McArdle.

Close shot. Mother silently watching; thinking.

Another angle. (*Time passage.*) *Karras is entering the living-room, pulling on his raincoat. He has his valise. He comes to Mother and observes her sadly for a moment. Regret. He leans over and kisses her cheek tenderly. He starts to leave, remembers something, tunes the radio to all-news station.*

EXT. FORDHAM UNIVERSITY. DAWN

Establishing shot.

INT. JESUIT RESIDENCE HALL. SMALL CHAPEL. DAWN

Karras wears trousers and a T-shirt. He vests and prepares for Mass, and then steps back facing the altar, blesses himself, and begins:

KARRAS

(*with poignant longing*)

'I will go to the Altar of God,
Unto God who gives joy to my youth.'

INT. HALL OF BELLEVUE HOSPITAL. DAY

The camera is fixed at one end of the hall, and Karras and his Uncle are approaching from far down the opposite end; however, their dialogue is clearly audible at all times, and their voices metalically reverberant. Karras has his head down, sorrowful and dismayed, as he listens to the Uncle, who speaks with a thick, immigrant accent. Karras is ruefully shaking his head, and the Uncle is gesturing helplessly, defensively, as:

UNCLE

But, Dimmy, da edema affected her *brain*! You understand? She don't let any doctor come *near* her! She was all da time screamin', even talkin' to da radio! Listen, regular hospital not gonna put *up* wit' dat, Dimmy! Un'erstan'? So we give her a shot an' bring her here 'til da doctors, day fix up her leg! Den we take her right out, Dimmy. Two or t'ree month, and she's out, good as new.

Another angle. Karras and his Uncle have halted outside a locked door above which is posted the legend: Neuro-Psychiatric: Ward 3, and Uncle pushes buzzer to summon Nurse.

You go in, Dimmy. I wait out here.

Karras nods. Now the Uncle has his head down in ironic thought.

Dat's funny. You know, if you wasn't be priest, you be famous psychiatrist now on Park Avenue, Dimmy. Your mother, she be livin' in a penthouse instead of da –

INT. WARD 3 AT PADDED ENTRY DOOR. DAY

As a corpulent Nurse waddles into frame and uses a large iron key to unlock door, off-screen, we hear the demented screams, moans and fragmented statements of mental patients. The door comes open, disclosing Karras and Uncle. Karras slowly lifts his head at the off-screen sounds.

INT. WARD 3. INVALIDED PATIENTS' ROOM. DAY

Karras walks down the aisle of an enormous ward containing eighty beds. The Patients are mostly elderly, and we hear their cries of pain and demented chatter. Karras stops before a bedded patient far down the row: his Mother. Gaunt and hollow-eyed, looking confused and helpless; disoriented; she has spied her son and is gripping at the sidebars of the bed, trying to raise herself as the camera now moves forward again, trained on Mother. By the time Karras halts by her, Mother, looking frightened and pathetic, eyes wide with pleading, has raised herself up, pulling weakly, hands trembling.

MOTHER

Why you do dis to me, Dimmy? Why?

INT. BELLEVUE HALL. DAY

Karras and Uncle walking. Behind them, Ward 3 entry door. Karras is fumbling for his cigarette pack. His eyes are wet with tears.

KARRAS

Couldn't you have put her someplace else?

UNCLE

Like what? Private hospital? Who got da money for dat, Dimmy? You?

INT. GYM. DAY

Karras in boxer shorts and shirt works savagely at a punching bag of the man-sized, stuffed variety. Eyes wet with tears, he slams at the bag with a mixture of sorrow, rage and frustration.

INT. DR KLEIN'S OFFICE. ROSSLYN BUILDING. DAY

Chris sits in the reception room. A few other Mothers and Children are present.

INT. DR KLEIN'S EXAMINING-ROOM. DAY

Brief montage of shots.

Klein administering a physical to Regan. Should include ophthalmoscope, tuning fork and simple coordination test. Also blood sample in centrifograph, and urine sample under microscope. Final shot has a Nurse leaning with her back against the examining table, her expression partly puzzled, partly disturbed as she observes Regan, who is in her slip and in constant motion; stepping, twirling, touching, making nervous movements while aimlessly humming. Klein is not present.

INT. DR KLEIN'S OFFICE. DAY

Chris is seated on the edge of a chair. Klein is behind his desk, writing a prescription.

KLEIN

A disorder of the nerves. At least we think it is. We don't know yet exactly how it works, but it's often seen in early adolescence. She shows all the symptoms: the hyperactivity; the temper; her performance in math.

CHRIS

Yeah, the math. Why the math?

KLEIN

It affects concentration.
(*rips the prescription from the small blue pad and hands it over*)
Now this is for Ritalin. Ten milligrams a day.

CHRIS

(*eyes prescription*)

What is it? A tranquilizer?

KLEIN

A stimulant.

CHRIS

*Stim*ulant? She's higher'n a kite right *now*!

KLEIN

Her condition isn't quite what it seems. Nobody knows the cause of hyperkinetic behaviour in a child. The Ritalin seems to work to relieve the condition, but we really don't know how or why, frankly. Your daughter's symptoms could be an overreaction to depression – but that's out of my field.

CHRIS

Depression?

KLEIN

Well, you mentioned her father . . . the divorce.

CHRIS

Do you think I should take her to see a psychiatrist?

KLEIN

Oh, no. I'd wait and see what happens with the Ritalin. I think that's the answer. Wait two or three weeks.

CHRIS

And those lies she's been telling?

KLEIN

Lies?

CHRIS

Ya know, those things to get attention, like saying that her bed shakes and stuff.

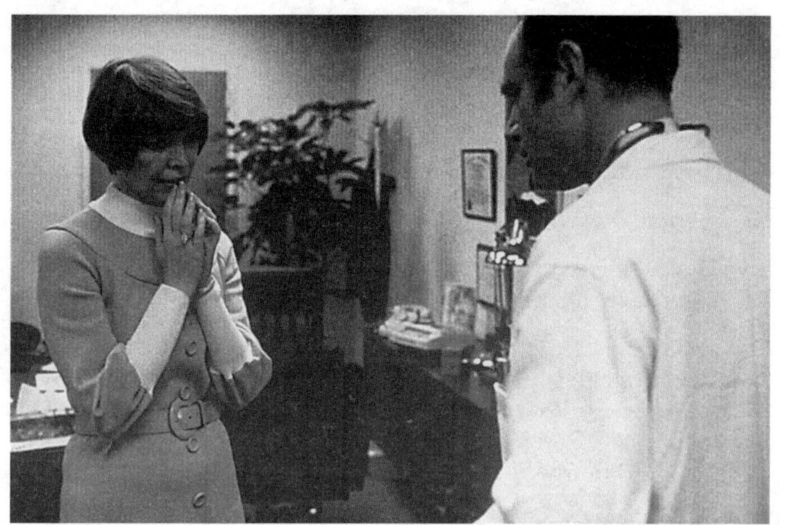

KLEIN

Have you ever known your daughter to swear and use obscenities?

CHRIS

Never.

KLEIN

Well, you see, that's quite similar to things like her lying – uncharacter –

CHRIS

(*interrupting, perplexed*)

Wait a minute. What are you talking about?

KLEIN

Well, she let loose quite a string while I was examining her, Mrs MacNeil.

CHRIS

You're kidding! Like what?

KLEIN

(*looking evasive*)

Well, I'd say her vocabulary's rather extensive.

CHRIS

Well, what, for example? I mean, give me a for instance!

Klein shrugs. No reply.

Hey, come on; I'm grown-up. What'd she *say*? I mean *specifically*, Doctor.

KLEIN

Well, specifically, Mrs MacNeil, she advised me to keep my fingers away from her 'goddam cunt'.

CHRIS

(*shocked*)

She used those words?

KLEIN

She used those words. Look, I doubt that she even understood what she was saying.

CHRIS

Yeah, I guess. Maybe not. You don't think a psychiatrist – ?

KLEIN

The best explanation is always the simplest one. Let's wait. Let's wait and see.

(*smiling encouragingly*)

In the meantime, try not to worry.

CHRIS

How?

INT. MACNEIL HOME. LIVING-ROOM. NIGHT

Full shot: party in progress. A few Jesuits and some of the cast and crew of the motion picture are present. Vibrant hum of conversation. Then a closer angle featuring Burke Dennings. Burke, an empty glass in hand, stands chatting with a silver-maned Senator and the Senator's Wife. Back of them, and to the side, Chris is visible, chatting with the Jesuit

Dean of the college. Karl is approaching the latter with a drinks tray. Burke seems irritable and tautly drunk.

DENNINGS

No, no, *her* part is finished; all the parts with the principal actors, you see; but I'm staying to finish other scenes.

SENATOR

I understand.

Karl has searched Burke's group.

DENNINGS

Oh, how splendid.

(*reaching for a fresh drink*)

Let's have another for the road.

CHRIS

(*brief over-the-shoulder at Dennings*)

The Lincoln Highway?

DENNINGS

(*to Chris*)

Oh, now, don't be so silly.

SENATOR'S WIFE

(*to Chris*)

Fun party.

CHRIS

(*to wife*)

Thanks, Martha.

And Chris returns to conversation with the Dean. During the above, the Senator has mutely refused another drink, but Burke now takes one in his other *hand as well as:*

DENNINGS

(*to Karl*)

Karl, oh, now tell me, was it *Public* Relations you did for the Gestapo, or *Community* Relations? I believe there's a difference.

KARL
(*grimly uptight*)
I am Swiss.

DENNINGS
Yes, of course. And you never went bowling with Goebbels, I suppose.

Front tracking shot. Karl, his face impassive; yet his eyes are angry, as we hear:

(*to Karl as latter moves on*)
So superior, aren't you? Nazi!

The camera follows Karl but holds – as he passes them – on Sharon and Mary Jo Perrin, who are seated somewhere in the room. A bubbly personality, Mary Jo is reading Sharon's palm.

PERRIN
Well, yes, your work line is longer than your heart line. There, you see? And you've recently broken up with a boyfriend. Am I right?

SHARON
No.

PERRIN
I'm really famous for predictions, not palms.
(*dropping Sharon's palm*)
Where's the bathroom?

SHARON
(*rising*)
Upstairs. I'll go with you.

As they move, the camera follows:

PERRIN
Oh, by the way, I brought that witchcraft book you asked for.

SHARON
Oh, thanks.

PERRIN
And another one on Russian ESP. They're in the study.

They walk out of frame as the camera holds on Dennings, the Senator and his Wife. The Senator is turned away from Dennings, conversing in low tones with Wife. Dennings is now composed and as he stares down into his gin glass:

DENNINGS

There seems to be an alien pubic hair in my gin.

SENATOR

(*turning to Dennings, as his Wife splits*)

I beg your pardon?

DENNINGS

(*defensive*)

Never seen it before in my *life*!

SENATOR

(*a murmur*)

Yes, I'm sure.

DENNINGS

(*now accusatory*)

Have you?

Angle on Chris, Jesuit Dean, Mary Jo Perrin. Mary Jo is seated on the sofa with Jesuit Dean. Chris is on the floor in front of the coffee table facing them, as all eat dinner.

PERRIN

On, come on, every family's got one black sheep.

DEAN

Yes, I know, but we were pushing our quota with the Medici Popes.

CHRIS

Say, Father, there's something I've been meaning to ask you. Do you know that sort of wing that's in back of the church over there? The red brick one, I mean.

(*pointing in direction*)

DEAN

St Mike's.

CHRIS

Yeah, right. St Mike's. What goes on in there, Father?

DEAN

Oh, that's where we say Black Mass.

CHRIS

(*as Perrin chuckles*)

What's that?

PERRIN

Oh, he's kidding.

CHRIS

I wasn't. I'd still like to know what it is.

DEAN

Oh, well, basically, I guess, it's a travesty of the Catholic Mass. It's connected to witchcraft. Devil worship cults.

(*looking around for someone*)

Gee, where's Joe? He knows all about this stuff.

He is indicating Father Dyer, who is standing at the buffet, heaping a second helping on to his plate.

Hey, Joe!

DYER

(*turning*)

You called, Great Dean?

Dean beckons him over.

DEAN

(*to Chris*)

They had a couple of cases of desecration in Holy Trinity last week, and Joe said something about one of them reminding him of some things they used to do at Black Mass, so I expect he knows something about the subject.

PERRIN

What happened at the church?

DEAN

Oh, it's really too disgusting.

DYER

Listen, give me just a minute. I think I've got something going over there with the astronaut.

DEAN

What?

DYER

(*raising eyebrows*)

First missionary on the moon?

They burst into laughter as he moves off to join the Astronaut.

CHRIS

He's fun.

(*to Dean*)

You haven't told me what goes on yet in back of St Mike's. Big secret? Who's that priest I keep seeing there? You know, sort of dark? Do you know the one I mean?

DEAN

(*lowered tone, trace of regret*)

Father Karras.

CHRIS

What's he do?

DEAN

He's our counselor, Chris. A psychiatrist. The back of St Mike's is our couch.

CHRIS

Oh, I see.

DEAN

Had a pretty rough knock last night, poor guy. His mother passed away.

CHRIS

(*sensation of grief*)

Oh, I'm sorry.

DEAN

He seems to be taking it pretty hard. She was living by herself, and I guess she was dead for a couple of days before they found her.

PERRIN

(*murmur*)

Oh, how awful.

DEAN

The superintendent of her apartment building found her at four in the morning. They wouldn't have found her even then except . . . Well, the next-door neighbors complained about her radio going all the time.

Two shot. Dyer and Astronaut. The Astronaut is breaking up as:

DYER

No, I'm really not a priest. I'm actually a terribly avant-garde rabbi.

INT. MACNEIL HOUSE. KITCHEN. NIGHT

Chris is bursting in as Dennings continues to rave at a stolid, expressionless Karl who stands immobile, arms akimbo, watching Dennings.

DENNINGS

Cunting *Hun*! You bloody damned butchering Nazi *pig*!

CHRIS

(*over Dennings*)

Karl! Will you get out of here! Get out!

Sharon enters now and Chris has started pushing Karl out. The latter, defiant, permits it only reluctantly.

DENNINGS

What the hell makes you think you're so fucking superior? Goddamned cunting Heinrich Himmler! Get the hell back to – !

Karl is out and now Dennings, in a remarkable performance, is instantly composed and as Chris turns to him after shoving Karl out of the door, Dennings turns to her genially and rubs his hands together with:

Now, then, what's dessert?

CHRIS

Des*sert*!

DENNINGS

(*whining*)

Well, I'm hungry.

Chris reacts, incredulous and exasperated, then turns and exits. Passing Sharon:

CHRIS

Feed him!

INT. REGAN'S BEDROOM. NIGHT

Regan is in bed. Chris is tucking her bedcovers in. The room lights are out and Regan is turned on her side. She has her eyes closed. Chris, finished, looks down at her.

CHRIS

You okay, hon?

No response. Chris waits. Regan appears to be asleep. Chris leans over, kisses her cheek.

(*whisper*)

Sleep tight.

INT. MACNEIL HOUSE. ANGLE AT MAIN STAIRCASE. NIGHT

Dyer and Dean are singing and playing, 'Oh, Lindberg (What a Flyin' Fool Was He)'. Camera goes to Chris holding the front door open for Sharon and the Assistant Director with a barely conscious Dennings being carried between them, heading for the open front door.

CHRIS

Night, Burke. Take it easy.

DENNINGS

(*eyes still closed; a mutter*)

Fuck it!

Chris shakes her head. Then the camera follows her to the piano group, which now includes the Astronaut. Dyer is just finishing the song. Group applauds. Dyer spots Chris.

DYER

Hi, Chris. Great party.

CHRIS

Thanks, Father. Keep goin'.

DYER

(*playing chords*)

I don't need the encouragement. My notion of heaven is a solid white nightclub with me center stage for all the rest of eternity.

(*after amused reaction from group*)

Does anyone else know the words to 'I'll Bet You're Sorry Now, Tokyo Rose'.

Chris starts singing as Dyer delightedly joins her. Then abruptly he stops, staring expressionlessly at something off-screen. Chris, too, stops as Dyer nods his head toward spot off-screen.

I believe we have a visitor, Mrs MacNeil.

On Chris and Astronaut. Chris looks where Dyer has indicated, and as sudden silence falls on the group, Chris gasps in shock and dismay, hand flying to her cheek, a small whimper coming up in her throat. The camera moves to tight on the Astronaut's face as he, too, looks down and we hear:

REGAN

(*off-screen*)

You're going to die up there.

As the Astronaut's face turns gray with dismay and chilling apprehension, we hear:

CHRIS

(*off-screen; anguished*)

Oh, my God! Oh, –

Astronaut's POV: On Regan. Regan, in nightgown, is staring up at the Astronaut (camera), and is urinating gushingly on to the rug.

CHRIS

(*off-screen; continuing*)

– my God. Oh my baby!

The angle widens out to disclose Chris rushing up to Regan and leading her away toward the stairs.

Oh, come on, Rags, come with me, come upstairs!

(*over shoulder to the Astronaut*)

Oh, I'm so sorry! She's been sick, she must be walking in her sleep! She didn't know what she was saying!

Close on Astronaut, staring, shaken.

INT. REGAN'S BATHROOM. NIGHT

Regan sits in the tub like someone in a trance while Chris rapidly bathes her.

CHRIS

Honey, why did you say that? Why?

INT. REGAN'S BEDROOM. NIGHT

Moonlight streams in through open window. Regan, turned toward the wall, is in bed, dully staring at a point in space. Chris sits on edge of bed. Through the window, from the street below, we hear off-screen sounds and voices of departing guests.

CHRIS

Howya feelin', honey? Better?

No response.

Would you like me to read to you?

Regan shakes head slightly, still staring at the wall.

Okay, then. Try to sleep.

She leans over, kisses Regan, rises.

'Night, my baby.

Chris leaves and is almost out the door when she is arrested by Regan calling to her in a low, despairing, haunted tone:

REGAN

Mother, what's wrong with me?

CHRIS

Why, honey, it's nerves. That's all. I mean, it's just like the doctor said. You keep taking those pills and you'll be fine. Just fine.

A long wait for reaction, but Regan neither moves nor speaks.

Okay, Rags?

Chris waits. Still nothing. Troubled and despondent, Chris starts out of room.

INT. SECOND-FLOOR HALL OF MACNEIL HOUSE. NIGHT

The camera is fixed at one end of the hall, and we see Chris exit at the other from Regan's bedroom. Head down, thoughtful, she starts toward us; then remembers something and moves back to lean over the balustrade railing and observe something below for a moment or two. We hear off-screen a scraping sound, like a brush against carpeting: Willie brushing out the urine stains.

CHRIS

(*softly*)

Comin' out, Willie?

WILLIE

Yes, madam. I think so.

CHRIS

(*slight nod*)

Good.

She continues to stare for a moment more, then comes toward the camera again until she reaches the door to her bedroom and enters. She closes the door. A beat. Then, from off-screen, within Regan's bedroom, we hear metallic sounds, like bedsprings violently quivering. They are tentative at first, then insistent. Then:

REGAN

(*off-screen; calling with burgeoning apprehension and surmise*)

Mother?

Two beats. The bedspring sounds. Then, much louder, and filled with terror:

(*off-screen*)

Mother, come *here*! Come *here*!

Chris's door has already shot open, and she's burst out into the hall, racing for Regan's bedroom.

CHRIS

Yes, I'm coming! All right, hon! I'm coming!

REGAN

(*off-screen*)

Mothhheerrrrrrr!

CHRIS

Oh, my baby, what's –

INT. REGAN'S BEDROOM. DOOR. NIGHT

Chris bursts in, continuing as she reaches for the light switch and we hear massive metallic sounds now:

CHRIS

– wrong, hon? What is it? What's – ?

The lights are on, and as Chris stares at Regan's bed off-screen, she breaks off, electrified.

Jesus! Oh, Jesus!

POV: At Regan. She lies taut on her back, face stained with tears and contorted with terror and confusion as she grips the sides of the narrow bed. It is savagely quivering back and forth!

REGAN

Mother, why is it *shaking*? Make it stop! Oh, I'm scared! Make it stop! Oh, I'm scared, Mother, please make it stooooooooooo –

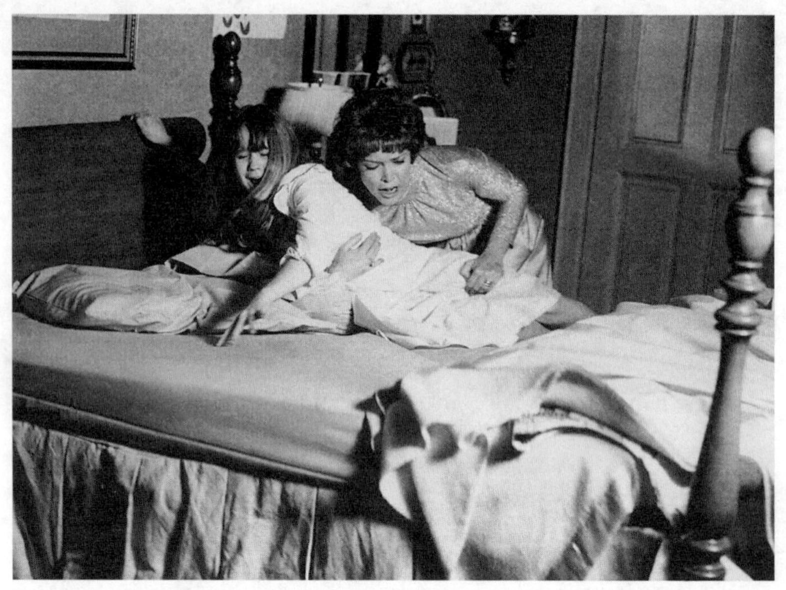

And on her elongated, fearful cry, we break it off before the 'p' sound as we:

CUT TO:

INT. JESUIT RESIDENCE HALL. NIGHT

Dyer enters.

INT. CORRIDOR IN RESIDENCE HALL. NIGHT

Follow Dyer to Karras's room.

INT. KARRAS'S ROOM. NIGHT

Dim desk-lamp lighting. Dyer sits back of Karras's desk wearing a Snoopy T-shirt. Karras is sitting on the edge of his cot, his eyes fixed low in a haunted stare. They are red and raw from weeping. In his hand is a cup containing a small amount of Scotch, and his eyes and voice are fogged by heavy drinking and chronic sleeplessness. Dyer is pouring from a bottle of Chivas Regal into Karras's cup.

KARRAS

Where'd you get the money for Chivas Regal, Joe? The poorbox?

DYER

Don't be an asshole, that would be breaking my vow of poverty.

KARRAS

Where did you get it then?

DYER

I stole it.

KARRAS

I believe you.

DYER

College presidents shouldn't drink. It tends to set a bad example. I figure I relieved him of a terrible temptation.

Karras is nodding slightly, smiling, when suddenly he bursts into sobs.

KARRAS

Ah, Joe.

DYER

(*with comforting gestures*)

I know. I know.

Karras cries it through, the sobbing gradually subsiding.

KARRAS

(*a whisper*)

Ah, God.

Karras at last exhales an enormous sigh, closing his eyes, outstretched on the cot.

DYER

Do you think you can sleep now, Damien?

Karras nods his head along with a throat sound of affirmation. Dyer moves to the foot of the bed, undoes laces and removes Karras's shoes.

KARRAS

Gonna steal my shoes now?

DYER

No, I tell fortunes by reading the creases. Now shut up and go to sleep.

KARRAS

You're a Jesuit cat-burglar.

DYER

Listen, someone's got to worry about the bills around this place.

(*moving softly to desk*)

All you other guys do is just rattle your beads and pray for the hippies down on 'M' Street.

Dyer flicks off the desk light.

KARRAS

Stealing is a sin.

A beat. Then, tenderly, Dyer touches a hand to Karras's shoulder in good night, but as he starts to move toward the door, Karras's hand reaches out and grips Dyer's wrist, squeezing, and giving a little shake in a gesture of gratitude and deep friendship. At this moment, the camera is tight on the hands, but then goes to Dyer, as he nods in acknowledgement. Then Dyer stares down and the camera follows his gaze to tight at the hands again, as healing sleep at last comes to Karras and his grip slackens and his hand falls.

DYER

(*off-screen; whisper*)

Good night, Damien.

INT. HOLY TRINITY CHURCH. VERY EARLY MORNING

Only two or three Worshippers in the church. Karras, in his black vestments, is at the main altar saying Mass. While washing hands at a small table to the side of the altar:

KARRAS

O Lord, I have loved the beauty of Thy house and the place

where Thy glory dwelleth. Take not away my soul, O God, with the wicked, nor my life with men of blood . . .

Another angle. (*Time lapse.*) *Now Karras's eyes are moistening with tears as:*

Remember also, O Lord, Thy servant, Mary Karras . . . who has gone before us with the sign of faith, and sleeps the sleep of peace. To her, O Lord, and to – all –

(*he's fighting tears*)

– who rest in Christ, grant her – we pray Thee, a place of – refreshment – of light – and . . .

(*striking his breast*)

To us also, Thy sinful servants . . .

Another angle. (*Time lapse.*)

Peace I leave you; my peace I give you. Look not upon my sins but upon the faith of your church . . .

Another angle. (*Time lapse.*)

(*hands extended*)

O Lord, I am not worthy. Speak but the word and my soul shall be healed.

INT. DR KLEIN'S EXAMINING-ROOM. DAY

While Klein attempts to administer an injection, Chris and Nurse forcibly restrain a struggling, kicking Regan who is shrieking as:

CHRIS

Please, honey! It's to *help* you!

REGAN

I don't *want* it! I don't – !

Klein leans over, injects needle.

Son of a bitch *bastard*!

She spits in Klein's face.

INT. HALL OF DR KLEIN'S SUITE OF OFFICES. DAY

KLEIN

Well, it's sometimes a symptom of a type of disturbance in the chemico-electrical activity of the brain. In the case of your daughter, in the temporal lobe.

(*a hand to side of his skull*)

Up here, in the lateral part of the brain. Now it's rare, but it does cause bizarre hallucinations and usually happens just before a convulsion. It –

CHRIS

(*frowning over the 'it'*)

Convulsion.

KLEIN

(*faintly evasive*)

Well, the shaking of the bed. That was doubtless due to muscular spasms.

CHRIS

To muscular spasms? Hey, I was on the bed and it even shook with me on it.

KLEIN

Look, Mrs MacNeil – your daughter's problem isn't her bed. It's in her brain.

CHRIS

Yeah, okay. So what causes this . . .?

(*she can't find the term*)

KLEIN

Lesion of the temporal lobe. It's a kind of . . . well, seizure disorder.

CHRIS

Yeah. Look, I'll tell you the truth, Doc; I don't understand how her whole personality could change.

KLEIN

In temporal lobe, that's very common, and can last in some cases for several days. It isn't rare to find destructive, even criminal behavior.

Chris closes her eyes and lowers her forehead on to a fist.

CHRIS

(*murmuring*)

Listen, tell me somethin' good.

KLEIN

Well, now, don't be alarmed. If it's a lesion, in a way, she's fortunate. Then all we have to do is remove the scar.

INT. RADIOLOGICAL LAB. DAY

Series of shots. Regan having her brain X-rayed (arteriogram). Chris and Radiologist present.

CUT TO:

INT. SMALL MEDICAL LAB AND X-RAY ROOM. DAY

We begin close on the X-ray of Regan's skull, then disclose Klein and a consulting neurologist (Dr Tanney) thoughtfully studying several of them.

Tanney, shaking his head, removes his eyeglasses and tucks them into the breast pocket of his jacket with:

TANNEY

There's just nothing there. No vascular distortion at all.

KLEIN

(*frowning, still studying X-rays*)

Doesn't figure.

TANNEY

Want to run another series?

KLEIN

(*turning away from X-rays*)

I don't think so.

We hear telephone buzzer simultaneous with:

(*picking up wall phone*)

I'd like you to see her again.

(*into phone*)

Yes.

RECEPTIONIST'S VOICE

(*urgent phone*)

Chris MacNeil's on the line! Says it's urgent!

INT. MACNEIL HOUSE. SECOND-FLOOR HALL. DAY

The camera is by the door to Regan's bedroom, from which emanate Regan's moans of pain and screams of terror. Rushing up from steps on the landing is Sharon, followed by Klein and Tanney. At the door, Sharon cracks it open and calls in:

SHARON

Chris, Doctors!

Chris immediately comes to the door, opening it. She is extremely distraught and bewildered.

INT. REGAN'S BEDROOM DOOR. DAY

Karl stands beside the door, staring numbly at off-screen sounds, and as the doctors enter, we hear the off-screen sound of something slamming on to bedsprings repeatedly (in addition to Regan's cries).

REGAN

(*off-screen; hysterical wail*)

Moooooootheeeee*rrrrr*!

POV: On Regan flailing her arms; her body seems to be flinging itself up horizontally about a foot into the air above her bed, and then is slammed down savagely on to the mattress, as if by an unseen person, and causing wrenching of Regan's breath. It happens repeatedly and rapidly as:

Oh, Mother, make him stop! Please *stop* him! *Stop* him! He's trying to kill me! He's – ! Oh, please stoopppppppppp himmmmmmmmmm, Motherrrrrrrrrrr!

On Chris and doctors.

CHRIS

Doc, what *is* it? What's *happening*?

He shakes his head, gaze fixed on Regan.

POV: on Regan. The up-and-down movements briefly; then they abruptly cease, and Regan twists feverishly from side to side, her eyes rolling upwards, into their sockets so that only the whites are exposed, while her legs keep crossing and uncrossing rapidly.

REGAN

(*moaning*)

Oh, he's burning me! I'm burning! I'm – ! *Uhh*!

With this sudden sound of pain, Regan has abruptly jerked her head back, disclosing a bulging, swollen throat, and she begins to mutter incomprehensibly in a strangely deepened, guttural tone.

Another angle as the doctors approach. Reaching the bedside, Klein reaches down to take Regan's pulse.

KLEIN

(*soothingly*)

All right, now let's see what the trouble is, dear. I'm just going to –

And abruptly Klein is reeling, stunned and staggering, across the room from the force of a vicious backward swing of Regan's arm as she suddenly sits up, her face contorted with hideous rage. Now, in a coarse and powerful, deep male voice:

REGAN

The sow is *mine*! *Mine*! Keep *away* from her!

On Klein. He stares off-screen, stunned, as Karl and Tanney kneel to his assistance.

KLEIN

I'm all right.

They look toward Regan as we hear from off-screen a yelping laugh gushing up in her throat.

On Regan. Her head is tilted back. The laugh continues, demonic. Then she falls to her back as if someone has pushed her down. She pulls back her nightgown with:

REGAN

Fuck me, fuck –

On Regan. Sitting up, she begins to caress her own arms sensually as she croons in that guttural, coarse, male voice:

Ah, my flower . . . my pearl . . .

Abruptly she falls on to her back again as if from a shove, and cries out with a wrench of breath. Then abruptly she is sitting up again, as if pulled by the hands, and:

(*normal voice*)

Oh, Mother! Mother – !

Another sudden cry, and then she is bending at the waist, whirling her torso around in rapid, strenuous circles.

(*weeping*)

Oh, *stop* him, please *stop* him! It hurts! Make him *stop*! Make him *stop*! I can't breaaaaaaathe!

On Chris.

CHRIS

Oh, my God, oh, my – !

On Regan. Before she finishes her cry, she again appears to be shoved savagely on to her back, and as Tanney comes beside the bed and observes, her eyes roll upward into their sockets and again she begins muttering incomprehensibly in that thickened voice. Tanney leans closer to try to make it out, frowning.

On Klein. He is by the large window overlooking steps, preparing a hypodermic injection.

KLEIN

Sam!

He beckons Tanney over to him with a move of the head and continues preparing the hypodermic. We hear the off-screen, fevered gibberish from Regan. Tanney comes into frame.

I'm giving her Librium. You're going to have to hold her.

They look quickly toward:

REGAN

(*off-screen; terrified*)

Oh, no! No! Captain Howdy, – !

Regan slamming up and down off the bed again.

Mother! Mother! Motherrrrrrrr!

QUICK CUT TO:

On Chris. Over Regan's prolonged scream of pain and terror, Chris, with fists to her temples, turns to shriek at doctors:

CHRIS

God almighty, will you *do* something! Help her! Help – !

On doctors. Klein is ready. And over:

(*off-screen; continuing*)

– herrrrrrrrrrrrrr . . . !

and Regan's continuing scream from off-screen, Klein grimly nods to Tanney. And as they start toward bed with both Chris and Regan's cries persisting we

QUICK CUT TO:

INT. MACNEIL HOUSE. SECOND-FLOOR HALL. DAY

Blessed silence. Chris and Sharon have heads lowered waiting by the balustrade. Klein and Tanney exit Regan's room and approach them. Chris dabs at her nose with a moist, balled-up handkerchief, her eyes red from crying.

KLEIN

She's heavily sedated. She'll undoubtedly sleep right through until tomorrow.

CHRIS

Doc, how could she jump off the bed like that?

TANNEY

There's a perfectly rational explanation. Technically speaking, pathological states can induce abnormal strength and accelerated motor performance. You know the story – a ninety-pound woman sees her child pinned under the wheel of a truck, runs out and lifts the wheels half a foot up off the ground. Same thing here.

CHRIS

Yeah, okay.

TANNEY

Same principle, I mean.

CHRIS

So what's wrong with her? What do you think?

KLEIN

Well, we still think it's temporal lobe, and –

CHRIS

(*erupting*)

What the hell are you talking about? She's been acting like some kind of a psycho, like a split personality! What do you –

(*recovering*)

Guess I'm all uptight. I'm sorry. You were saying?

TANNEY

There haven't been more than a hundred authenticated cases of so-called dual or split personality, Mrs MacNeil. Now I know the temptation is to leap to psychiatry, but any reasonable psychiatrist would exhaust the somatic possibilities first.

CHRIS

Okay, so what's next?

TANNEY

A pneumoencephelogram, I would think, to pin down that lesion . . . outline the cavities of her brain. It *will* involve another spinal.

CHRIS

Oh, Christ.

TANNEY

It's vital. What we missed in the EEG and the arteriograms could conceivably turn up there. At the least, it would exhaust certain other possibilities.

INT. MEDICAL LABORATORY. DAY

Lab Technician completes check of spinal fluid protein content.

INT. KLEIN'S OFFICE. DAY

Klein is looking at lab reports and seems baffled.

KLEIN

Dr Tanney says the X-rays are negative. In other words, normal.

Chris sighs, bowing head.

CHRIS

Well, –

(*bleak murmur*)

here we are again, folks.

Klein stares down, shaking his head and frowning in perplexity. Then he looks up at Chris.

KLEIN

Do you keep any drugs in your house?

CHRIS

Huh?

KLEIN

Amphetamines? LSD?

CHRIS

Gee, no. Look, I'd tell you. No, there's nothing like that.

Klein nods and stares at his shoes; then looks up again.

KLEIN

Are you planning to be home soon? LA, I mean.

CHRIS

No. No, I'm building a new house and the old one's been sold. We were going to Europe for a while after Rags finished up with her school here. Why'd you ask?

KLEIN

I think it's time we started looking for a psychiatrist.

EXT. CHRIS'S CAR. NIGHT

As she drives back across Key Bridge.

INT. CHRIS'S CAR. NIGHT

Angle from driver's seat – 'M' Street and 36th. Through the windshield, dead ahead, a crowd has gathered by the base of the steep steps beside the house, and an ambulance is pulling out into traffic. White-coated Medics are running around in a panic. Police car lights are flashing. As Chris rounds off the bridge on to Prospect, the ambulance pulls out and gets just ahead of her, siren wailing. We follow the ambulance for two beats, then:

CUT TO:

EXT. MACNEIL HOUSE. REGAN'S WINDOW – CURTAINS BLOWING. NIGHT

INT. MACNEIL HOUSE FRONT DOOR. NIGHT

Chris enters despondently. Closing door behind her, she leans back against it, looking down in thought, her hand still clutching the doorknob. A beat. The lights in the house blink out for a beat. Chris looks up. They blink out again, this time longer.

CHRIS

Sharon?

The lights come back on.

Shar?

Still no response. Chris starts up the staircase, frowning apprehensively.

INT. MACNEIL HOUSE. SECOND-FLOOR HALL. NIGHT

The camera is fixed by the door to Regan's bedroom. As Chris reaches the landing, the lights blink out again, briefly, then on. Chris has halted, her eyes warily scanning around, then she continues down the hall toward us, and opens the door to Regan's bedroom.

INT. REGAN'S BEDROOM. NIGHT

Full shot. Silence as Chris stands by the door a moment; then she goes to Regan's bedside, and rubs at her arms, as if from extreme cold. She examines Regan, who is still sound asleep.

Closer angle on Chris hugging herself, shivering.

CHRIS
(*perplexed; whisper*)

Shit!

Then she looks toward window; frowns in consternation.

The room. Full shot. The window is open. Chris moves to it and stares for a moment. She closes and locks it. But she still feels cold. She hears the front door opening from off-screen, below, through the open door to Regan's bedroom, and turns toward the sound. We follow her out into:

INT. MACNEIL HOUSE. SECOND-FLOOR HALL. NIGHT

As Chris exits and softly closes Regan's door. She starts toward stairs.

CHRIS
(*calling softly*)

Sharon?

INT. MACNEIL HOUSE. FOYER. LIVING-ROOM AREA. NIGHT

Sharon enters the house with a white paper pharmacy bag in hand.

CHRIS

Hey, what the hell's wrong with you, Sharon? You go out and leave Rags by herself? Where've you been?

SHARON

Oh, didn't he tell you?

CHRIS

Oh, didn't *who* tell me?

SHARON

Burke. Isn't he here? Where is he?

CHRIS

He was here?

SHARON

You mean he wasn't when you got home?

CHRIS

Listen, start all over.

SHARON

Oh, that nut. I couldn't get the druggist to deliver. Karl and Willie are off, so when Burke came around, I thought, fine, he can stay here with Regan while I go get the Thorazine. Guess I should have known.

CHRIS

Yeah, you should've.

SHARON

What happened with the tests?

CHRIS

Not a thing. I'm going to have to get Regan a shrink.

INT. FOYER AREA OF MACNEIL HOUSE. NIGHT

Chris is answering the door. It is the Assistant Director, ashen-faced.

CHRIS

Oh, Chuck. How ya doin'? Come on in.

ASSISTANT DIRECTOR

(*stepping inside gravely*)

You haven't heard?

CHRIS

Heard what?

Sharon enters scene, listening.

ASSISTANT DIRECTOR

Well, it's bad.

CHRIS

What's bad?

ASSISTANT DIRECTOR

Burke's dead.

CHRIS

Oh, no!

SHARON

What happened?

ASSISTANT DIRECTOR

I guess he was drunk. He fell down from the top of the steps right outside. By the time he hit 'M' Street, he'd broken his neck.

Chris puts a hand to her mouth stifling a sob.

Yeah, I know.

(*exiting*)

See you later.

He closes door behind him. Chris leans against door crying while Sharon moves despondently to the foot of the staircase.

CHRIS

Oh, Burke! Poor Burke!

SHARON

I can't believe it.

Chris lowers her brow into her hand, leaning against the door. She shakes her head, exhales.

CHRIS

I guess everything –

She breaks off, staring with horror at something descending the stairs behind Sharon. It is Regan on all fours. She is gliding, spiderlike, noiselessly and swiftly, down the staircase, her tongue flicking rapidly in and out of her mouth like a snake. She halts directly beside Sharon.

(*numbly*)

Sharon?

Sharon stops, as does Regan. Sharon turns and sees nothing; and then screams as she feels Regan's tongue snaking out at her ankle.

Call that doctor and get him the hell over here, Sharon! Get him *now*!

INT. RECEPTION AREA. DISTRICT MORGUE. DAY

A young Attendant has his feet propped up on a desk. He is munching at a sandwich while working a newspaper crossword puzzle. He looks up off-scene at:

Police Detective Kinderman, a portly, middle-aged man; he shows his ID.

KINDERMAN

Dennings.

INT. MORGUE AREA. DAY

Kinderman and the Attendant walk down between the banks of metal lockers used for the filing of sightless eyes. They stop at the other end where the Attendant finds the proper locker and then pulls it out full length. Kinderman removes his hat, staring down.

KINDERMAN

Pull the sheet back.

Up angle on Kinderman and the morgue Attendant, as the Attendant leans over and we hear the rustling sound of the sheet being pulled back. Never changing his expression, Kinderman mutely shakes his head.

ATTENDANT

Could that have happened from the fall?

KINDERMAN

Only from the one at the beginning of time.

INT. CHRIS'S BEDROOM. DAY

Shutters are closed and the room is dark. Klein stands by the bureau, watching. Chris sits on the edge of the bed, as does a Psychiatrist. He is swinging a bauble on a chain back and forth, hypnotically, in front of Regan. He shines a penlight on the bauble so that it glows in the dark. He halts, inclining the penlight beam up, and we see Regan's eyes are closed and she appears to be in a trance. He turns off the penlight.

PSYCHIATRIST

Are you comfortable, Regan?

REGAN

(*voice soft and whispery*)

Yes.

PSYCHIATRIST

How old are you?

REGAN

Twelve.

PSYCHIATRIST

Is there someone inside you?

REGAN

Sometimes.

PSYCHIATRIST

Who is it?

REGAN

I don't know.

PSYCHIATRIST

Captain Howdy?

REGAN

I don't know.

PSYCHIATRIST

If I ask *him* to tell me, will you let him answer?

REGAN

No!

PSYCHIATRIST

Why not?

REGAN

I'm afraid!

PSYCHIATRIST

If he talks to me, I think he will leave you. Do you want him to leave you?

REGAN

Yes.

PSYCHIATRIST

Let him speak, then. Will you let him speak?

REGAN

(*a pause; then:*)

Yes.

PSYCHIATRIST

(*firmly; new tone*)

I am speaking to the person inside of Regan, now. If you are there you too are hypnotized and must answer all my questions. Come forward and answer me now. Are you there?

No response, and after three beats, we hear Regan's breath coming loud and raspily, like a rotted, putrid bellows. The Psychiatrist sniffs, as if at a horrid smell, and then flicks on a laser lamp and shines it up into Regan's face. Chris gasps. We do not see Regan's face, but play off reactions of Chris and the Psychiatrist. Chris lowers her head into a hand, the sight too unbearable for her, and she grips the Psychiatrist's arm with the other in a tight vise. This causes him to extinguish the laser lamp.

Are you the person inside of Regan?

REGAN

(*in the coarse and guttural voice*)

Say.

PSYCHIATRIST

Did you answer?

REGAN

Say.

PSYCHIATRIST

If that's yes, nod your head.

Regan nods.

Who are you?

REGAN

Nowonmai.

PSYCHIATRIST

That's your name?

REGAN

Say.

PSYCHIATRIST

Are you speaking in a foreign language?

REGAN

Say.

PSYCHIATRIST

Are you someone whom Regan has known?

REGAN

One.

PSYCHIATRIST

That she knows of?

REGAN

One.

PSYCHIATRIST

Part of Regan?

REGAN

One.

PSYCHIATRIST

Do you like her?

REGAN

One.

PSYCHIATRIST

Do you hate her?

REGAN

Say.

PSYCHIATRIST

Are you punishing her?

REGAN

Say.

PSYCHIATRIST

You wish to harm her?

REGAN

Say.

PSYCHIATRIST

To kill her?

REGAN

Say.

PSYCHIATRIST

But if Regan died, wouldn't you die, too?

REGAN

One.

PSYCHIATRIST

Is there something she can do to make you leave her?

REGAN

Say.

PSYCHIATRIST

Do you blame her for her parents' divorce?

His question elides into a prolonged gasp of startled pain and horrified incredulity as we go quickly to full at Regan, mad, evil glee in the eyes as now the light drops from the Psychiatrist's hand.

Close on Psychiatrist. In the darkness, we see his mouth agape in horrible pain, his eyes wide-staring. What has happened is that Regan has gripped his scrotum in a hand that is squeezing like an iron talon.

PSYCHIATRIST

Marc! Marc, help me!

Quickly on Chris leaping up and away from the Psychiatrist struggling to wrench Regan's hand away, a hand with incredible strength.

CHRIS

Jesus!

Klein races forward toward the bed; Chris is running, panicked, for the light switch; Psychiatrist, in agony, struggling; Regan 'creature' with head tilted back is cackling demoniacally and then howls like a wolf as Chris slaps at the light switch. The lights come on and we see:

On bed. Regan, cackling demoniacally, is rolling around on the bed in savage struggle with Klein and Psychiatrist, who are still attempting to dislodge her hand from its grip. Grimaces. Gasps. Curses. The bedstead is quivering violently from side to side.

Another angle. Regan jerks upright. Her eyes roll upward into their sockets and she wrenches up a keening shriek of terror torn raw and bloody from the base of her spine as her face becomes her own. Then she falls backwards in a faint.

View of bed. Stillness. Regan unconscious. Two beats. One of the doctors makes a small move at extricating himself from the tangle. Chris crumples in a dead faint.

EXT. OUTDOOR TRACK IN HOLLOW OF GEORGETOWN UNIVERSITY CAMPUS. DAY

In shorts and T-shirt, Karras is running laps. Parked on the road near the track is a police squad car, and seated on a bench at the edge of the track, watching Karras, is Kinderman. From off-screen the sounds of football practice. Karras seems curious, if not disturbed, by Kinderman's presence. When Karras slows to a walk, hands on hips, head down, panting, Kinderman rises and moves to catch up with him.

KINDERMAN
(*calling*)

Father Karras?

Karras turns, squinting into the sun, his breath coming in great gulps. He waits for Kinderman to reach him, then beckons him to follow as Karras resumes his walk.

KARRAS

Do you mind? I'll cramp.

KINDERMAN

Yes, of course.

KARRAS

Have we met?

KINDERMAN

No, we haven't, but they said I could tell; that you looked like a boxer. Some priest from the barracks. I forget. I'm so terrible, awful with names.

(*flashing ID*)

I'm William F. Kinderman, Father.

KARRAS

'Homicide'. What's this about?

KINDERMAN

You know, you *do* look like a boxer. Excuse me, but that scar there by your eye? Just exactly Marlon Brando, it looks, in *On the Waterfront*. People ever tell you that, Father?

KARRAS

People tell you that you look like Paul Newman?

KINDERMAN

Always. Incidentally, you're busy? I'm not interrupting?

KARRAS

Interrupting what?

KINDERMAN

Well, mental prayer, perhaps.

KARRAS

(*stopping*)

Is this about the desecrations?

KINDERMAN

Excuse me?

Karras gives him a skeptical look, then moves on, shaking his head.

Ah, well. A psychiatrist. Who am I kidding? I'm sorry, it's a habit with me, Father. Schmaltz. That's the Kinderman method.

KARRAS

(*stopping*)

Look, Lieutenant, if you want a sick priest, I can help you. I suggest you take a look in the Jesuit Infirmary and at one of the Jebbies there who's ninety years old and is convinced the Holy Spirit keeps hiding his socks to test his faith in the underlying order of the universe.

(*moving on*)

Thank you. That's the Damien Karras method.

KINDERMAN

People tell you for a priest you're a little bit smart-ass?

KARRAS

Always.

KINDERMAN

Maybe always isn't enough.

EXT. UNIVERSITY QUADRANGLE AREA. DAY

KINDERMAN

You know that director who was doing the film here, Father? Burke Dennings?

KARRAS

Yes, I've seen him.

KINDERMAN

You've seen him. You're familiar how he died?

KARRAS

Well, the papers . . .

KINDERMAN

No, the papers, that's just part of it. Part. Only part. Listen, what do you know on the subject of witchcraft, Father? From the witching end, please, not the hunting.

KARRAS

Well, I once did a paper on it.

KINDERMAN

Oh, really? Oh, that's wonderful! Great!

KARRAS

(*drily*)

You never knew that till this moment, I suppose.

KINDERMAN

Father, people can suppose what they want.

KARRAS

Go ahead.

KINDERMAN

It's a free country, Father.

KARRAS

Go *ahead.*

KINDERMAN

These desecrations . . . they remind you of anything to do with witchcraft?

KARRAS

Maybe. Some rituals used in Black Mass.

(*stopping*)

What's that got to do with Dennings?

KINDERMAN

Burke Dennings, good Father, was found at the bottom of those steps down to 'M' Street with his head turned completely around and facing backwards.

Karras is floored; then he turns to meet Kinderman's steady gaze.

KARRAS

It didn't happen in the fall?

KINDERMAN

Oh, yes, it's possible . . . possible. However . . .

KARRAS

Unlikely.

Kinderman nods mutely. They resume walking.

KINDERMAN

And so what comes to mind in the context of witchcraft?

KARRAS

Well, supposedly, demons broke the necks of witches that way.

KINDERMAN

They did. So, on the one hand, a murder, and on the other, desecrations in the church identical with rituals used in devil worship.

KARRAS

You think the killer and the desecrator are the same?

KINDERMAN

Maybe somebody crazy, Father Karras; maybe someone with a spite against the Church, some unconscious rebellion, perhaps.

INT. HEALY BUILDING. GROUND FLOOR. DAY

Karras and Kinderman are approaching us down the long hallway as:

KINDERMAN

And so who fits the bill, also lives in the neighborhood, knows Latin, and also has access to the church in the night?

KARRAS

Sick priest.

KINDERMAN

Listen, Father, this is hard for you – please, I understand. But for priests on the campus here, you're the psychiatrist; you'd know who was sick at the time, who was not. I mean, *this* kind of sickness. You'd know that.

KARRAS

Look, I really know of no one who fits the description.

KINDERMAN

Ah, of course, doctor's ethics. If you knew, you wouldn't tell.

KARRAS

No, I wouldn't.

KINDERMAN

Incidentally – and I mention it only in passing – this ethic at the moment is maybe illegal. Not to bother you with trivia and legal minutiae, but lately a psychiatrist in sunny California was thrown into jail for not telling the police what he knew about a patient.

KARRAS

(*slight smile*)

That a threat?

KINDERMAN

Don't talk paranoid, Father. I mention it only in passing.

KARRAS

I mention it only in passing, but I could always tell the judge it was a matter of confession.

KINDERMAN

Want to go into business, Father? What 'Father'? You're a Jew who's trying to pass; though, let me tell you, I think you've gone a little bit far.

HEALY BUILDING. TOP OF STEPS. DAY

Kinderman and Karras are coming through doors to the top of the steps overlooking the entry circle, the front gates, the squad car below.

KINDERMAN

Listen, Father. Listen, *doctor*. Am I crazy? Could there maybe be a witch coven here in the District? Right now, I mean? Today?

KARRAS

I don't know.

KINDERMAN

(*linking arms with Karras*)

Come on, we'll take you where you're going.

KARRAS

That's all right, thanks. It's just a short walk.

KINDERMAN

Never mind. Enjoy. You can tell all your friends you went riding in a squad car.

KARRAS

Been there, done that.

Kinderman shakes his head ruefully.

EXT. GEORGETOWN STREET. SQUAD CAR. DAY

The car pulls up to the Jesuit Residence Hall and parks.

INT. SQUARD CAR. KARRAS AND KINDERMAN. DAY

KINDERMAN

You like movies, Father Karras?

KARRAS

Yes, I do.

KINDERMAN

I get passes for the very best shows. I always hate to go alone. You know, I love to talk film; to discuss, to critique. Would you like to see a movie with me sometime, Father? I've got passes for the Biograph this week. It's *Othello*.

KARRAS

Who's in it?

KINDERMAN

Who's *in it?*

KARRAS

Yes, who's starring?

KINDERMAN

Debbie Reynolds, Desdemona, and Othello, Groucho Marx. You're happy? What's the difference who's starring, who's not?

KARRAS

I've seen it.

KINDERMAN

You are difficult, Father.

KARRAS

Yes.

As Karras is about to exit, Kinderman grabs his arm.

KINDERMAN

Listen, one more time: Can you think of some priest who fits the bill?

KARRAS

Oh, come on, now!

KINDERMAN

Just answer the question, please, Father Paranoia.

KARRAS

Look, you want me to tell you who I really think did it?

KINDERMAN

Oh yes, who?

KARRAS

The Dominicans. Go pick on them.

KINDERMAN

I could have you deported, you know that?

KARRAS

What for?

KINDERMAN

A psychiatrist shouldn't piss people off. Plus also the goyim, plainly speaking, would love it. Who needs it, a priest who wears T-shirts and sneakers?

KARRAS

(*smiling, exiting car*)

Thanks a lot for the ride.

KINDERMAN

I lied! You look like Sal Mineo!

EXT. BARRINGER CLINIC. DAY

Establishing shot.

INT. ROOM IN BARRINGER CLINIC. DAY

Regan in another fit, in bed and restrained by straps. Clinic Director is in the room with other Doctors observing. They are baffled.

Hospital corridor. Nurse walking to the door to Regan's room. She pauses outside as she hears a curious rapping sound from within. She enters the room. Dim night-light illumination. The rappings have ceased. Regan is sleeping. Nurse checks her pulse, then frowns in wonderment as she spots something on Regan's chest. She parts Regan's pajama top to see better, and as she leans closer, she looks mystified. We now see that on Regan's chest, faintly, the letter 'L', followed by a separation, then the letter 'M', having risen up in blood-red, light bas-relief lettering on her skin.

INT. CLINIC DIRECTOR'S OFFICE. DAY

The room is glass enclosed on two sides, so that we have a view in the background of a traffic of doctors and nurses. Clinic Director and two of the Doctors from earlier clinic scenes are present. Chris sits in a chair, taut and drawn. In the room, a closed-circuit TV monitor showing Regan in the hospital room, in a fit, as:

CLINIC DIRECTOR

People with very, very sensitive skin can just trace with a finger, and then a little while later it shows up. Not abnormal. Why an 'L' and an 'M', of course, we don't understand. In the meantime . . .

Another angle. (*Time lapse.*)

It looks like a type of disorder that you rarely ever see any more, except among primitive cultures. We call it somnambuliform possession. Quite frankly, we don't know much about it except that it starts with some conflict or guilt that eventually leads to the patient's delusion that his body's been invaded by an alien intelligence; a spirit, if you will. In times gone by, the entity possessing the victim is supposed to be a so-called demon, or devil.

Full at TV monitor. (Time lapse.)

CHRIS

Look, I'm telling you again and you'd better believe it, I'm not about to put her in a goddamn asylum!

CLINIC DIRECTOR

It's –

CHRIS

I don't care *what* you call it! I'm not going to put her away!

CLINIC DIRECTOR

Well, I'm sorry.

CHRIS

Yeah, sorry. Christ, eighty-eight doctors and all you can tell me with all of your bullshit . . .

Another angle. (Time lapse.)

CLINIC DIRECTOR

There *is* one outside chance of a cure. I think of it as shock treatment. As I say, it's a *very* outside chance. But then since you're so opposed to your daughter being hospitalized –

CHRIS

Will you *name* it, for God's sake? What *is* it?

CLINIC DIRECTOR

Have you any religious beliefs?

CHRIS

No, I don't.

CLINIC DIRECTOR

And your daughter?

CHRIS

Why?

CLINIC DIRECTOR

Have you ever heard of exorcism, Mrs MacNeil?

CHRIS

Come again.

CLINIC DIRECTOR

It's a stylized ritual in which rabbis and priests try to drive out a so-called invading spirit. It's pretty much discarded these days, except by the Catholics who keep it in the closet as a sort of embarrassment. It has worked, in fact, although not for the reason they think, of course. It was purely the force of suggestion. The victim's *belief* in possession helped cause it; and in just the same way this belief in the power of exorcism can make it disappear.

CHRIS

Are you telling me to take my daughter to a witch doctor?

EXT. STREET IN FRONT OF MACNEIL HOUSE. DAY

Full shot. A limo has pulled up and Karl is exiting the driver's seat and opening the rear door while Sharon exits on the right rear side. Karl reaches in and picks up a small figure (Regan) wrapped in a blanket from Chris in the back seat. While Karl carries Regan toward the door of the MacNeil house where Willie is standing, anxiously watching, Chris exits the car in deep depression.

INT. REGAN'S BEDROOM. DAY

Regan is faced to the side. Sharon is adjusting a Sustagen flask used for a naso-gastric feeding. Karl is affixing a set of restraining straps to the bed. Chris enters, stands by the door and observes. Karl lets the straps hang loose, nods to Sharon. Sharon starts out of the room, pausing for a moment by the door to look at Chris.

Chris moves slowly forward to the bedside and looks down at Regan.

We see now that Regan's face is torn and bloated with numerous scratch marks and scabs. Projecting hideously from her nostrils is the naso-gastric tubing. Karl has finished adjusting the straps. He, too, now looks down at Regan. Two beats. He looks up at Chris.

KARL

She is going to be well?

CHRIS

(*after a beat*)

I don't know.

Another angle. A beat. Then Chris leans and tenderly adjusts Regan's pillow. In the process, she discovers a crucifix under it made of white bone. She lifts it out, examining it, frowning. Then, at Karl:

Who put this crucifix under her pillow?

EXT. HOUSE. DAY

Camera behind Kinderman looking up to Regan's window.

INT. MACNEIL HOUSE. KITCHEN. DAY

Sharon, her coat still on, listless, sorts through a mound of mail and messages. Willie is slicing carrots for a stew. Chris enters with the crucifix.

CHRIS

(*to Sharon*)

Was it you put this under her pillow?

SHARON

(*fuddled*)

Whaddya mean?

CHRIS

You didn't?

SHARON

Chris, I don't even know what you're talking about. Listen, I told you . . .

CHRIS

(*interjecting*)

Yeah.

SHARON

All I've ever said to Rags is maybe 'God made the world', and maybe things about –

CHRIS

Fine, Sharon. Fine. I believe you, but –

WILLIE

Me, I don't put it.

CHRIS

This fucking cross didn't just walk up there, dammit! Now –

She is interrupted by the entrance of Karl.

KARL

Please, madam, there is man here to see you.

CHRIS

What man?

INT. MACNEIL HOUSE. ENTRY HALL. DAY

Kinderman stands waiting with hat in hand as Chris approaches. He shows his ID.

KINDERMAN

I'd know that face in *any* line-up, Mrs MacNeil.

CHRIS

Am I in one?

INT. MACNEIL HOUSE. KITCHEN. DAY

Chris and Kinderman. On the breakfast table sits Regan's sculpt of the bird. It is set among the salt and pepper shakers and is now a decorative piece.

KINDERMAN

(*to Chris*)

Might your daughter remember if perhaps Mr Dennings was in her room that night?

CHRIS
(*vague apprehensiveness*)
Why do you ask?

KINDERMAN
Might your daughter remember?

CHRIS
Oh, no, she was heavily sedated.

KINDERMAN
It's serious?

CHRIS
Yes, I'm afraid it is.

KINDERMAN
May I ask . . .?

CHRIS
We still don't know.

KINDERMAN
Watch out for drafts. A draft in the fall when a house is hot is a magic carpet for bacteria.

CHRIS
Why are you asking all this?

KINDERMAN
Strange . . . strange . . . so baffling. The deceased comes to visit, stays only twenty minutes without even seeing you, and leaves all alone here a very sick girl. And speaking plainly, Mrs MacNeil, as you say, it's not likely he would fall from a window. Besides that, a fall wouldn't do to his neck what we found except maybe a chance in a thousand. My hunch? My opinion? I believe he was killed by a powerful man: point one. And the fracturing of his skull – point two – plus the various things I have mentioned, would make it very probable – probable, not certain – the deceased was killed and then afterwards pushed from your daughter's window. But no one was here except your daughter. So how could this be? It could be one way: if someone came calling between the time Miss Spencer left and the time you returned.

CHRIS
(*hoarsely; stunned*)
Judas Priest, just a second.

KINDERMAN
The servants? They have visitors?

CHRIS
Never. Not at all.

KINDERMAN
You expected a package that day? Some delivery?

CHRIS
Not that I know of.

KINDERMAN
Dry-cleaning, maybe? Groceries? Liquor? A package?

CHRIS
I really wouldn't know. Karl handles all of that.

KINDERMAN
Oh, I see.

CHRIS

Want to ask him?

KINDERMAN

Never mind, it's remote. You've got a daughter very sick, and – well, never mind.

Chris rises.

CHRIS

Would you like another cup of coffee?

Kinderman acknowledges in the affirmative.

INT. MACNEIL KITCHEN. DAY

Kinderman follows Chris toward Sharon's working area. He notices Regan's artwork.

KINDERMAN

Cute . . . It's so cute. Your daughter. She's the artist?

Chris nods.

Incidentally, just a chance in a million, I know; but your daughter – you could possibly ask her if she saw Mr Dennings in her room that night?

CHRIS

Look, he wouldn't have a reason to be up there in the first place.

KINDERMAN

I know that. I realize; that's true, very true. But if certain British doctors never asked 'What's this fungus?' we wouldn't today have penicillin. Correct?

CHRIS

When she's well enough, I'll ask.

KINDERMAN

Couldn't hurt. In the meantime . . .

(*at the front door Kinderman falters, embarrassed*)

Look, I really hate to ask you; however . . .

CHRIS

(*tensing*)

What?

KINDERMAN

For my daughter . . . you could maybe give an autograph?

He has reddened, and Chris almost laughs with relief.

CHRIS

Oh, of course. Where's a pencil?

KINDERMAN

Right here!

He has whipped out the stub of a chewed-up pencil from the pocket of his coat while he dipped his other hand in a pocket of his jacket and slipped out a calling card.

She would love it.

CHRIS

What's her name?

Chris presses the card against the door and poises the pencil stub to write. There follows a weighty hesitation.

KINDERMAN

(*eyes desperate and defiant*)

I lied. It's for me.

(*fixes gaze on card and blushes*)

Write 'To William F. Kinderman' – it's spelled on the back.

Chris eyes him with a wan and unexpected affection, checks the spelling of his name and writes on the card as:

You know that film you made called *Angel*? I saw that film six times.

CHRIS

If you were looking for the murderer, arrest the director.

KINDERMAN

You're a very nice lady.

CHRIS

You're a very nice man.

Kinderman exits. Chris leans against the door, thoughtful, for a moment. Then she moves on.

EXT. PROSPECT STREET. DAY

About to enter police squad car, Kinderman notices it's parked in front of a fire hydrant. He shakes his head.

INT. SQUAD CAR. DAY

Kinderman enters, closes door, stares sourly at the Driver.

KINDERMAN

In front of a hydrant you parked?

DRIVER

I'm in the car.

KINDERMAN

So am I. Proving what? The existence of God or that the hydrant isn't there? You're talking Zen.

The Driver moves the car forward a few feet and it stops with a lurch. Kinderman eyes the Driver dismally, then opens the glove compartment, extracts an evidence envelope, scrapes out something from under his fingernail – paint from the little sculpt he picked up in the MacNeil house – hands it to the Driver. During this:

And now take this to the lab for a spectrum analysis and have them compare it with the paint from the desecrated statue in the church.

INT. MACNEIL HOUSE. KITCHEN. DAY

Chris enters, moves to counter, feels at coffee pot. It's cold. She takes her hand away, stares down, pensive. Then, drawn by the sound of the washing-machine, she looks up toward the open door to basement, then moves to it. Calling down:

CHRIS

Willie.

WILLIE

Oh, yes, madam.

CHRIS

Look, never mind dinner tonight. I'm not hungry, and if anyone –

Her eye has fallen to a book that is lying open, face down, on top of the dryer. In an insert we see the title: A History of Witchcraft. *Picking it up:*

You reading this?

WILLIE

I try, but very difficult, madam.

CHRIS

Some illustrations.

WILLIE

I find in Miss Regan bedroom.

Chris looks up at her. The dryer stops spinning and Willie turns away to take out the clothes. Chris resumes thumbing through the book. Abruptly she freezes, turning ashen. She holds the gaze on the book for a beat; then, numbly:

CHRIS

Willie – you found this in Regan's bedroom?

WILLIE

Yes, madam. Under bed.

Still numb, Chris runs a finger along the edge of a right-hand page, and in an insert, we see that a narrow strip – in the manner of Burke Dennings – has been surgically shaved from along its length.

Another angle. Willie and Chris look up at a sound from above, in Regan's bedroom, of a blow, of someone staggering across the room, of someone crashing to the wall and falling heavily to the ground. This is followed, as Chris races upstairs, by an at-first-indistinct altercation between a tearful and terror-stricken Regan and someone else – a man – with a powerful and incredibly deep bass voice. Regan is pleading; the man commanding in obscene terms.

Angle on Chris from top of steps (second floor). Rushing up, frenzied, while Willie and Sharon stare up from bottom of steps. We hear:

REGAN
(*off-screen*)
No! Oh, no, don't! Don't –!

MALE VOICE
(*off-screen*)
Do it, damned piglet! You'll –!

REGAN
(*off-screen*)
No! Oh, no don't! Please, don't –

And in this manner, the voices continue – and never overlapping – while the camera tracks with Chris to the door to Regan's bedroom.

INT. REGAN'S BEDROOM. DAY

Chris bursts in, then stands rooted in shock, as we hear the sound of the bed shaking violently, and the continuation of dialogue between Regan and the thundering deep Male Voice.

REGAN
(*off-screen*)
Please! Oh, please don't m[-*ake*] –!

MALE VOICE
(*off-screen*)
You'll do as I tell you, filth! You'll –!

Chris has turned her head to stare at:

POV: On Karl. Blood trickling down from his forehead, he lies unconscious on the floor near the bureau. The camera goes to the bed disclosing Regan sitting up in a side view to camera, her legs propped wide apart and the bone-white crucifix clutched in raw-knuckled hands that are upraised over her head. She seems to be exerting a powerful effort to keep the crucifix up, away from her vagina, which we cannot (and will not) see, her nightgown pulled up to precisely that point. We see that her face alters expression to match each voice in the argument, both of which are coming from her! When the deep Male Voice speaks through her mouth, the features instantaneously contort into a demonic grimace of malevolence and rage. Blood trickles down from Regan's nose. The naso-gastric tubing has been ripped out. During the above:

REGAN

Oh, no don't make me! Don't!

REGAN/DEMON

You'll do it!

REGAN

No! No – !

REGAN/DEMON

Do it, stinking bitch! You'll do it! You'll do it or I'm going to kill you!

REGAN

Nooooo!

REGAN/DEMON

Yes, *do* it, *do* it, do – !

QUICK CUT TO:

Close down angle on Regan showing nothing from the waist down as with eyes wide and staring she seems to be flinching from the rush of some hideous finality, her mouth agape and shrieking in terror as she stares up at the upheld crucifix. Then the shriek ends as the demonic face once again takes over her features, and the piercing cry of terror elides into a yelping, guttural laugh of malevolent spite and rage triumphant as the crucifix is plunged down and out of sight at Regan's vagina. The demonic face looks down, and we hear Regan/Demon roaring in that coarse deafening voice as the crucifix is repeatedly brought up and plunged down again, blood now spotting it as:

REGAN/DEMON

Yes, now you're *mine*, you stinking cow! You're *mine*, you're *mine*, you're – !

Chris has raced in, screaming, grappling to take hold of the crucifix. We see blood on Regan's thighs, but never the vagina. The Demon first turns on Chris with a look of mindbending fury. Then:

Ahhh, little pig-mother!

The Demon pulls Chris's head down, rubbing her face sensually against the pelvic area, then lifts her head and smashes Chris a blow across the chest that sends her reeling across the room and crashing to a wall with stunning force while Demon laughs with bellowing spite. Chris crumples against the wall near Karl. Willie arrives, staring in confusion and horror. Chris begins to pick herself up. She stares toward the bed, her face bloodied, and begins to crawl painfully toward it.

Ah, there's my pearl, my sweet honey piglet!

Chris's POV: Moving shot on bed as she crawls closer. Regan now has her back to camera, looking down, and we know the crucifix is being used for masturbation.

Ah! Yes, mine, you are mine, you are –!

It breaks off and Regan/Demon abruptly looks over her shoulder at camera (and Chris), which halts at the sight. The features of Regan's face seem to be those of Burke Dennings. Then it speaks in the British-accented giggly voice of the dead director.

REGAN/DENNINGS

Do you know what she *did*, your cunting daughter?

Close on Chris screaming in horror.

QUICK CUT TO:

EXT. 35TH STREET BRIDGE AND CANAL AREA. DAY

Chris. She wears oversized dark glasses and is leaning over the bridge railing.

Another angle as Chris sees a large, powerfully built man wearing khakis, sweater and sturdy, scuffed white tennis shoes approaching her. She quickly looks away. Though she doesn't recognize him, we see it is Karras. Coming up beside her:

KARRAS

Are you Chris MacNeil?

CHRIS

Keep movin', creep.

KARRAS

I'm Father Karras.

Chris reddens, jerks swiftly around.

CHRIS

Oh, my God! Oh, I'm – ! *Jesus!*

She is tugging at her sunglasses, flustered, and immediately pushing them back as the sad, dark eyes probe hers.

KARRAS

I suppose I should have told you that I wouldn't be in uniform.

CHRIS

Yeah, it would've been terrific. Got a cigarette, Father?

KARRAS

(*reaching into pocket of shirt*)

Sure.

Chris lights up. After a deep exhalation of smoke:

CHRIS

How'd a shrink ever get to be a priest?

KARRAS

It's the other way around. The Society sent me through medical school and psychiatric training.

CHRIS

Where?

KARRAS

Oh, well, Harvard, Johns Hopkins, Bellevue, then –

CHRIS

(*over him*)

You're a friend of Father Dyer's, that right?

KARRAS

Yes, I am.

CHRIS

Pretty close?

KARRAS

Pretty close.

CHRIS

Did he talk about the party?

KARRAS

Yes.

CHRIS

About my daughter?

KARRAS

No, I didn't know you had one.

CHRIS

Yeah, she's twelve. He didn't mention her?

KARRAS

No.

CHRIS

He didn't tell you what she did?

KARRAS

He never mentioned her.

CHRIS

Priests keep a pretty tight mouth, then. That right?

KARRAS

That depends.

CHRIS

On what?

KARRAS

On the priest.

CHRIS

I mean, what if a person, let's say, was a criminal, like maybe a murderer or something, you know? If he came to you for help, would you have to turn him in?

KARRAS

If he came to me for spiritual help, I'd say, no.

CHRIS

You wouldn't.

KARRAS

No, I wouldn't. But I'd try to persuade him to turn himself in.

CHRIS

And how do you go about getting an exorcism?

KARRAS

Beg pardon?

CHRIS

If a person's possessed by some kind of a demon, how do you go about getting an exorcism?

KARRAS

Well, first you'd have to put him in a time machine and get him back to the sixteenth century.

CHRIS

(*puzzled*)

Didn't get you.

KARRAS

Well, it just doesn't happen anymore, Miss MacNeil.

CHRIS

Since when?

KARRAS

Since we learned about mental illness, about paranoia, dual personality, all of those things that they taught me at Harvard.

CHRIS

You kidding?

KARRAS

Many educated Catholics, Miss MacNeil, don't believe in the devil anymore, and as far as possession is concerned, since the day I joined the Jesuits I've never met a priest who's ever in his life performed an exorcism. Not one.

CHRIS

Oh, really.

(*a shaking hand to her sunglasses*)

Well, it happens, Father Karras, that someone very close to me is probably possessed. She needs an exorcism. Will you do it?

She has slipped off the glasses and Karras feels momentary, wincing shock at the redness, at the desperate pleading in the haggard eyes.

Father Karras, it's my *daughter!*

KARRAS

(*gently*)

Then all the more reason to forget about exorcism and –

CHRIS

(*outburst in a cracking voice*)

Why? God, I don't under*stand*!

Karras takes her wrist in a comforting hand.

KARRAS

To begin with it could make things worse.

CHRIS

But *how*?

KARRAS

The ritual of exorcism is dangerously suggestive. And secondly, Miss MacNeil, before the Church approves an exorcism, it conducts an investigation to see if it's warranted. That takes time. In the meantime, you –

CHRIS

Couldn't you do the exorcism yourself?

KARRAS

Look, every priest has the power to exorcise, but he has to have Church approval, and frankly, it's rarely ever given, so –

CHRIS

Can't you even *look* at her?

KARRAS

Well, as a psychiatrist, yes, I could, but –

CHRIS

She needs a *priest*! I've taken her to every goddamn fucking doctor psychiatrist in the world and they sent me to *you*! Now you send me to *them*?

KARRAS

But your –

CHRIS

(*shrieking*)

Jesus *Christ*, won't somebody *help her*!

She crumples against Karras's chest, moaning, with convulsive sobs.

Help her! Help her! Oh, somebody . . .

The final 'help' elides into deep, throaty sobbing.

INT. MACNEIL HOUSE STAIRCASE. DAY

Chris and Karras are ascending the staircase, Karras frowning in consternation at the off-screen sound, from Regan's bedroom, of the demonic voice threatening and raging. When they reach the door to Regan's bedroom, we pick up Karl leaning against the opposite wall, arms folded, head bowed.

KARL

It wants no straps, still.

Karras stares at him; looks at door; exchanges looks with Chris. Then he grasps the doorknob and starts to open the door. He reacts, as if to a noxious odor; then steels himself.

INT. REGAN'S BEDROOM. DAY

Close shot on door. Karras.

He enters, scanning the room; then he freezes, seeing:

POV: On bed – Regan. Arms held down by a double set of restraining straps, it seems no longer entirely Regan but something somehow demonic that now lies on the bed and turns its head to stare at the camera. The

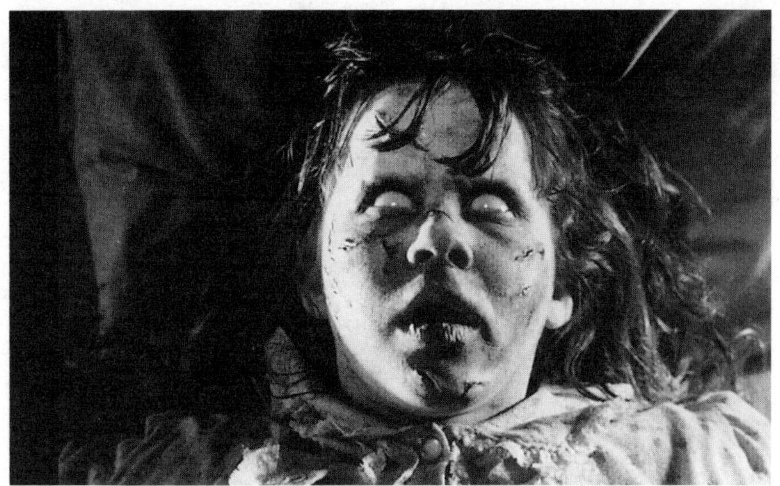

eyes bulge wide in wasted sockets, shining with a mad and burning intelligence. The hair is tangled and thickly matted, the legs and arms spider-thin, a distended stomach jutting up grotesquely. Her face is puffy, scratched and bruised from self-mutilation. In that husky voice:

REGAN/DEMON

So it's you. After all, they sent you.

The Regan/Demon entity throws back its head and roars with yelping, spine-chilling laughter. Karras is momentarily taken aback. Then, reining in his revulsion, he slowly and warily closes the door behind him and we follow closely as he fetches a chair to the bedside.

KARRAS

Hello, Regan. I'm Damien Karras. I'm a friend of your mother's and I've come here to help you.

REGAN/DEMON

Well, then kindly have the goodness to undo these straps.

KARRAS

I'm afraid you might hurt yourself, Regan.

REGAN/DEMON

I'm not Regan.

KARRAS

Then who are you?

REGAN/DEMON

I'm the Devil.

KARRAS

Is that so?

REGAN/DEMON

Oh, I assure you.

KARRAS

Well, then why don't you just make the straps disappear?

REGAN/DEMON

That's much too vulgar a display of power, Karras. Too crude. After all, I'm a prince.

KARRAS

But you won't give me proof.

REGAN/DEMON

Parlor magic? Saw the Devil in half?

KARRAS

Just make the straps disappear.

REGAN/DEMON

It's unworthy. And besides, it would deprive you of the opportunity of performing a charitable act.

KARRAS

Then let's try a different test. Let's test your knowledge.

REGAN/DEMON

How bizarre.

KARRAS

If you're the Devil, you know everything, right?

REGAN/DEMON

No, not quite. *Almost* everything. There. They say I'm proud. As you can see, I am not.

KARRAS

Let's try a question. Where is Regan?

REGAN/DEMON

In here. With us.

KARRAS

Who is 'us'?

REGAN/DEMON

Loose the straps. I can't talk. I'm accustomed to gesturing. I spend most of my time in Rome. In the meantime, I've passed your preposterous test.

KARRAS

Yes, if Regan's really in there.

REGAN/DEMON

Oh, she is.

KARRAS

Then let me see her.

REGAN/DEMON

Very sly. Put her back in control and push me out, is that it?

KARRAS

Oh, well, it's clear you're not the Devil.

REGAN/DEMON

Who said that I was?

KARRAS

Well, didn't you?

REGAN/DEMON

I don't know. Perhaps I did. I'm not sure. I'm not well.

KARRAS

Christ drove demons out of people, not the Devil.

REGAN/DEMON

Ah, that's it, then. Yes, of course. It makes sense. I'm a demon.

KARRAS

Which one?

REGAN/DEMON

(*ominous*)

I do not think you'd want to know that, Priest.

KARRAS

Priest?

Karras starts to say something else, then abruptly half-turns his head as if reacting to an invisible, chilling force at the back of his neck.

REGAN/DEMON

Yes, Karras. Icy fingers at the back of your neck? And now colder? Gripping tighter . . . tighter . . . ?

Karras jerks out of an apparently hypnotic state. The Demon laughs.

Yes, of course, Karras. Autosuggestion. Whatever would we do without the unconscious mind?

KARRAS

(*now wary; uneasy*)

Who are you? What's your name?

REGAN/DEMON

Call us 'Legion', Karras. We are many. A little gathering of poor lost homeless souls.

KARRAS

What's your reason for coming into Regan?

REGAN/DEMON

Ah, yes, that's the mystery, isn't it?

KARRAS

How long are you planning to stay?

REGAN/DEMON

How long? Until she rots and lies stinking in the earth! Until the worms have curled festering garlands in her hair and come crawling through the pus-oozing sockets of her eyes, the little – !

The Demon breaks off, trembling with rage; then falls back on the bed.

There, you see how these straps have upset me, Karras? Take them off.

KARRAS

Well, as I said, I'll con–

Abruptly, Karras breaks off, transfixed upon seeing:

Karras's POV: Push to close angle on Regan. The features more authentically Regan's, her eyes filled with terror, her mouth gaping open in an electrifying shriek of agony that is simulated by a piercing stab of the dramatic score. A succession of different personalities, beings – including Dennings – flash across her countenance.

Close on Karras reacting. He bends head, pinches bridge of nose, as if shaking off a visual illusion. The shriek ends and now we hear the voice of the Derelict in the subway station:

DERELICT

(*voice-over*)

Couldya help an old altar boy, Faddah? I'm a Cat'lic.

Then mocking laughter as Karras looks up in wonder.

Back to scene.

REGAN/DEMON

Incidentally, your mother's in here with us, Karras. Would you like to leave a message? I'll see that she gets it.

The Demon laughs.

KARRAS

(*hooked; a pause before*)

If that's true, then you must know my mother's maiden name.

Regan nods, emitting a teasing groan of assent.

What is it?

Regan shakes her head, her eyes closed, and she lies back with a long and rattling exhalation of breath.

What is it?

Regan's lips begin to move, and she whispers something over and over, a single word we cannot make out. Karras slowly leans his head down close, his ear to her mouth trying to make it out. And suddenly jerks away with a cry as from Regan's mouth there erupts a deafening, angry bellowing, as of an alien steer, that shivers through the walls of the room.

On Regan still bellowing, her eyes roll up in her sockets, exposing the whites. Her neck grows elongated, an enormous goiter bulging in it.

INT. CHRIS'S BATHROOM AND HALL OFF BEDROOM. LATE DAY

Karras's sweater is draped over the shower pole as he washes his hands at the sink. Chris sits on the edge of the tub, anxiously fidgeting with a towel in her lap as she watches Karras. From down the hall, off-screen, we hear varied animal sounds.

KARRAS

But your daughter doesn't say she's a demon, Miss MacNeil, she says she's the Devil himself and if you've seen as many psychotics as I have, you'd know that's like saying you're Napoleon Bonaparte.

CHRIS

Look, I'll tell you something, Father. You show me Regan's identical twin: same face, same voice, same smell, same everything down to the way she dots her 'i's, and still I'd know in a second that it wasn't really her! I'd know it! I'd know it in my gut and I'm telling you that thing up there is not my daughter!

(*she leans back, drained*)

Now you tell me what to do. Go ahead: you tell me that you know for a *fact* there's nothing wrong with my daughter except in her head; that you know for a *fact* that she doesn't need an exorcism; that you know it wouldn't do her any good. Go ahead! You tell me! You tell me that!

For long troubled seconds, the priest is still. Then he answers softly:

KARRAS

Well, there's little in this world that I know for a fact.

Chris stares at him a brief beat, then rises and moves quickly out of the bathroom. Karras frowns, hearing Regan howling like a wolf. Chris returns with a framed photo of Regan and shows it to him.

CHRIS

That's her. That's Regan. That was taken four months ago.

Karras is deeply affected.

KARRAS

Look, I'm only against the chance of doing your daughter more harm than good.

CHRIS

But you're talking now strictly as a psychiatrist, right?

KARRAS

No, I'm talking now also as a priest. If I go to the Chancery office to get permission to perform an exorcism, the first thing I'd have to have is a pretty substantial indication that your daughter's condition isn't a purely psychiatric problem. After that, I'd need evidence the Church would accept as signs of possession.

CHRIS

Like what?

KARRAS

Well, like her speaking in a language that she's never known or studied.

CHRIS

And what else?

KARRAS

I don't know. I'm going to have to look it up.

CHRIS

I thought you were supposed to be an expert.

KARRAS

There *are* no experts. You probably know more about demonic possession right now than most priests.

EXT. MACNEIL HOUSE. NIGHT

Chris opens the door for Karras. He steps out on to the stoop carrying the witchcraft book and a slender box containing a tape-recording.

KARRAS

Did your daughter know a priest was coming over?

CHRIS

No. No, nobody knew but me.

KARRAS

Did you know that my mother had died just recently?

CHRIS

Yes, I'm very sorry.

KARRAS

Is Regan aware of it?

CHRIS

Why?

KARRAS

Is she aware of it?

CHRIS

No, not at all.

Karras nods.

Why'd you ask?

KARRAS

(*shrugging*)

Not important. I just wondered.

He studies Chris for a moment without expression, then quickly moves away. Chris watches from the doorway. Karras crosses the street. At the corner, he drops the book and stoops quickly to retrieve it, then rounds the corner and vanishes from sight. Chris closes the door. And now the camera discloses Kinderman observing the house from an unmarked car parked a little down the street, toward the campus library.

EXT. PROSPECT STREET. NIGHT

Kinderman frowns in puzzlement as he sees something: in the window of Regan's bedroom (the shutters are partially open), a suggestion of a slender figure (Regan?) quickly ducking away from sight. We go back to Kinderman, thoughtful. He does not see the shutter slowly pulled shut.

EXT. GEORGETOWN UNIVERSITY CAMPUS. NIGHT

Low ground fog. We hear a soft, low, eerie wind.

INT. UNIVERSITY LIBRARY. NIGHT

Karras is alone, seated at a small table in an alcove on the lower floor. A single reading lamp is the sole illumination. The table now has several books stacked on it. He is reading from one of them:

KARRAS

(*voice-over*)

'Of the four Jesuit exorcists sent to deal with an outbreak of demonic possession at the Ursuline Convent in Loudon, France, three – Fathers Lucas, Lactance and Tranquille – not only became possessed themselves but also died while in that state of either shock or cardiac exhaustion. The fourth exorcist, Father Surin, whose age was only twenty-eight and who was France's foremost intellectual –

(*a beat as Karras absorbs what's next*)

– became insane and so remained for the last thirty years of his life.

A beat. Then from somewhere in the library an odd, slow creaking sound, like a surreptitious footfall, is heard. Karras looks up warily. He sees nothing.

INT. GEORGETOWN UNIVERSITY JESUIT RESIDENCE HALL. NIGHT

Karras comes toward us, knocks on a door.

KARRAS

Hey, Joe, pal?

From within we hear a chair sliding, then footsteps. Dyer opens the door.

DYER

You wish to make your confession, my son?

KARRAS

I need a tape-recorder, Joe. A cassette player. Think you can get me one?

DYER

(*holding out his hand, palm up*)

Lemon drop.

And as Karras shakes his head ruefully and reaches into a pocket:

Make it two. You want to shake your head some more? We'll make it three.

EXT. GEORGETOWN CAMPUS. KARRAS'S WINDOW. NIGHT

Through the window, we see Karras hunched over a tape-recorder on his desk. He wears stereo earphones.

INT. KARRAS'S ROOM. NIGHT

The tape-recorder is running and we hear:

REGAN

(*voice-over*)

Hello . . .

Whining feedback. Then:

CHRIS

(*voice-over*)

Not so close to the microphone, honey. Hold it back.

REGAN

(*voice-over*)

Like this?

CHRIS

(*voice-over*)

No, more.

REGAN

(*voice-over*)

Like this?

(*muffled giggling; then*)

Hello, Daddy? This is me.

(*giggling; then a whispered aside*)

I can't tell what to say.

CHRIS
(*voice-over*)
Oh, just tell him how you are, Rags, and what you've been doin'.

Karras looks more and more shaken as he listens.

REGAN
(*voice-over*)
Ummm, Daddy – well, ya see; I mean I hope you can hear me okay and – let's see. Umm, well, first we're – No, wait, now . . . See, first we're in Washington, Daddy, ya know? It's – No, wait, now, I better start over.

INT. CUBICLE. DAY

On Karras. In a tiny room used by the Jesuits for the saying of their daily Mass. Standing at the altar, informally dressed, Karras lifts the communion host in consecration.

KARRAS
'Then he broke the bread, blessed it, gave it to his disciples, and said: "Take this, all of you, and eat it. For this – is – My body."'

His fingers, holding the host, tremble with a hope he dares not hope: that the words he has just spoken might be literally true.

INT. REGAN'S BEDROOM. DAY

Close on tape-recorder. A full reel is just beginning to wind on to an empty reel. A microphone is propped in position. Karras sits at the foot of the bed. He is in his clerical robes.

REGAN/DEMON
Hello, Karras. What an excellent day for an exorcism. Do begin it soon.

KARRAS
(*puzzled*)
You would like that?

REGAN/DEMON

Intensely.

KARRAS

But wouldn't that drive you out of Regan?

REGAN/DEMON

It would bring us together.

KARRAS

You and Regan?

REGAN/DEMON

You and us.

Karras stares and then reacts as he feels something cold and unseen at his neck. Then he jerks his head around at a loud, sudden banging sound. Off-screen a bureau drawer has popped open, sliding out its entire length. The Demon bursts into hysterical, gleeful laughter.

KARRAS

You did that?

REGAN/DEMON

Assuredly.

KARRAS

Do it again.

REGAN/DEMON

In time, in time. But *mirabile dictu*, don't you agree?

KARRAS

(*startled*)

You speak Latin?

REGAN/DEMON

Ego te absolvo.

The Demon chuckles.

KARRAS

(*excitedly*)

Quod nomen mihi est?

REGAN/DEMON

Bon jour.

KARRAS

(*persistent*)

Quod nomen mihi est?

REGAN/DEMON

Bon nuit. La plume de ma tante.

The Demon laughs full and mockingly. Karras holds up a small vial of water that he has had cupped in his hand. The Demon abruptly breaks off the laughter.

(*warily*)

What is that?

KARRAS

Holy water.

Karras has uncapped the vial and now sprinkles its contents over Regan. Instantly, Regan/Demon writhes to avoid the spray, howling in pain and terror.

REGAN/DEMON

Ahhhhhhhhhhhh! It burns me! It burns! It burns! Ah, cease, priest, bastard! Cease! Ahhhhhhhh!

Karras looks disappointed. The howling ceases and Regan's head falls back on to the pillow. Regan's eyes roll upward into their sockets, exposing the whites. Regan/Demon is now rolling her head feverishly from side to side muttering an indistinct gibberish:

I'drehtellteeson. Dobetni tee siti. Leafy. Tseerpet reef. Emitsuvig.

Karras is intrigued and moves to the side of the bed. He turns up the volume on the recorder, then lowers his ear to Regan's mouth to pick it up. He listens. The gibberish ceases and is replaced by deep and raspy breathing. Karras straightens up.

KARRAS

Who are you?

REGAN/DEMON

Nowonmai . . . Nowonami . . .

KARRAS

Is that your name?

The lips move. Fevered syllables, slow and unintelligible. Then it ceases.

Are you able to understand me?

Silence. Only the eerie sound of breathing. Karras waits a little; then he shakes his head, disappointed. He grips Regan's wrist to check her pulse; then he draws back Regan's nightgown top and looks with a pained expression at the sight of her skeletal ribs. He shakes his head.

INT. MACNEIL HOUSE. STUDY. DAY

Chris is at the bar. Karras enters.

KARRAS

I'm not hopeful I could ever get permission from the Bishop.

CHRIS

Why *not*?

He holds up the empty vial.

KARRAS

I just told her this was holy water; when I sprinkled it on her, she reacted very violently.

CHRIS

And so?

KARRAS

It's just ordinary tap water.

CHRIS

Christ, who *gives* a shit! She's *dying*!

KARRAS

Where's her father?

CHRIS

In Europe.

KARRAS

Have you told him what's happening?

CHRIS

No!

KARRAS

Well, I think it would help if he were here. It's –

CHRIS

(*over him*)

I've asked you to drive a demon *out*, goddamnit, not ask another one *in*! What the hell good is *Howard* right now? What's the *good*?

KARRAS

There's a strong possibility that Regan's disorder is caused by her guilt over –

CHRIS

(*hysterical*)

Guilt over *what*?

KARRAS

It could –

CHRIS

Over the divorce? All that psychiatric bullshit?

KARRAS

It's –

CHRIS

She's guilty 'cause she killed Burke Dennings! She killed him!

INT. LANGUAGE LAB. NIGHT

Karras and the language lab director, Frank, are listening to the tail-end of the recording of Karras's last session with Regan. Karras is tense.

KARRAS

Well, all right, is it a language or not?

FRANK

Oh, I'd say it was a language all right. It's English.

KARRAS

It's *what*?

Frank is threading another tape on to the recorder.

FRANK

I thought you were putting me on. It's just English in reverse. I've pulled your questions, flipped the responses, and respliced them in sequence.

(*pushing playback button*)

Here, you just play it backwards.

INT. KARRAS'S ROOM. NIGHT

Karras sits in front of the tape-recorder listening to an eerie, unearthly series of various whispered voices.

FIRST VOICE

(*on tape-recorder*)

Let her die!

SECOND VOICE

(*on tape-recorder*)

No, no, sweet! It is sweet in the body! I feel!

THIRD VOICE

(*on tape-recorder*)

Fear the priest.

SECOND VOICE

(*on tape-recorder*)

Give us time.

THIRD VOICE

(*on tape-recorder*)

He is ill.

FOURTH VOICE

No, not this one. The other. The one who will –

SECOND VOICE

(*on tape-recorder; interrupting*)

Ah, the blood! Feel the blood! How it sings!

KARRAS'S VOICE
(*on tape-recorder*)

Who are you?

FIRST VOICE
(*on tape-recorder*)

I am no one.

KARRAS'S VOICE
(*on tape-recorder*)

Is that your name?

SECOND VOICE
(*on tape-recorder*)

I have no name.

FIRST VOICE
(*on tape-recorder*)

I am no one.

THIRD VOICE
(*on tape-recorder*)

Many.

FOURTH VOICE
(*on tape-recorder*)

Let us be. Let us warm in the body.

SECOND VOICE
(*on tape-recorder*)

Leave us.

THIRD VOICE
(*on tape-recorder*)

Let us be, Karras.

FIRST VOICE
(*on tape-recorder*)

Merrin . . . Merrin.

Phone rings. Karras leaps for it.

KARRAS
(*urgently*)
Hello, yes? . . . Be right over.

EXT. PROSPECT STREET. NEAR THE HOUSE. NIGHT

Very late. No traffic noise. Karras is hastily crossing, throwing on a sweater.

INT. ENTRY OF MACNEIL HOUSE. NIGHT

Sharon, wearing a sweater and holding a flashlight, has the door open, waiting as Karras comes up the steps. At the door, she puts a finger to her lips for quiet. She beckons him in and closes the door silently and carefully.

SHARON
(*whispering*)
I don't want to wake Chris. I don't think she ought to see this.

She beckons Karras to follow.

INT. SECOND-FLOOR HALL BY REGAN'S DOOR. NIGHT

The house is darkened. Karras and Sharon are silently approaching. Sharon carefully opens the door, enters, and beckons Karras into the room.

INT. REGAN'S BEDROOM AT DOOR. NIGHT

As he enters and Sharon closes the door, Karras reacts as if to extreme cold. His breath, like Sharon's, is frostily condensing in the chill air of the room. He looks at Sharon with wonder.

Another angle as Karras and Sharon approach the bedside. The room is dark except for a night-light glow. Sharon has the flashlight on now, trained low. They stop by the bed. Regan seems to be in a coma, the whites of her eyes glowing eerily in the dim light. Heavy breathing. Karras takes her wrist to check her pulse. The naso-gastric tube is in place, Sustagen seeping into Regan's motionless body. Beads of perspiration on Regan's forehead. Sharon is bending, gently pulling

Regan's pajama tops wide apart, exposing her chest. Karras wipes a little perspiration off Regan's forehead, then stares at it on his fingers, rubbing them together with deeper consternation. Then he looks up at Sharon, feeling her gaze upon him.

SHARON

(*whispering*)

I don't know if it's stopped. But watch. Just keep looking at her chest.

Karras follows her instruction. One beat. Two. Then, flipping flashlight beam on to Regan's chest:

(*whispering*)

There! There, it's coming!

Karras leans his face closer to observe, then halts, shocked at:

POV: Regan's chest. Rising up slowly on her skin in blood-red, bas-relief script are two words: HELP ME.

Close on Sharon and Karras reacting.

INT. HEALY BUILDING. GROUND-FLOOR HALLWAY. DAY

Karras walks down the hallway toward the stairs.

INT. HEALY BUILDING MAIN STAIRWAY. DAY

Karras climbs stairs and enters Cardinal's outer office.

INT. CARDINAL'S OFFICE. DAY

In the room, Karras and the Cardinal.

CARDINAL

You're convinced that it's genuine.

Karras looks down, thinking for a moment.

KARRAS

I don't know. No, not really. But I've made a prudent judgment that it meets the conditions set forth in the Ritual.

CARDINAL

You would want to do the exorcism yourself?

Karras nods.

How's your health?

KARRAS

All right.

CARDINAL

Well, we'll see. It might be best to have a man with experience. Maybe someone who's spent time in the foreign missions. Let's see who's around. In the meantime I'll call you as soon as I know.

INT. GEORGETOWN UNIVERSITY PRESIDENT'S OFFICE. DAY

PRESIDENT

Well, he does know the background. I doubt there's any danger in just having him assist. There should be a psychiatrist present, anyway.

CARDINAL

And what about the exorcist? Any ideas? I'm blank.

PRESIDENT

Well, now, Lankester Merrin's around.

CARDINAL

Merrin? I had a notion he was over in Iraq. I think I read he was working on a dig around Nineveh.

PRESIDENT

That's right. But he finished and came back around three or four months ago, Mike. He's at Woodstock.

CARDINAL

What's he doing there? Teaching?

PRESIDENT

No, he's working on another book.

CARDINAL

Don't you think he's too old, though, Tom? How's his health?

PRESIDENT

Well, it must be all right or he wouldn't be running around digging up tombs, don't you think?

CARDINAL

Yes, I guess so.

PRESIDENT

And besides, he's had experience, Mike.

CARDINAL

I didn't know that.

PRESIDENT

Maybe ten or twelve years ago, I think, in Africa. Supposedly the exorcism lasted for months. I heard it damn near killed him.

EXT. PROSPECT STREET IN FRONT OF MACNEIL HOUSE. NIGHT

A cab pulls up to the house in long shot. Out of the cab steps a tall, old priest (Merrin), carrying a battered valise. A hat obscures his face. As the cab pulls away, Merrin stands rooted, staring up at the second floor of the MacNeil house like a melancholy traveler frozen in time.

INT. REGAN'S BEDROOM. NIGHT

Regan is apparently unconscious, her features recomposed into her own in the normal state (as happens whenever she's unconscious). Sharon is winding sphygmomanometer wrappings around Regan's arm while Karras pinches Regan's Achilles tendon, checking her sensitivity to pain. During this:

SHARON

Four hundred milligrams in less than two hours! That's enough to put an *army* out!

Karras nods; silently takes Regan's blood pressure.

KARRAS

Ninety over sixty.

INT. ENTRY TO MACNEIL HOUSE. NIGHT

Chris opens the door, disclosing Merrin, face still shaded by the hat, and Roman collar by coat buttoned at the top.

CHRIS

Yes?

MERRIN

(*reaching for hat*)

Mrs MacNeil? I'm Father Merrin.

And now we see it is the Old Man in khaki from the opening sequence.

CHRIS

(*flustered*)

Oh, my gosh, please come in! Oh, come *in*!

Suddenly, Chris flinches at a sound from above: the voice of the Demon, booming, yet muffled, like amplified premature burial.

REGAN/DEMON

(*off-screen*)

Merriiiinnnnnnnnn!

CHRIS

God almighty!

REGAN/DEMON

(*off-screen*)

Merriiinnnnnnn!

Karl steps, incredulous, from the study and Karras comes out from the kitchen. Merrin turns and puts a hand out to Karras.

MERRIN

(*warmly; serene*)

Father Karras.

KARRAS

Hello, Father. Such an honor to meet you.

Merrin takes Karras's hand in both of his, searching Karras's face with a look of gravity and concern while upstairs the demonic laughter segues into vicious obscenities directed at Merrin.

MERRIN

Are you tired?

KARRAS

No, Father.

MERRIN

I should like you to go quickly across to the residence and gather up a cassock for myself, two surplices, a purple stole, some holy water, and your copy of *The Roman Ritual*. The large one. I believe we should begin.

KARRAS

Don't you want to hear the background of the case, first?

MERRIN

Why?

EXT. RESIDENCE HALL AREA. NIGHT

Karras, in his cassock, is crossing swiftly toward the house carrying a cardboard laundry box.

EXT. MACNEIL HOUSE. NIGHT

Karras enters.

INT. MACNEIL HOUSE. STUDY. NIGHT

Karras and Merrin are dressing in vestments taken out of the laundry box.

MERRIN

Especially important is the warning to avoid conversations with the demon. We may ask what is relevant, but anything beyond that is dangerous. Extremely. Especially, do not listen to anything he says. The demon is a liar. He will lie to confuse us, but he will also mix lies with the truth to attack us. The attack is psychological, Damien. And powerful. Do not listen. Remember that. Do not listen.

(*as Karras hands him his surplice*)

Is there anything at all you would like to ask now?

KARRAS

No. But I think that it might be helpful if I gave you some background on the different personalities that Regan has manifested. So far, I'd say there seem to be three.

MERRIN

There is only one.

INT. SECOND-FLOOR LANDING, AT STAIRS. NIGHT

Merrin and Karras, fully vested, Roman Rituals *in their hands, slowly come to the stairs and ascend in single file, Karras after Merrin.*

Angle down hall from outside room as the priests approach. Chris and Sharon, bundled in sweaters, watch them. The priests halt by them; look at them a moment, then:

MERRIN

What is your daughter's middle name?

CHRIS

Theresa.

MERRIN

What a lovely name.

He nods; then looks to the door. The others follow suit.

(*continuing; nods to Karras*)

All right.

Karras opens the door, disclosing Karl sitting in a corner wearing a heavy hunting jacket, a look of bewilderment and fear on his face as he looks toward us. Merrin hangs motionless for a moment.

INT. REGAN'S BEDROOM. NIGHT

Merrin, just outside the door, staring in at:

Regan/Demon lifting head from pillow, staring at Merrin with burning eyes.

Another angle as Merrin steps into the room, followed by Karras, Chris and Sharon. Karras sees door is open, closes it. Merrin goes to side of bed while Karras moves to its foot. They halt. (*Note: The room is freezing. Breath is condensing throughout.*) *A beat. Regan licks a wolfish, blackened tongue across dried lips with a sound like parchment being smoothed over. Then:*

REGAN/DEMON

Proud scum! This time you are going to lose!

Regan tilts back head and laughs gleefully. Merrin traces the sign of the cross above her, then repeats the gesture at Karras and Karl, and as he plucks the cap from the holy water vial in his hand, the demonic laughter breaks off. Merrin begins sprinkling the holy water on Regan, and she jerks her head up, mouth and neck muscles trembling as she bellows inchoately with hatred and fury. Then:

MERRIN

Be silent!

The words have flung forth like bolts. Karras has flinched and jerked his head around in wonder at Merrin, who stares commandingly at Regan. The Demon is silent, returning his stare with eyes now hesitant, blinking and wary. Merrin caps the holy water vial routinely and

returns it to Karras, who slips it in his pocket and watches as Merrin kneels down beside the bed and closes his eyes in murmured prayer:

'Our Father, who art in . . .'

Regan spits and hits Merrin in the face with a yellowish glob of mucus that oozes slowly down the exorcist's cheek. His head still bowed, Merrin plucks a handkerchief out of his pocket and serenely, unhurriedly wipes away the spittle as:

'. . . heaven, hallowed be Thy name. Thy kingdom come, Thy will be done, on earth, as it is in heaven. Give us this day, our daily bread, and forgive us our trespasses, as we forgive those who trespass against us. And lead us not into temptation.'

KARRAS

'And deliver us from the evil one.'

Karras briefly looks up. Regan's eyes are rolling upwards into their sockets until only the whites are exposed. Karras looks uneasy, then returns to his text to follow as Merrin now stands, praying reverently:

MERRIN

'God and Father of our Lord Jesus Christ, I appeal to your holy name, humbly begging your kindness, that you may graciously grant me help against this unclean spirit now tormenting this creature of yours; through Christ our Lord.'

KARRAS

'Amen.'

As Merrin continues reading, Karras again glances up as he hears Regan hissing, sitting erect with the whites of her eyes exposed while her tongue flicks in and out rapidly, her head weaving back and forth like a cobra's. During this:

MERRIN

'God, Creator and Defender of the human race, who made man in your image, look down in pity on this your servant, Regan Teresa MacNeil, now trapped in the coils of man's ancient enemy, sworn foe of our race.'

After another look of disquiet, Karras looks down again to his text as:

'Save your servant.'

KARRAS

'Who trust in you, my God.'

MERRIN

'Let her find in you, Lord, a fortified tower.'

KARRAS

'In the face of the enemy.'

MERRIN

'Let the enemy have no power over her.'

On bed. The front legs are gently, rockingly rising up off the floor!

On Karl rising and hastily blessing himself.

On Chris.

On bed. It comes up jerkily, inches at a time, until the front legs are about a foot off the ground, at which point the back legs come up also. Then the bed hovers, bobbing and listing gently in the empty air as if floating on a stagnant lake, Regan still undulating and hissing.

On Karras, transfixed.

(*off-screen, gently*)

Father Karras.

Karras doesn't hear it. A beat.

Damien.

Karras turns to Merrin. We see him eyeing Karras serenely as he motions with his head at the copy of the Ritual in Karras's hands.

The response, please, Damien.

Karras, still dumbfounded, glances again to the bed. Then he collects himself and looks down at his text.

KARRAS

(*excited*)

'And the son of iniquity be powerless to harm her.'

MERRIN

'Lord, hear my prayer.'

KARRAS

'And let my cry come unto Thee.'

Here Merrin reaches up his hand in a workaday manner and traces the sign of the cross unhurriedly three times on Regan's brow while:

MERRIN

(*continuing to read aloud*)

'. . . Almighty Father, everlasting God, who sent your only begotten Son into the world to crush that roaring lion . . .'

The hissing ceases and from the taut-stretched 'O' of Regan's mouth comes the nerve-shredding lowing of a steer, growing shatteringly louder and louder as:

'. . . snatch from ruination and from the clutches of the noonday devil this human being made in your image.'

Merrin reaches his hand up again (still reading aloud) and presses a portion of his purple stole to Regan's neck. Abruptly, the bellowing ceases and in the ringing silence a thick and putrid greenish vomit begins to pump from Regan's mouth in slow and regular, sickening spurts that ooze like lava over her lip and flow in waves on to Merrin's hand, which he does not move as we now hear:

'God and Lord of all creation, by whose might Satan was made to fall from heaven like lightning, strike terror into the beast now laying waste your vineyard. Let your mighty hand cast out this cruel demon from this creature. Drive out this persecutor of the innocent . . .'

The bed begins to rock lazily, and then to pitch, and then suddenly is violently dipping and yawing. During this, the vomit is still pumping from Regan's mouth and Merrin routinely makes adjustments, keeping the stole firmly to Regan's neck.

During the latter part of the prayer, the bed has ceased its movements and floated with a cushioned thud to the rug, and Karras now stares mesmerized at Merrin's hand buried under the thick and mounded vomit.

Damien?

Karras turns to him blankly.

'Lord, hear my prayer.'

KARRAS

(*turning to the bed*)

'And let my cry come unto Thee.'

Now Merrin takes a step back and jolts the room with the lash of his voice as he commands:

MERRIN

'I cast you out, unclean spirit, along with every satanic power of the enemy! Every specter from hell! Every savage companion! It is Christ who commands you, He who flung you headlong from the heights of Heaven! You robber of life! You corrupter of justice! You inventor of every obscenity!'

As Merrin speaks, Regan ceases vomiting, Karras moves slowly around to bedside and reaches down, checking Regan's pulse. She is silent and unmoving. Into icy air, thin mists of vapor waft upward from the vomit like a reeking offering. And now Karras lifts his eyes, staring, as with nightmare slowness, a fraction at a time, Regan's head turns toward

him, swiveling like a mannequin's and creaking with the sound of a rusted mechanism until the dread and glaring whites of the eyes are fixed directly on Karras. And now Karras glances up warily as the lights in the room begin flickering, dimming, then fade to an eerie, pulsing amber. Regan turns back toward Merrin, and now a muffled pounding jolts the room; then another; and another, and then steadily, the splintering sound of throbbing at a ponderous rate like the beating of a heart that is massive and diseased.

(*off-screen*)

'Why do you stand and resist, knowing as you must that Christ the Lord brings your plans to nothing. He has already stripped you of your powers and laid waste your kingdom. He has cast you forth into the outer darkness. To what purpose do you brazenly refuse? For you are guilty before almighty God, whose laws you have transgressed. You are guilty before His Son, our Lord Jesus Christ, whom you dared to nail to the cross. You are guilty before the whole human race.'

(*oblivious*)

'Depart, you monster! Your place is in solitude! Your abode is in a nest of vipers! Get down and crawl with them! It is God Himself who commands you . . . '

Merrin continues and now the poundings begin to come steadily louder, faster, until Sharon cries out, pressing fists against her ears as the poundings grow deafening and now suddenly accelerate to a terrifying tempo. And then abruptly the poundings cease and Merrin's prayer comes through clear in the silence.

'Oh, God of heaven and earth, God of the angels and archangels . . .'

Over the continued recitation, we hear the return of the Demon as the flickering haze grows gradually brighter.

REGAN/DEMON
(*raging at Merrin*)
Hypocrites!

Liar! Proud bastard! Go back to the mountain top and speak to your only equal!

MERRIN
(*off screen*)
'God who has power to bestow life after death and rest after toil. I humbly entreat you to deliver this servant of yours, Regan Teresa MacNeil, from the unclean spirit.'

On Merrin.

MERRIN

'I adjure you, ancient serpent, by the judge of the living and the dead, by your . . .'

Angle on Regan. As Merrin continues, off-screen, Regan begins to emit various animal noises, and Karras, a hypodermic syringe in one hand, moves to the bedside, nodding for Chris and Sharon to approach. As he does, the Dennings personality takes over in Regan, turning to plead with Karras:

REGAN/DENNINGS

Good Christ, Karras! What in thunderation are you *doing*? Can't you see the little bitch should be in hospital? She belongs in a madhouse! Now *really*! Let's stop all this mumbo-jumbo! If she dies, you know, it's *your* fault! Just because *he's* stubborn –
(*indicating Merrin*)
– doesn't mean *you* should behave like a snot! And anyway, it simply isn't fair to drive us out! I mean, speaking for myself,

it's only justice I should be where I am. The little bitch! I was minding my business at the bar that night when I thought I heard the little slut moaning, so I went upstairs to see what was the matter – swear to God, it was for no other reason! *None*! – and she bloody well took me by my bloody ruddy throat! Christ, I've never in my *life* seen such strength! Screamed I'd diddled her mother or some such, and saying that I'd caused the divorce. It wasn't clear. But I tell you, love, she pushed me out the window! Yes, she did. Now you really think it's fair to chuck me out? You think it's – ?

The entity breaks off, jerking her head toward Chris, as Chris and Sharon come to the bedside.

REGAN/DEMON

Ah, the mother of piglet! Yes, come see your handiwork, sow!

While Sharon and Chris pin Regan's arms, Karras administers the injection.

(*to Chris*)

See the puke! See the murderous bitch! Are you pleased! It is *you* who has done it! Yes, you with your career before her, before *husband*, before – !

KARRAS	REGAN/DEMON
(*to Chris*) All right, swab it! Swab the arms! Over here! (*as Chris moves*) And don't listen! Don't – !	– anything! The *divorce* is the cause of her illness! Go to priests, will you! Priests will not help! She is mad! You have driven her to madness and to murder! You have driven her into her grave! She – !

And now the Demon has jerked its head around to Karras, eyes bulging with fury.

REGAN/DEMON

And *you*, bastard! *You!*

Chris has swabbed Regan's arm and as Karras flicks the needle into wasted flesh:

KARRAS
(*to Chris*)

Now get out!

As Chris flees the room we are:

On Demon.

REGAN/DEMON

Yes, we *know* of your kindness to *mothers*!

On Karras. His head is lowered as he extracts the needle, and we hear the off-screen mocking laughter of the Demon. Karras blanches and for a moment does not move.

MERRIN
(*continuing adjuration*)

'The mystery of the Cross commands you! The faith of the saints and the martyrs commands you! The blood of Christ commands you! The prayers of – '

Merrin breaks off and looks up at hearing the Demon cry in sudden pain, as well as anger. He repeats the line that produced this effect:

'The blood of Christ commands you!'

Same reaction; greater.

'The blood of Christ commands you.'

Midway through the word 'command', however, a prolonged howl of pain and rage from:

REGAN/DEMON

Daaaammmmn youuuuu, Merrrriiinnnn!

But the cry of 'Merrin' gives way to a prolonged exhalation of breath, almost as in death. And now from Regan comes the slow, lilting singing – in a sweet clear voice like a choirboy's – of a hymn sung at Catholic benediction: 'Tantum Ergo'.

On Regan/Demon. The whites of the eyes are exposed. The singing.

A full angle on Regan, Karras as Merrin appears with a towel. He wipes the vomit from Regan's face with tender, weary movements. Sharon enters the room and comes to the bed. She takes the towel from Merrin's hands.

SHARON

I'll finish that, Father.

Karras checks Regan's pulse.

KARRAS

(*to Sharon*)

Clean her up, please, and give her half of a twenty-five milligram Compazine suppository.

EXT. HALL OUTSIDE REGAN'S BEDROOM. NIGHT

From within the bedroom we hear the sweet singing of another hymn: 'Panis Angelicus', and in the dimness, Merrin and Karras lean wearily against the wall opposite the door to the room. Karras is staring at it. Then, he begins a hesitant dialogue that will continue in hushed tones, almost whispers:

KARRAS

If it's possession, why her? Why this girl?

MERRIN

Who can know? Who can really hope to know. Yet I think – the demon's target is not the possessed; it is us . . . the observers . . . every person in this house. And I think – I think the point is to make us despair, to reject our own humanity, Damien, to see ourselves as ultimately bestial, as ultimately vile and putrescent; without dignity, ugly and unworthy. And there lies the heart of it, perhaps: in worthiness. For I think belief in God is not a matter of reason at all; I think that it is finally a matter of love: of accepting the possibility that God could love *us*.

Merrin looks up at the door and listens to the singing for a moment. Then he continues:

Yet even from this . . . from evil . . . will come good. In some way. In some way that we may never understand or ever see. Perhaps evil is the crucible of goodness . . . so that perhaps even Satan . . . Satan, in spite of himself . . . somehow serves to work out the will of God.

It has an impact. Karras thinks. Then:

KARRAS

Once the demon is driven out – what's to keep it from coming back in?

MERRIN

I don't know. Yet it never seems to happen. Never.

He puts a hand to his face, tightly pinching at the corners of his eyes.

Damien . . . what a wonderful name.

There is exhaustion in his voice. And something else, something like repression of pain. Abruptly, Merrin pushes himself away from the wall, and with his face still hidden in his hand:

(*softly*)

Please excuse me.

Merrin hurries down the hall out of sight of Karras, then takes out a pill box, extracts a nitroglycerine tablet and places it under his tongue. Karras turns to the door as Sharon emerges with a bundle of fouled bedding and clothing. Karras takes a deep breath and enters.

INT. REGAN'S BEDROOM. NIGHT

Regan sleeps but Karras's frosty breath tells us the air in the room is still icy. He shivers. Then he walks to the bedside, reaches down and grips Regan's wrist to take her pulse. As he stares at the sweepsecond hand of the wristwatch, we are close at Karras and we hear the voice of Karras's Mother.

REGAN/MOTHER

(*off-screen*)

You leave me to be priest, Dimmy. Send me institution. Why? Why you do dis?

Karras is almost trembling with the effort to keep from looking at Regan's face. And now the voice grows frightened and tearfully imploring.

You always good boy, Dimmy. Please! I am 'fraid! Please don't chase me outside, Dimmy! *Please!*

KARRAS

(*vehement whisper*)

You're not my mother!

REGAN/MOTHER

Dimmy, *please*!

KARRAS

You're not my – !

Intercut: Regan and Karras as the demonic entity now returns, raging:

REGAN/DEMON

Won't you face the truth! You believe what Merrin tells you? You believe him to be holy? Well, he is not! And I will prove it! I will prove it by killing the piglet!

(*grinning*)

Feel her pulse, Karras! Feel it!

Karras looks down at the wrist still gripped in his hand.

Somewhat rapid, Karras? Yes. But what else? As, yes, feeble.

As Karras leans quickly to his medical bag and extracts a stethoscope.

(*a laugh; then as Karras puts instrument to chest*)

Listen, Karras! Listen! Listen, well!

Karras looks very worried. Demon laughs. Then, as Merrin enters:

I will not let her sleep!

The Demon puts its head back in prolonged, hideous laughter, Karras staring numbly. Merrin comes to the bedside and looks at Regan, then at Karras's stunned expression.

MERRIN

What is it?

KARRAS

Her heart's begun to work inefficiently, Father. If she doesn't get rest soon, she'll die from cardiac exhaustion.

MERRIN

(*alarmed*)

Can't you give her something? Drugs?

KARRAS

No, she might go into coma. If her blood pressure drops any more . . .

EXT. HOUSE ACROSS POTOMAC. SUNRISE

INT. REGAN'S BEDROOM. DAWN

Merrin is fighting sleep. Regan is grunting like a pig, whites of eyes exposed. Karras is checking Regan's heartbeat, and then her pulse, and then wraps black sphygmomanometer cloth around Regan's arm to take a blood-pressure reading. Both priests have blankets draped over their shoulders. Their breath is condensing in the frosty air of the room.

REGAN/MOTHER

I not good to you, Dimmy? Why you leave me to die all alone?

Merrin is at Karras's side, clutching at his arm and trying to draw him away, Karras resisting, his gaze fixed trancelike on the off-screen face.

MERRIN

Damien!

REGAN/MOTHER

Why, Dimmy?

MERRIN

Go and rest for a while!

On Regan. The features and eyes are subtly reminiscent of Karras's mother, but vividly evident is the large, circular mole that the mother had on her right cheek.

REGAN/MOTHER

Dimmy, *please*!

MERRIN

Go and rest!

Reluctantly, Karras leaves. Merrin, after a beat, turns to Regan. The demonic entity reappears.

REGAN/DEMON

(*seething whisper*)

You will lose!

INT. MACNEIL HOUSE. KITCHEN. LATE DAY

Chris is sitting at the breakfast nook looking at an album of photographs. She's on the verge of tears. Karras enters the kitchen, pauses as he sees Chris.

CHRIS

(*a sniffle*)

There's coffee there, Father.

Chris moves quickly past Karras with her face averted.

Excuse me.

She exits the kitchen. Karras's gaze shifts to the album. We see that these are candid photos of Regan. In one photograph, she is blowing out candles on a birthday cake. In another, she is sitting on a lake-front dock in shorts and T-shirt with 'Camp Brown Ledge' stencilled on the front. Karras is deeply affected. Close to a breakdown, he puts a trembling hand to brow, with a fervently whispered, desperate:

KARRAS

God . . . God help . . .

The camera follows him as he leaves the kitchen. Passing the living-room, he hears sobbing from within. Looking in, he sees Chris on the sofa convulsively weeping. Sharon, beside her, is comforting her.

INT. MACNEIL HOUSE. FOYER. LATE. DAY

Chris hears the front-door chimes. She reacts; waits. They ring again. She goes to answer. She opens the door, disclosing Kinderman.

KINDERMAN

I'm so sorry to dis–

He halts, eyeing her bruise. Chris knows what he's staring at. She puts a hand to the bruise. He stares for a beat. Then:

Look, I'm sorry to disturb you at this hour of the night, but

I'm afraid that I'm going to have to talk to your daughter, Mrs MacNeil, and I'd like to take a look at her room, if you don't mind.

CHRIS

Regan's bedroom?

KINDERMAN

Yes, immediately, please. I have a warrant.

CHRIS

Oh, please, not now! She's gotten worse, Lieutenant. Please! Please, not now!

INT. MACNEIL HOUSE. SECOND-FLOOR HALL. NIGHT

Karras enters Regan's bedroom and walks wearily to the chair where he had been sitting beside Merrin. During the above moves:

REGAN/DEMON

(*off-screen*)

. . . would have lost! Would have lost and you *knew* it, Merrin! *Bastard!*

Regan on bed. Merrin, limp and disjointed, lies sprawled face-down on floor on far side of bed and beside it. Regan/Demon cranes head over side of bed at him, croaking inchoately with rage and frustration.

Another angle as Karras rushes to Merrin, kneeling beside him, and turning him over, disclosing bluish coloration of Merrin's face.

(*off-screen*)

Die, will you? Die? Karras, heal him! Heal him! Bring him back that we may finishhhhhh itttttt!

And now inchoate croakings and moans of rage and frustration from off-screen, as Karras feels for Merrin's pulse and in a wrenching, stabbing instinct of anguish realizes that Merrin is dead.

KARRAS

(*groaning in a whisper*)

Ah, God no!

Karras sags back on his heels, an aching moan of grief rising up in his

throat as he shuts his eyes fiercely and shakes his head in despair. Then:

No!

Karras's eyes fix on something on the floor around Merrin: the pill box and a scattering of nitroglycerine pills. Karras begins gently and tenderly to place Merrin's hands on his chest in the form of a cross. An enormous, mucoid glob of yellowish spittle hits the dead man's eye.

On Regan/Demon.

REGAN/DEMON
(*mocking*)

The last rites!

Then it puts back its head and laughs long, and wildly, through:

KARRAS

You son-of-a-bitch! You murdering bastard!

A projectile stream of vomit from off-screen strikes his face, but he is oblivious.

Yes, you're very good with children! Well, come on! Let's see you try something bigger!

Karras has his hands out like great fleshy hooks, beckoning, challenging.

Come on! Try me! Take *me*! Come into *me*!

On Regan/Demon. In the demonic features now, a trembling, wild-eyed rage; a fearsome struggle over some irresistibly tempting decision that the Demon is fighting against.

On Karras as he breaks off, his body jerking as if seized suddenly by some inner force alien to him. Yet his features do not change as his hands go to his throat and he struggles to his feet. His actions are those of a man who either has been possessed by or thinks he has been possessed by the Demon, but who also is fighting for control of his own organism. And now here, suddenly, on a move toward the bed and Regan (who, if she is in shot, is unconscious, her face in shadow), Karras's features briefly contort into those of the Demon Pazuzu, but then return to normal again on a backward jerk by Karras as:

No!

The Demon – in Karras's body – had moved to kill Regan; but Karras has won control now long enough to reach the window, rip the shutters off their hinges and leap out.

EXT. MACNEIL HOUSE. NIGHT

Karras hurtles out of the window.

Angle from near Regan's bedroom door as Chris, Sharon and Kinderman rush toward us.

INT. REGAN'S BEDROOM. NIGHT

Chris, Sharon and Kinderman burst in, halt. Sharon rushes forward toward window.

On Merrin as Chris rushes to him, kneels down by him, then reacts with shock.

CHRIS

Sharon! Come here! Quick, come – !

On Sharon and Kinderman staring down from the window. Hands to the sides of her face, Sharon is screaming.

POV: On Karras in street below.

Angle to include Chris and Kinderman as Sharon runs toward the door.

CHRIS

Shar, what is it!

SHARON

(*running out*)

Father Karras!

Chris rises and runs trembling toward the window.

On Chris and Kinderman from exterior window. Looking down, Chris freezes at what she sees. Then from behind her, in a small, wan voice calling tearfully:

REGAN

(*off-screen*)

Mother?

Chris half turns her head.

Mother, what's happening?

On Chris and Kinderman from interior room as they turn toward Regan.

(*off-screen*)

Oh, please! Please, come here!

On Regan. The real Regan, weeping in helpless confusion and fear.

Mother, please! I'm afraid!

Another angle as Chris rushes forward to Regan, arms outstretched, and weeping:

CHRIS

Rags! Oh, my baby, my baby!

She is on the bed and embracing her daughter.

EXT. 'HITCHCOCK' STEPS AREA ON 'M' STREET. NIGHT

Gathering of Passers-by at an accident scene. A Policeman shepherds them back. Dyer, followed by Sharon, is frantically pushing through as:

FIRST PASSER-BY

What happened?

SECOND PASSER-BY

Some guy fell down the steps.

POLICEMAN

Come on, now, move it back, folks. Give him air. Let him breathe.

Dyer has pushed through almost to the Policeman.

DYER

Let me through, please! Coming through! Coming –!

POV: On Karras. He lies crumpled and twisted in a pool of blood. Dyer kneels to him.

On Dyer and Karras. Low angle.

Damien . . . Can you talk?

Karras slowly and painfully reaches out his hand to Dyer's wrist and grips it, briefly squeezing. Fighting back the tears, Dyer leans his mouth close to Karras's ear.

Do you want to make your confession now, Damien?

Karras squeezes Dyer's wrist.

Are you sorry for all of the sins of your life and for having offended almighty God?

A squeeze. And now Dyer leans back and slowly traces the sign of the cross over Karras, reciting the words of absolution:

Ego te absolvo in nomine Patris, et Filii, et Spiritus Sancti. Amen.

On Dyer as he again leans over with his mouth close to Karras's ear.

Are you – ?

He halts, slightly turning his head towards his wrist.

Close on Dyer's wrist gripped by Karras. The grip slackens, the hand slowly opening, then falling limp.

Angle on Dyer and Karras. Slowly and tenderly, Dyer slips the eyelids down as we hear the wailing siren of an approaching ambulance. Dyer weeps . . .

SLOW FADE OUT:

FADE IN:

EXT. PROSPECT STREET FEATURING THE HOUSE. DAY

Full shot. Sharon exits the house carrying a suitcase which she places in the trunk of the limo parked in front of the house.

INT. MACNEIL HOUSE. SECOND-FLOOR HALL. DAY

Chris is coming toward Regan's bedroom.

CHRIS
(*calling*)

Hey, Rags, how ya comin'?

INT. REGAN'S BEDROOM. DAY

Looking a little wan and gaunt, dark sacs beneath her eyes, Regan stands by her bed, holding two stuffed animals in her grip as she stares down with indecision and a child's discontent at an overpacked, open suitcase.

CHRIS

How ya comin', hon? We're late.

REGAN

There's just not enough *room* in this thing!

CHRIS

Well, ya can't take it all, now, sweetheart. Just leave it and Willie'll bring it later on. Come on, babe, we've got to hurry or we're going to miss the plane.

Doorchime sound.

REGAN
(*mildly pouting*)

Okay, okay.

CHRIS

That's my baby.

Chris exits the scene, heading for the stairs. Regan sighs with resignation, looking down at the animals.

INT./EXT. MACNEIL HOUSE. FRONT-DOOR AREA. DAY

Chris is opening the door, disclosing Dyer in cassock and Roman collar saying goodbye to Sharon, the latter going to the limo at the curb and getting in as Chris steps outside and:

CHRIS

Oh, hi, Father.

DYER

Hi, Chris. Just came by to say 'so long'.

CHRIS

I was just about to call. We're just leaving.

DYER

Going to miss you.

CHRIS

Me too.

DYER

How's the girl?

CHRIS

Oh, she's great, really great.

Karl passes between them with two suitcases heading for Chris's car which is parked in front of house. Dyer nods a little glumly.

DYER

I'm glad.

CHRIS

She still can't remember.

DYER

Well, that's good.

CHRIS

Funny. He never even knew her.

Dyer looks up, and then so does Chris, their gazes meeting.

DYER

What do *you* think happened. Do you think she was really possessed?

CHRIS

Oh, yeah, you bet I do. I mean, if you're asking if I believe in the Devil, the answer is yes – yeah, that I believe.

DYER

But if all of the evil in the world makes you think that there might be a Devil – then how do you account for all of the good?

Chris's reaction reveals that this is a telling point. Then into the scene comes Regan, dressed to go.

REGAN

Okay, I finished.

CHRIS

Honey, this is Father Dyer.

REGAN

Hi, Father.

DYER

Hi.

(*tousles her hair*)

All set to go?

Regan has begun to stare oddly up at Dyer's Roman collar, some tugging remembrance in her eyes. Willie passes them with Regan's luggage, which she takes to the car to load in the trunk.

KARL

Ready, mizzes?

CHRIS

Okay, Karl.

(*taking Dyer's hand*)

Bye, Father. I'll call you from LA.

DYER

Goodbye, Chris.

Suddenly, impulsively, in a quick and unexpected move, Regan reaches up to Dyer, pulls his head down and kisses his cheek; a quick smack. Then, looking puzzled herself at what she has done:

REGAN

Goodbye.

DYER

Goodbye, dear.

Chris remembers the medal still in her hand. She offers it to him.

CHRIS

Oh, I forgot. Here.

Dyer, who instantly recognizes the medal, stares at it a moment. Then:

DYER

Why don't *you* keep it?

A beat. Dyer sees that Chris's eyes are clouding with tears.

It's all right, Chris. For him, it's the beginning.

Chris holds his gaze, then nods.

CHRIS

C'mon, Rags. Gotta hurry.

As Chris and Regan leave the frame, the camera stays on Dyer, turning to watch them. Then:

(*off-screen*)

Bye, Father!

POV: on car pulling away and moving quickly down Prospect Street.

On Dyer watching. Willie goes back inside the house. Off-screen sound of squeal of car brakes.

POV: on squad car. Kinderman is emerging, hurrying toward Dyer.

KINDERMAN

I came to say goodbye.

DYER

You just missed them.

Kinderman stops. A beat. Then:

KINDERMAN

How's the girl?

DYER

She seemed fine.

KINDERMAN

Ah, that's good. Very good. Well, that's all that's important. Back to business. Back to work. Bye now, Father.

He turns and takes a step toward the squad car, then stops and turns back to stare speculatively at Dyer.

You go to films, Father Dyer?

DYER

Sure.

KINDERMAN

I get passes.

(*hesitates for a moment*)

In fact, I've got a pass for the Crest tomorrow night. You'd like to go?

DYER

What's playing?

KINDERMAN

Wuthering Heights.

DYER

Who's in it?

KINDERMAN

Heathcliff, Jackie Gleason, and in the role of Catherine Earnshaw, Lucille Ball.

DYER

(*expressionless*)

I've seen it.

Kinderman stares limply for a moment, then looks away.

KINDERMAN

(*murmuring*)

Another one.

Then Kinderman steps up to the sidewalk, hooks an arm through Dyer's and slowly starts walking him down the street. Camera tracking front.

(*fondly*)

I'm reminded of a line in the film *Casablanca*. At the end Humphrey Bogart says to Claude Rains, 'Louie – I think this is the beginning of a beautiful friendship.'

Rear shot: Kinderman and Dyer.

DYER

You know, you *look* a little bit like Bogart.

KINDERMAN

You noticed.

The camera stays behind, but is rising. The street becomes busy as classes empty out at the university; students begin to appear in throngs, their laughter and chatter gradually growing as Kinderman mutely puts his arm around Dyer's shoulder and we:

FADE OUT.

The cast and crew for *The Exorcist* include:

CHRIS MACNEIL	Ellen Burstyn
FATHER MERRIN	Max von Sydow
LIEUTENANT KINDERMAN	Lee J. Cobb
FATHER KARRAS	Jason Miller
REGAN	Linda Blair
SHARON	Kitty Winn
BURKE DENNINGS	Jack MacGowran
FATHER DYER	Reverend William O'Malley, S.J.
DR KLEIN	Barton Heyman
CLINIC DIRECTOR	Peter Masterson
VOICE OF THE DEMON	Mercedes McCambridge

Costume Designer	Joseph Fretwell
Production Designer	Bill Malley
Set Decorator	Jerry Wunderlich
Sound	Chris Newman
Special Effects	Marcel Vercoutere
Make-up Artist	Dick Smith
Supervising Film Editor	J. Leondopoulos
Film Editors	Evan Lottman Norman Gay
Director of Photography	Owen Roizman
Director of Photography (Iraq Sequence)	Billy Williams
Associate Producer	David Salven
Executive Producer	Noel Marshall
Produced by	William Peter Blatty
Screenplay by	William Peter Blatty (based on his novel)
Directed by	William Friedkin

Legion

FADE IN:

EXT. WASHINGTON, D.C. SUNRISE SHOT

Centered in the huge orange ball of a mist-shrouded sun, three police helicopters whir toward us hazily in slow motion like giant, apocalyptic insects. At the same time we hear the calm voice of Father Joseph Dyer saying Mass:

DYER'S VOICE

'A light shall shine upon this day, for the Lord has been born unto us.'

EXT. POTOMAC RIVER. DAWN

We are on the Virginia shore looking across the river to Georgetown. Quietly slipping through the other-worldly fog that shrouds the face of the mud-brown waters is a Georgetown University crew team scull. Beyond it, on the opposite shore, the red lights atop massed police cars rotate, flashing red, beside and upon the Potomac Boathouse dock where police and photographers move about, recording and measuring a crime scene.

DYER'S VOICE

'And He shall be called wonderful . . . God . . . the Prince of Peace.'

INT. POLICE HELICOPTER. DAWN

As the jarring sound of the chopper's blades shatters the quiet of the previous moment. We are moving low and fast over the Georgetown University campus, heading for the river, as, talking into his communicator:

CHOPPER PILOT

Hello, Dockside Hunter, sweep completed.

EXT. GEORGETOWN CAMPUS QUADRANGLE AREA. DAWN

Dahlgren Chapel. Its doors are open, and through them we see Dyer saying Mass as the choppers overfly the chapel, zooming past our frame with a tremendous roar. As they do, we hear, continuing through crackling static:

CHOPPER PILOT

Negative finding. Over.

A male voice responds, Police Sergeant Atkins:

ATKINS

Roger. River Repeater, acknowledge.

CHOPPER PILOT

Chopper One confirming, Dockside. River Repeater. Over.

ATKINS

Roger.

INT. DAHLGREN CHAPEL. DAWN

Dyer on the altar saying Mass, assisted by an Altar Boy. With the chopper sounds fading:

DYER

'The Lord is my light and my salvation. Whom shall I fear? The Lord is the Defender of my life.'

EXT. POTOMAC RIVER. DAWN

We are in a high, very long angle from the parapet of Key Bridge. The police helicopters whir in a search pattern over the river, very low, two of them moving in tandem, each along the opposite shore, while the third moves counter to them down the center of the river. On the right, the university spires; the scene on the dock.

EXT. POLICE DREDGEBOAT. DAWN

On dredge mechanism churning the waters. The sound is pounding, grating, fearful – the engines of doom.

Shot inside dredge main cabin.

On the right, a shivering Police Frogman sips coffee. On the left, head down in somber thought, is Police Sergeant Atkins. He wears a black leather jacket, turtleneck sweater and woolen seaman's cap. Through windows between the men we see we are slowly inching under a great arch of Key Bridge, heading for the boathouse and the police activity on the dock.

EXT. POTOMAC BOATHOUSE DOCK. DAWN

The chopper sounds are close by, but their transmissions are low and indistinct, and throughout the sequence we will hear the griefstricken sobbing of a woman as we see, in series:

Massed police cars, rotating red lights flashing.

On the dock – two Paramedics resting against an ambulance, watching. One, emotionally overcome, is dragging on a cigarette, his hand trembling as he lowers it, his eyes welling up.

Crime Team Member (Ryan) collecting hair and dust samples from dock floor with a tiny vacuum cleaner.

Crime lab wagon: standing by it, studying a sketch on a large sketchpad, is police pathologist Stedman. His expression is shadowed by puzzlement and foreboding. He looks up toward the sound of sobbing. The sketchpad shows a crude zodiacal sign of the Gemini.

On Policewoman (white) and black woman (Mrs Kintry). Mrs Kintry is well dressed, refined, early middle age. It is she whom we have heard sobbing throughout this sequence, as we now see. Her face is buried in the shoulder of the Policewoman, whose arms are around her consolingly.

Lt William F. Kinderman, the world-weary homicide detective, is on one knee as he holds up the edge of a canvas tarp while he studies something beneath it which we cannot see. A strobe light's wink washes him as an off-screen police Photographer shoots the lump beneath the tarp. Kinderman's look is one of stunned horror. He can't take much of it, drops the tarp and looks away.

On Mrs Kintry and the Policewoman. Mrs Kintry looks up toward off-screen dredge and begins a prolonged, heart-stopping cry of grief and awful realization.

MRS KINTRY

Ohhhhhhhhhh!!

On Kinderman as he looks up at off-screen dredge, his eyes filled with tears and rage. Mrs Kintry's scream is rising in pitch, building, as we:

Zoom at dredgeboat. The 'catcher' mechanism is rising up out of the waters with a heavily encrusted severed head as:

Tommyyyyyyy!!

The heart-stopping shriek builds, pouring into the engine sound, overcoming it, then bleeds into the sudden quiet of:

EXT. DAHLGREN CHAPEL. DAWN

Faint sounds of activity in the university refectory.

ALTAR BOY

(*off-screen*)

How'd I do on my theology quiz?

DYER

(*off-screen*)

I recommend you change your name to Rajneesh.

INT. DAHLGREN CHAPEL SACRISTY. DAWN

Through door from main altar we see Dyer and the Altar Boy folding and putting away the Mass vestments as:

ALTAR BOY

Father, everything's relative.

DYER

It is?

ALTAR BOY

(*shrugging*)

Or maybe not. Well, that's it. I gotta hurry now, Father.

Extreme close-up: single red rose in slender flower holder.

DYER

(*off-screen*)

Speed kills.

ALTAR BOY

(*off-screen*)

Who's to say?

DYER

(*off-screen*)

Not me.

The Altar Boy turns at door to exterior.

ALTAR BOY

You know, Father, you mentioned a Damien Karras in your prayer for the dead.

DYER

(*sad and haunted*)

Yes, I did.

ALTAR BOY

Father, isn't he – ?

DYER

Yes.

ALTAR BOY

The one who died in a fall on those steps?

DYER

That's right, Tim. Fifteen years ago today.

ALTAR BOY

You hear all kinds of – [stories]

DYER

Philbin, get lost.

ALTAR BOY

(*turning to go*)

I am Flight.

Close on holy water font as Altar Boy's hand dips into it.

DYER

(*off-screen*)

Please drive carefully, Tim.

ALTAR BOY

(*off-screen*)

Maybe so.

We've heard the door open. Now:

On Dyer. He is standing at the preparation table and cupboards, the chalice just used at the memorial Mass glowing softly on white linen beneath him as he looks up at the sound of the door closing, and then down into the chalice and his sadness.

EXT. PROSPECT STREET. VERY EARLY MORNING

Dyer forlornly crosses the deserted street and comes toward us as a Georgetown University crew team – some of them carrying a scull atop their shoulders – come pounding up the steps beside the old Chris MacNeil house, shouting out a cadence and crossing Dyer's path as he arrives at the uppermost landing and stops, then stares down sadly. And now we see, from the priest's point of view, the sinister, sharply angled flight of stone steps that plunge precipitously far down to 'M' Street below, the steps where Damien Karras met his end. A soft gust of wind rises up and blows a section of newspaper into our view down below, then up the steps and out of frame. Like a ghost.

INT. JESUIT DINING HALL. EARLY MORNING

After an establishing cut or two of the activity, we settle on a table where Dyer sits with the university President, an ex-navy chaplain. Around them, a scattering of other priests in various attire, most in their clericals, but a few dressed informally in civvies. While Dyer breakfasts, the President smokes and stirs his coffee, the better drily and inscrutably to react to Dyer's quirkiness. Dyer wears a comic T-shirt. The university President is the only Jesuit dressed in clerical suit and Roman collar. Camera is circling table from rear as:

PRESIDENT

Joey, what did you say that offended Tom Lowry? He's our biggest benefactor.

DYER

Oh, he is?

PRESIDENT

What'd you say to him?

DYER

'Jesus loves you. Everyone else thinks you're an asshole.'

With a soft groan, the President lowers his brow to a propped hand. Here the camera is now front on them and stops as a bespectacled Elderly Jesuit in sweat-soaked jogging attire passes closely by, a towel draped from his neck. His shuffling steps are agonizingly slow, and one hand rests on a hip. With a nod of acknowledgment:

ELDERLY JESUIT

Father President.

PRESIDENT

(*weak and despairing*)

Good morning, John.

ELDERLY JESUIT
(*to himself*)

Back aches.

DYER
(*with a sidelong glance at the Elderly Jesuit*)

Do we *really* have to have our own Olympics?

PRESIDENT

Any plans today, Joe?

DYER

What's up?

PRESIDENT

We need to kick around some names for a speaker at commencement.

DYER

Pee-Wee Herman's out the window, then?

PRESIDENT

What's good for you?

DYER

This morning or tonight.

PRESIDENT

Tonight's fine.

DYER

This afternoon I'm at the flicks. *It's a Wonderful Life.*

PRESIDENT

Very nice.

DYER

I've seen it thirty-seven times.

PRESIDENT

That's commendable.

DYER

I'm taking Bill Kinderman with me.

PRESIDENT

The cop?

DYER

Every year he gets depressed on this day so I try to cheer him up.

PRESIDENT

Oh, it's today.

Dyer nods.

I'd forgotten.

INT. PRECINCT SQUAD ROOM. DAY

We are shooting from the doorway of Kinderman's office. Activity. Stedman is walking toward us briskly, and a Desk Officer looks up toward the office as we hear:

KINDERMAN

I cannot believe that you just said that!

INT. KINDERMAN'S OFFICE. DAY

Present are Ryan and Atkins.

On Kinderman. From behind his desk, the detective is fuming at Ryan, who is off-screen.

KINDERMAN

Do you know what *Macbeth* was about?

On Atkins standing impassively, arm resting on top of a tall filing cabinet next to coat hooks, coats. He still wears the black seaman's cap and leather jacket over black turtleneck.

I'll tell you!

On Ryan. He is seated on a couch, his gaze down and averted, sullen and defiant as Stedman enters frame and sits on the couch beside him, casting a puzzled, interrogatory glance to the off-screen Kinderman as:

It's a play about the numbing of the moral sense!

Master shot from doorway of the scene.

(*to Stedman*)

I tell Ryan we've got nothing to go on in this case –

Medium close on Kinderman.

– and you know what he says to me? 'Win some, lose some.'

Close on Atkins turning to look at the off-screen Ryan.

(*off-screen*)

You are a racist, Ryan, did you know that?

Close on Kinderman.

On the entrance exam for new policemen they ask, 'What are rabies and what would you do for them?'

On sofa – Ryan and Stedman. Ryan knows what's coming, looks away from Stedman as:

Ryan said, 'Rabies are Jewish priests and I would do anything I possibly could for them.'

On 'priests', Stedman has turned an expressionless stare at Ryan.

Close on Kinderman.

What was the murder weapon, Stedman?

Close on Stedman.

STEDMAN

I'd be guessing.

Close on Kinderman.

KINDERMAN

If not us, who?

Close on Atkins.

If not now, when?

Close on Stedman.

STEDMAN

All right, something like garden shears, maybe.

Close on Kinderman as he tosses some object – a letter opener? – he's been gesturing with on to the desk despairingly.

KINDERMAN

(*low aside*)

We're abandoned.

Close on Stedman.

STEDMAN

Didn't get you.

Full shot from doorway as Kinderman heads for Atkins and coat rack, turning a significant, black look on Ryan.

KINDERMAN

I was signaling beings on Mars.

Close on Ryan glowering up sullenly as Kinderman passes.

(*off-screen*)

Sometimes they answer.

Slightly side angle – full on Atkins but favoring Kinderman as he walks into shot, takes his coat from the hook and puts it on, his glance taking in Atkins's seaman's dress as:

You're enjoying your luxury cruise on the *Patna*, Lord Jim? Now please telex right away and most urgently for the file on the 'Gemini Killer'.

RYAN

The Gemini's been dead for fifteen years.

KINDERMAN

Who was talking to you?

RYAN

But he's dead.

KINDERMAN

He should live so long!

(*moving closer to Stedman*)

And the autopsy? When, please?

STEDMAN

Tomorrow.

KINDERMAN

'And tomorrow.'

(*turns, heads for door*)

I am leaving you. Ryan and Stedman, go home. Go home to your families and talk about Jews.

INT. KINDERMAN'S KITCHEN. DAY

We are in a country kitchen. At a kitchen counter, mixing batter the old-fashioned way for a cake or strudel, is Mary Kinderman, the detective's wife. Seated in a rocking chair is Mary's sour, elderly mother, Shirley.

SHIRLEY

What kind of a job is that, detective? All hours he's keeping bad company!

As we hear the front door open:

MARY

Mama, when you're right you're right.

INT. KINDERMAN HOME FOYER. DAY

Kinderman is slipping off his coat and hanging it on the coathook as:

SHIRLEY

(*off-screen*)

Mary, please don't patronize me. It hurts old people when they vomit.

As Kinderman shakes his head ruefully:

MARY

(*off-screen*)

That you, honey?

INT. KINDERMAN'S KITCHEN. DAY

As he enters, he heads for Mary, kisses her cheek, picks up a piece of Danish pastry in its package sitting on the counter before heading for the breakfast table and sitting.

KINDERMAN

Hello, sweetheart. Yeah, a piece of me.

MARY

(*wiping hands on apron*)

You starving?

KINDERMAN

No, not really. Just some coffee.

MARY

You've been up since five o'clock.

KINDERMAN

(*holding up the Danish*)

I've got this. Tell me, how was your brunch in Virginia?

MARY

Terrific. Instead of potatoes they gave Mama grits and she says right out loud, 'These Jews are crazy!'

SHIRLEY

They are! They're fahblondjet!

MARY

Real loud. How was *your* day?

By now, Mary has followed Kinderman to the table with his coffee, where she sits with him.

KINDERMAN

An incredible triumph. Our trackers at long last brought in Mushkin, the Georgetown terrorist and scourge of society who breaks into houses and completely redecorates.

Down the stairs and heading for the front door has come Julie, Kinderman's eighteen-year-old daughter. She is dressed for dance class, carries pointe shoes, and wears her hair in a single long, thick ponytail.

Mary reads the depression behind Kinderman's façade, puts a hand on his arm, leans in to him.

MARY

(*quietly; concerned*)

Something wrong, Bill?

KINDERMAN

No, I'm fine.

JULIE

Hi, Daddy.

Julie gives Kinderman a quick peck on the cheek, heads for the front door as Shirley stares at her with hooded eyes.

SHIRLEY

Pocahontas with the hair.

JULIE

Off to dance class.

And Julie exits.

KINDERMAN

Watch out for red shoes.

MARY

Julie wants to change her name. You know, a stage name.

KINDERMAN

Like what?

MARY

Well, like Kelly Febré.

SHIRLEY

Do you hear?

KINDERMAN

Kelly's nice.

SHIRLEY

It's *not* nice, it's the fiendish beginning! Then the next thing Dr Feinerman will spritz up her nose so it matches the name and after that comes the Bible and the Book of Febré and in the Ark there'll be nothing that looks like a gnu, only cleancut-looking animals named Melody and Tab, and then the Dead Sea Scrolls they'll rediscover in the Hamptons!

MARY

Could be worse.

SHIRLEY

How worse?

KINDERMAN

'The Psalms of Lance?'

As Shirley turns away with a dismissive wave of the hand:

MARY

So you're home now?

KINDERMAN

(*checking wristwatch*)

No, out again. It's the day I have to cheer up our friend, Father Dyer.

EXT. BIOGRAPH THEATER. DAY

Dyer is in front of the theater, looking this way, then that, for Kinderman, as we pull back from our featuring of the round Roman collar to a full shot disclosing the street beyond. He is dragging on a cigarette and turns to the sound of a police siren's approach.

Angle from inside lobby behind Ticket-taker. A police patrol car screeches to a rubber-burning halt in front of us, and Kinderman hastens out, scowling at Dyer, who is pointedly checking his wristwatch. Immediately taking the offensive, Kinderman pauses to confront Dyer:

KINDERMAN

And so what are you doing here – founding an order called 'Lurking Fathers'?

DYER

I've been standing here for centuries. Four new popes have been elected.

Full shot on ticket turnstile and Ticket-taker as Kinderman and Dyer hurry in. Kinderman is reaching for his wallet as:

That's a lot of white smoke.

KINDERMAN

(*flashing detective ID at Ticket-taker*)

Official business!

Following him in, Dyer's eyes roll upward to heaven as he mouths a silent 'I'm sorry.' Both men quickly pass out of frame as Ticket-taker stares after them.

Front tracking – Kinderman.

So all right, so I'm late. So I know it. I'm sorry. I . . .

He halts, abruptly noticing that Dyer isn't with him. He looks around for him, spots him off-screen.

Theater lobby – shot from behind refreshment counter. In the background, Kinderman frowns in consternation as he moves to Dyer, who is standing at the edge of a group of waiting Patrons at the theater refreshment counter. A lot of popcorn is being served.

COUNTER ATTENDANT

You want butter on it?

YOUNG THEATER-GOER

Yes, and two Cokes, please?

COUNTER ATTENDANT

Medium?

YOUNG THEATER-GOER

Large.

Kinderman has nudged in between Dyer and another Patron. Dyer has an anxious eye on the off-screen Counter Attendant.

KINDERMAN

What are you doing?

DYER

I need some lemon drops.

KINDERMAN

We'll be late for the start of the picture.

DYER

I once spent a year hearing children's confessions and I wound up a lemon-drop junkie. The little weirdos keep breathing it on you along with all that pot. Between the two I've got a feeling that it's probably addictive.

KINDERMAN

That's an interesting theory, Father Joe.

DYER

You agree with it?

KINDERMAN

I rush to find any common ground between our planets.

Full on movie screen. A scene from It's a Wonderful Life, *near the end of the film.*

Close on Kinderman and Dyer. Dyer seems not to be listening to the off-screen dialogue. He is pensive, far away, his gaze lowered. Kinderman is beaming with an innocent delight even as he brushes away a tear. He looks over at Dyer, sees the priest staring down sadly, doubtless thinking of Karras. It spoils Kinderman's enjoyment. He looks down, shakes his head.

EXT. BIOGRAPH THEATER. DAY

We are tracking with Kinderman and Dyer as they walk up the street. Kinderman has Dyer by the arm. Both men have the blues, but Dyer more obviously so.

KINDERMAN

Come on, let's go and get a bite. We'll critique, we'll discuss.

DYER

You look beat, Bill. Go home and get some rest.

As they halt and Kinderman checks wristwatch:

KINDERMAN

No, I can't go home.

DYER

Why not?

KINDERMAN

Never mind.

DYER

No, tell me. What is it?

Standing with his face in very close to Dyer's, and, looking deadly grim, if not dangerous:

KINDERMAN

The carp.

DYER

The – ?

Kinderman silences him with a gesture.

KINDERMAN

My Mary's mother is visiting, Father, and Tuesday she's cooking us a carp. It's a tasty fish. I'm not against it. But because it's supposedly filled with impurities, Mary's mother buys it alive and for three days now it's been swimming in my bathtub. Up and down. Cleaning out the impurities. And I hate it. I can't stand the sight of it moving its gills. Now you're standing very close to me, Father. Have you noticed? Yes. I haven't had a bath in days. So I never go home until the carp is asleep: I'm afraid that if I see it while it's swimming I'll kill it!

EXT. BELLS AND CROSS ATOP CHURCH. DAY

Below, the streets of Georgetown.

EXT. 36TH STREET. ENTRANCE TO HOLY TRINITY CHURCH. DAY

As the bells continue to ring, we see parishioners going up steps to evening Mass, a few students hurrying from across the street.

EXT. CORNER OF 36TH AND 'P' IN GEORGETOWN. DAY

We are gently zooming at the opposite corner, shooting toward Prospect Street, as Nurse Allerton comes toward us, gently guiding a very slow-moving Elderly Woman in black, who is reminiscent of the

'Vision of Death' in the Iraqi sequence of The Exorcist. *From her hat there falls a finely knit black veil. The face behind it is sweet and clear of all possibility of malice. Behind us, the sound of church bells continues. From the left, a cheerfully animated group of Georgetown students, two of them obviously basketball players, enter the frame, crossing the path of Allerton and the Old Woman. We hold as they wait at the corner while two or three automobiles pass. Now we are close on the women. Allerton's face is an unreadable mask of strength and shadow. The Old Woman grips the straps of a large shopping bag that is zippered at the top. From off-screen, the sound of the students' voices.*

INT. THE TOMBS RATHSKELLAR. EARLY EVENING

Booths, tables, rectangular bar. The walls are festooned with prints and lithographs of old Georgetown, the university's early days, bygone heroes and beloved faculty. The place is filled with students, some faculty, parents. A lively buzz of conversation and activity. We establish with a series of quick cuts of:

Bar activity – steins hanging from ceiling.

Shot of oars over fireplace.

John Thompson and staff in booth.

Waitress taking order from professor in booth.

And then we are on a group of lithos and photos on the wall. Among them, a smiling photo of Father Karras. We are very slowly panning them to arrive at the Karras photo as we hear:

KINDERMAN

No one could do that scene like a Jimmy Stewart, Father – no one. What a film! It's so innocent, so good. It fills your heart.

DYER

You said the same about *Eraserhead.*

Reverse angle: Kinderman and Dyer in booth. Beyond, the bustling activity. Dyer is smoking a cigarette, sipping coffee; before him a plate of untouched food, an omelet. In front of Kinderman, a half-eaten burger, fries.

KINDERMAN

Most Jews, they pick a priest to be a friend, it's always someone like Teilhard de Chardin. What do *I* get? A priest who calls children 'little weirdos' and treats all his friends like Rubik's Cube, always twisting them around in his hands to make colors. What's the matter? You're not eating.

DYER

(*downcast; eyes on tablecloth*)

Too spicy.

KINDERMAN

I've seen you dip Twinkies in mustard. Come on, eat something, Gandhi. Stop fasting. The teeming masses need your strength.

Dyer shakes his head, turns and looks into camera at the off-screen photo of Karras as:

You're so stubborn.

Kinderman briefly follows Dyer's gaze, then looks back down at the table.

(*nodding head; softly*)

I know. I know. Me too. The whole world is a homicide victim, Father. Would a God who was good invent something like death? Plainly speaking, it's a lousy idea. It isn't popular, Father. No, it isn't a hit, it's not a winner.

DYER

There you go, blaming God.

KINDERMAN

Who should I blame? Phil Rizzuto?

DYER

You wouldn't want to live for ever.

KINDERMAN

Yes, I would.

DYER

No, you wouldn't. You'd get bored.

KINDERMAN

I have hobbies. In the meantime, we have cancer and Mongoloid babies, and murderers, monsters, prowling the planet, even prowling this neighborhood, Father, this minute while our children suffer and our loved ones die and your God goes shtravansing through the universe blithely like some kind of cosmic Billie Burke while we're dropping like flies by the hundreds of millions. Tell me how such a God could be good? Please explain it. On this question your Pope always takes the Fifth Amendment.

DYER

So why should the Mafia get all the breaks?

KINDERMAN

Oh, enlightening words. Father. When are you preaching again? I feel keen to hear more of your spiritual insights.

DYER

It all comes out right, Bill.

KINDERMAN

When?

DYER

At the end of time.

KINDERMAN

That soon?

DYER

We'll be there, Bill. We all live for ever. We're spirits.

Kinderman is glum, depressed, a little bitter, as now he stares down for:

KINDERMAN

How I'd love to believe that.

DYER

It's that kid who got killed on the dock, Bill, isn't it? I heard it on the news.

Kinderman nods slightly.

Want to talk about it?

Kinderman shakes his head, averting his gaze. Dyer extracts a fresh pack of cigarettes, observing the quiet detective as he fiddles distractedly with a packet of matches. As he breaks the seal on the cigarette pack:

I heard you knew him.

Still downcast, Kinderman nods. Then after a beat:

KINDERMAN

A little. Police Boys' club.

Lighting his cigarette, Dyer nods, exhales smoke, watches. Kinderman waits. Then:

His name was Thomas – Thomas Kintry. A black boy. Twelve years old. The killer drove an ingot into each of his eyes, and then cut off his head.

A young Waitress hovers, indicates Dyer's omelet.

WAITRESS

This okay, Father?

Dyer nods tersely.

I can get you something else.

DYER

No, that's okay.

Kinderman watches the Waitress leave. Then:

KINDERMAN

In the place of his head was the head from a statue of Christ. Done up in blackface. You know? Like a minstrel show, with the mouth and the eyes painted white. 'Mr Bones.' Like an 'end man', Father.

Dyer looks up slowly and Kinderman meets his gaze.

The boy had been crucified on a pair of rowing oars.

On the bar as a stein of beer is passed to a customer.

Full shot on students sitting in booth. The students are spirited, merry.

Framed between them is a poster advertising the Georgetown–Virginia football game of April 1892. From the laughter of the students, we go quickly to the silence of:

INT. CATHOLIC CHURCH. CONFESSIONAL BOX. DAY

On the cut, a wooden panel slides back with a final, sharp thud, opening up a window between the confessor's and the penitent's boxes. We see the priest – Father Kanavan. His face is averted.

KANAVAN
(*nodding*)
Yes.

The Penitent speaks. The voice is a whisper, labored and raspy, and the voice is so husky and reminiscent of Mercedes McCambridge that we cannot tell whether it is that of a male or a female. It is extremely distinctive.

PENITENT
(*off-screen*)
I have – a scrupulous conscience, Father.

KANAVAN
Yes.

PENITENT
(*off-screen*)
This need – to confess so many things. If I step – on two straws in the shape of a cross, I feel – that I have to confess it.

KANAVAN
Yes.

PENITENT
(*off-screen*)
It torments me.

KANAVAN
Try to make a good confession, and remember, Christ forgives all our sins.

PENITENT
(*off-screen*)

Only little things.

Kanavan nods assent and understanding as:

Nothing. Seventeen of them, Father. The first was that waitress near Candlestick Park. I cut her throat and watched her bleed. She bled a great deal. It's a problem that I'm working on, Father: all this bleeding.

The Priest has begun to react. At first nonplussed, and then with a growing dreadful surmise in his eyes as the Penitent's eerie, raspy breathing grows louder and louder. A sound of something like shears cutting fabric.

INT. HOLY TRINITY CHURCH. DAY

We are full on the crucifix over the main altar as we hear a woman shrieking in horror, a general awed and shocked walla of off-screen church parishioners.

Angle on back of church – Elderly Woman in black. Her veil is down. She is walking to back, pushes open a door, disclosing Nurse Allerton in the background, leaning against the foyer wall with arms crossed. Allerton comes forward, stands beside the Elderly Woman as the latter turns to stare back at the commotion. Her face is very sweet, her expression a little helpless and confused. She doesn't understand what's going on. Allerton's face is emotionless, somehow implacable. The Elderly Woman still grips the shopping bag.

Angle on woman parishioner. She sobs hysterically while being supported by a male parishioner beside her. A muted uproar among the parishioners.

Angle on two children aged three and four. They stare toward the sobbing.

Full on the confessional box so that we can see the penitent's box as well; then we zoom to the confessor's box only. The door is open. Father Kanavan is seated, slumped against the confessional wall at a grotesque angle. Above his round, bloodstained Roman collar there is no head. The priest's head is on his lap, facing out to us and held in the dead priest's hands, as if being offered for display. The screaming in background grows to a crescendo, then abruptly cuts to the relative silence of:

INT. HOLY TRINITY CHURCH. NIGHT

On stained-glass window. Light rain falling against it. Ryan dusting for prints on sliding panel. He is on the penitent's side of the box.

Up angle at Crime Team Photographer shooting body (off-screen) with strobe. He is laconic, gum-chewing.

Shot of station of cross – Jesus falling.

Shot of empty confessor's box. Door open, empty, bloodstained.

Shot of single red rose below statue of the Virgin Mary. Same statue as in the original film, but prior to its desecration.

Through the series above, we hear a gurney being wheeled in, stopping.

High shot: Stedman and ambulance team as Stedman adjusts a sheet to cover the body of priest. Then the ambulance team starts to wheel the body out, but halt as Kinderman approaches.

KINDERMAN

Wait, please. Hold it up a moment.

As they halt, Ryan comes up to the gurney.

RYAN

I was thinking, Lieutenant –

KINDERMAN

(*glowering up at him*)

This is new. Do you want me to call United Press or should we keep this little miracle here in the church?

RYAN

Do we really need prints from inside the sliding panel? All you'd get is the prints of the priest.

KINDERMAN

Yes, I know that.

RYAN

What's the point of it?

KINDERMAN

I'm padding the job.

Ryan scowls and walks away under Kinderman's smoking, threatening gaze. Then Kinderman slowly stares down at the gurney. He pulls back enough of the sheet to reveal the priest's right hand. He examines it as if not for the first time. The index finger is missing, neatly severed at the stump. Now Kinderman walks around, pulls back enough of the sheet to allow his examination of the priest's left hand. We do not see what Kinderman sees; but it apparently has some ominous meaning for him. He replaces the hand, pulls the sheet over it, stares for a moment at the spot. Then:

Go ahead.

Slow zoom. As the medics leave the scene, we push in closer on Kinderman. He lifts one of his hands. It is trembling. He looks up with a chilling dread.

EXT. STREET. HOLY TRINITY. NIGHT

The angle is long, includes Holy Trinity and the Georgetown General Hospital building which is on the next corner, same side of the street. The restaurants are closed, the street dark. The only persons we see are two young and pretty Nurses walking up the street. A wind blows a section of newspaper. The Nurses are laughing.

INT. HOLY TRINITY. NIGHT

High, full shot. It is empty. The only light, the ghostly flickering of votive candles. In the silence, we hear an odd sound from the confessor's box; a sound that keeps repeating as the camera drifts to it.

INT. CONFESSOR'S BOX. NIGHT

Angle from penitent's section. We come up on a shot of the panel sliding full open, disclosing Kinderman seated in the murdered priest's place. He stares, thinking, then slides the panel almost shut.

Angle on Kinderman from confessor's section. Above the sliding panel section, a small crucifix. Kinderman's left hand still rests on the pull affixed to the panel. He is pensive, puzzled by something. As we come

in, the camera is in motion, slightly circling and inexorably closing on Kinderman. He drops his hand, shakes his head and lowers it, exhausted, pinching the bridge of his nose with thumb and fingertips. When we have closed to an extreme close-up of him:

KINDERMAN
(*a whisper*)
Madness.

And with a startling suddenness, we hear the panel as it is pulled back very swiftly with a shocking report. Kinderman jerks up his head.

Angle on Kinderman from penitent's section. Kinderman's head jerking up, staring at us.

Angle from confessor's section from Atkins's POV. Atkins stares in from the penitent's section, where he is kneeling.

ATKINS
(*quietly*)
We've got an autopsy report on the boy.

Angle to include Kinderman and Atkins as Kinderman unconsciously leans his head and his ear in close to Atkins's mouth, like a priest hearing confession. His face is to us; he does not look at Atkins as:

KINDERMAN
(*a whisper*)

Yes?

ATKINS

Kintry didn't die from the decapitation. He was injected with a drug called succinylcholine. They use it in electroshock therapy.

Kinderman listens, expressionless.

But injecting ten milligrams for each fifty pounds of body weight causes immediate and total paralysis. The kid couldn't move or scream while the killer was nailing and cutting him up.

KINDERMAN

Was he conscious?

ATKINS

Yes. He was fully aware. The drug attacks the respiratory system. He died from slow asphyxiation.

Close on Kinderman from Atkins's POV as the detective looks up at him.

High shot: the church from main altar POV. Atkins emerges from the confessional, leaves the church. We hear his footsteps fade away, a door open and close, creaking. Then Kinderman emerges from the confessional box and as we slowly push to him, he walks toward us, head down, exhausted, numbed by this horror. As we achieve him in a close shot, he halts, looking up in anger at the crucifix over the main altar.

KINDERMAN

I'd like to read you your rights.

Close on votive light burning. We hear very slow and deliberate footsteps echoing on the tiles of the church floor.

Close on face of Virgin Mary statue. The footsteps sound.

High crane shot of the church. It is empty save for Kinderman. The main lights have been turned off: there is only the highly focused light on the statues, and the flickering light from votive candles. Kinderman is slowly scanning the church, as if for clues, then puts his head down, a hand to his chin, deeply pondering as he ambles.

Close rear tracking shot on Kinderman. A step or two. But then he freezes in his tracks as he hears something from off-screen and behind him: a low, muffled giggle, a little girl's, but sardonic, evil – in fact, the demon's giggle on beholding Karras trying to resuscitate Father Merrin in The Exorcist. *That very image flashes on the screen subliminally. The sound is repeated, but breaks off abruptly as Kinderman turns. We track front with him as he walks, his eyes darting warily around, and then he stands still and, as he stares all around, the camera pulls up to achieve a high, full shot of the church, disclosing that there is no one there but Kinderman. He looks straight up into camera.*

EXT. HOSPITAL STREET. DAY

Establishing shot.

INT. HOSPITAL MAIN LOBBY. DAY

The long hall at left teems with activity: nurses pushing a gurney bearing a patient, etc. We pan off the hall to the information/reception desk at right, where Kinderman stands at the counter and the Reception Nurse points, directing him to elevators. Kinderman – carrying a large stuffed teddy bear and a sack of White Castle hamburgers – nods and crosses camera right. We follow, but hold on the main entry area activity while he moves and, at the last second, starts to run out of frame.

INT. HOSPITAL ELEVATOR BANK. DAY

Just past the elevators, in a corner, a life-sized statue of Christ or crucifix. Kinderman races into shot, hurrying to catch the elevator before the doors close. For a moment we hold on the statue as the doors close and we hear:

KINDERMAN
(*off-screen*)

You're going up?

INT. HOSPITAL CORRIDOR. KINDERMAN. DAY

Front tracking shot on Kinderman: he is checking room numbers.

Through an open door he sees merriment, a birthday cake, patient and visitors, a family. He pauses at one room number long enough for us to see the legend 'Neurology' painted on the wall. In the background, another large statue of Christ. Kinderman continues on. He looks into a room opposite the charge desk, almost passes, then takes a half-step back, stares into:

INT. PRIVATE ROOM IN NEUROLOGY WARD. DAY

The footsteps approach off-screen. Dyer is sitting up reading a newspaper. Kinderman enters and walks hurriedly to the bedside, agitated.

KINDERMAN

And so what is this nonsense?

DYER

Look, there's nothing really wrong. They're just doing some tests.

KINDERMAN

You mean they couldn't find a rabbit?

DYER

(*picking up paper and burying face in it*)

I don't know you.

Kinderman grabs top of paper and folds it back to see banner:

KINDERMAN

(*incredulous*)

This is *Women's Wear Daily* you're reading?

DYER

So what! Am I supposed to give spiritual advice in a vacuum?

(*his gaze flicks to the bear*)

Is that for me?

KINDERMAN

(*as Dyer takes bear*)

I just found it in the street. I thought it might suit you.

Dyer embarks upon a fit of delicate coughing.

(*as he sits*)

Oh, so we're doing *Anastasia* today. I thought you told me that there's nothing really wrong with you.

DYER

There isn't. My brother Eddie had these same stupid symptoms for years.

KINDERMAN

(*exploding*)

Your brother Eddie died at thirty!

DYER

So what? He got killed in Vietnam.

KINDERMAN

There could be some connection!

DYER

(*incredulous*)

A *connection*?

Kinderman rubs a hand over face, abashed.

KINDERMAN

I'm just tired.

DYER

(*gesturing at phone*)

Call the desk and book a room.

A young nurse (Nurse Hara) has hurried down the hall and now pokes her head into the room.

NURSE HARA

Things okay in here, guys?

KINDERMAN

(*a little sharp and defensive*)

Yes, I'm fine!

And as Hara withdraws with raised eyebrows:

Now, you're sure it's not serious, Father.

DYER

Well, with Eddie –

KINDERMAN

Don't mention Eddie!

DYER

With my brother it was nerves.

KINDERMAN

Yes, you do make people nervous.

DYER

Only sinners.

KINDERMAN

*Every*body!

Kinderman glowers, reaches over and plops the bag of burgers on to the bed next to Dyer.

Here, I brought you a hamburger, Father.

DYER

I'm not hungry.

KINDERMAN

Eat half. It's White Castle.

DYER

Where'd the other half come from?

KINDERMAN

Space, your native country.

A short, stout nurse (Nurse Bierce) waddles into the room with a tourniquet and hypodermic needle. She is a veteran. Tough.

NURSE BIERCE

Come to take a little blood from you, Father.

DYER

Again?

NURSE BIERCE

What's 'again'?

DYER

Someone took it twenty minutes ago.

NURSE BIERCE

Are you kidding me, Father?

He points to a little round piece of tape on his inner forearm.

DYER

There's the hole.

She has already turned away, grim and gimlet-eyed as:

NURSE BIERCE

There it sure as hell goddamn ratshit is.

KINDERMAN

Eat the burger. It's got pickles.

DYER

I will.

KINDERMAN

Couldn't hurt.

Bierce stands outside the door to room and bellows down the hallway:

NURSE BIERCE

Who stuck this guy?

DYER

Nice and peaceful here, isn't it?

KINDERMAN

Idyllic.

DYER

I've been thinking.

KINDERMAN

This is new.

DYER

You'd better start being nice to me.

KINDERMAN

The bear is only garbage then, I gather.

Kinderman picks up the newspaper as:

DYER

I was thinking. Being here in the hospital . . .

KINDERMAN

Being here in the hospital with not a thing wrong with you.

DYER

I thought about things that I've heard about surgery.

KINDERMAN

(*staring at photo layout in paper*)

These people have almost no clothes on, did you know that?

As we hear the drug cart approaching in the hallway:

DYER

They say that when you're under anesthesia, your unconscious is aware of everything. It hears the doctors and nurses talking about you; it feels the pain of the scalpel. But when you wake up from the anesthesia it's as if it had never happened. So maybe when we all go back to God, that's how it will be with all the pain of the world.

Nurse Keating has entered, pushing a drug cart in before her. The cart's wheels are very squeaky and make a very distinctive ominous sound. She plucks a chart from the cart.

NURSE KEATING

Mr Horowitz?

As Kinderman gives Dyer an inscrutable look:

DYER

No.

NURSE KEATING

This is 402?

DYER

404.

Withdrawing cart and imitating Saturday Night Live'*s Emily:*

NURSE KEATING

'Never mind.'

Kinderman's gaze is fixed thoughtfully on the cart as:

DYER

Go in peace, and may the Schwartz be with you, my child.

Dyer has picked up the newspaper and is into it as:

KINDERMAN

That's a drug cart?

DYER

Why not?

KINDERMAN

Almost anyone could steal something from it.

DYER

I heard about what happened in the church.

KINDERMAN

(*playing dumb*)

Beg your pardon?

DYER

(*pretending absorption in the newspaper*)

Father Kanavan.

KINDERMAN

We found some kind of drug in him, Father. He didn't feel a thing. He had no pain.

DYER

Oh, well, that's good.

We know from his voice that he knows Kinderman is lying.

KINDERMAN

Don't you think you should be reading from the gospels or something?

DYER

They don't give you all the fashions.

KINDERMAN

This is true.

DYER

Damn right. Gooey gowns are getting boring. Could you get me something serious to read?

KINDERMAN

(*checking watch; getting up*)

I should be going.

DYER

Can't you pick me something up?

KINDERMAN

(*burying face in hand*)

My God, the grammar!

DYER

Be a pal. I want the *Star* and the *National Enquirer*.

INT. NEUROLOGY WING. HALLWAY. DAY

We are shooting long from outside Dyer's door. Kinderman rounds a far corner and strides toward us, red-faced and laden with trash newspapers. He enters.

INT. DYER'S ROOM. DAY

Angle through door from hallway. Kinderman marches to Dyer's bed, drops the armload of papers on to it.

KINDERMAN

As you ordered. *The Life of Monet* and *Conversations with Wolfgang Pauli*.

DYER

Thanks.

KINDERMAN

There are Jesuit missions in India, Father. Couldn't you find one to work in? The flies are not as bad as they say. They're very pretty. They're all different colors.

Dyer indifferently sorts through newspapers, magazines spread on his bed messily.

DYER

See, these are all last week's editions. I've read them.

KINDERMAN

You'll forgive me if I leave now this mystical discussion? Too much of esthetics always gives me a headache. Plus I'm visiting two patients in another ward, both priests: Joe DiMaggio and Jimmy the Greek.

(*turns and starts out*)

I am leaving.

DYER

Is it something I said?

KINDERMAN

Mother India is calling you, Father.

Dyer watches fondly as Kinderman disappears from view. Staring at empty open doorway:

DYER

'Bye, Bill.

INT. NEUROLOGY WARD. HALLWAY. DAY

We pick up Kinderman walking past the charge desk and follow him to the elevators. He pushes 'Down'. Another alcove in background. Elevator doors open. He steps in. Doors close. As Kinderman steps into the elevator, he gives us a clear view of what we previously couldn't see behind him in the alcove: a full-sized statue of Christ. This one's head is missing.

INT. DEN IN KINDERMAN'S HOME. NIGHT

A desk lamp is turned on. Kinderman is seated at his desk. He picks up a framed photo, and in an insert we see it's a photo of Damien Karras and Kinderman, both smiling happily, each with an arm around the other's shoulder. Kinderman is in shirtsleeves, Karras wears a T-shirt. Each holds a can of beer. Kinderman sighs.

KINDERMAN

(fond, sad whisper)

Damien.

INT. POLICE CRIME LAB. DAY

Kinderman, Stedman, Atkins and Ryan. On a blackboard, a sketch of the confessional box, suspects' names. There is also a scale mock-up of the sliding panel of the confessional box. Stedman is pale and unshaven. Kinderman is reading a lab report. Off-screen, the muted sound of a Telex machine; an occasional telephone ring. As we enter the scene:

STEDMAN

Father Kanavan's vocal cords were paralyzed. He couldn't make a sound. He couldn't cry out for help. So the killer was able to take his time.

KINDERMAN

Succinylcholine again.

STEDMAN

In precisely the proper dosage to cause the paralysis. A fraction too little has no effect, while a fraction too much causes instant death.

KINDERMAN

So the killer has medical expertise. Did we find a hypodermic syringe at the crime scene, or as usual only the *Crackerjack* prizes the rich kids are constantly throwing away?

RYAN

No syringe.

KINDERMAN

And the fingerprint analysis?

RYAN

Most of the prints were the priest's.

KINDERMAN

You said 'most'?

RYAN

Yeah, we got something else.

Close on blackboard sketch as Ryan walks into shot. He indicates the sliding panel on the right side of the sketch of the confessional booth.

Right here, on the inside pull of this panel. It's weird.

KINDERMAN

You're invoking supernatural causes?

RYAN

No one touches that pull except the priest.

KINDERMAN

And the killer.

On Stedman turning away from sketch to stare.

On Kinderman as he moves to the model of the sliding panel arrangement. Then, demonstrating:

You see? The killer wants the panel closed so the next in line to make his confession doesn't see that Father Kanavan is dead. And so he reaches in – slides it almost shut – and then he has to pull his hand out and finish the job from outside.

(*he demonstrates; turns to Ryan*)

So the prints on the oars from the crucified boy match the prints on the panel. Correct? They're the same.

Ryan and Atkins look at one another, then at Kinderman.

Well, aren't they?

After a long beat, Ryan shakes his head. Kinderman stares at him, then looks to Stedman and back to Ryan.

Two different people committed these murders?

EXT. KINDERMAN'S HOME. NIGHT

Up angle – wide-angle lens. Moonlight. A light on in the upstairs bedroom. We hear the ticking of the pendulum clock in the kitchen. Then:

KINDERMAN
(*off-screen*)

Where's Julie?

MARY

At dance class.

KINDERMAN

So late?

MARY

Bill, it's only ten o'clock.

KINDERMAN

It's very late.

INT. DYER'S ROOM IN HOSPITAL. NIGHT

We are close on Dyer in the darkened room. He is sitting up in bed reading his office under the narrowly focused beam of a reading light. From the hall we hear that slow squeaking sound of the drug cart. It stops outside the room. Dyer looks up pleasantly, and we see the shadow cast by someone – a nurse? – standing in the off-screen doorway.

DYER
(*peering over his reading glasses; pleasantly*)

Is this something to help me sleep?

INT. KINDERMAN'S KITCHEN. NIGHT

Moonlight seeps in, eerily illuminating the pendulum clock which shows the time to be 5:20. Now we fade up an overlay, another shot: Kinderman faced toward us, asleep in his bed. As we push in slowly to him, a rosary floats down through the scene in slow motion, then another, and we fade up the sound of a train departure announcement at a train station. Along with it, we are slowly fading up other sounds, bleeding them in from the next shot: a million murmurings; children's voices arguing over the rules of a game; the music of a spirited string trio; and, low but persistent under it all, an ethereal, atonal chorus of voices reminiscent of that in the 'Unearthed Monolith' sequence in 2001.

Throughout, the ticking of the pendulum clock has been growing gradually louder, and now we hear, reverberating over the boomy speakers of a train station's public announcement system:

PA ANNOUNCER'S VOICE

Your attention, please. The twelve-eighteen to Elsewhere now departing from track eleven. All passengers boarding, proceed to the gate.

On train arrival/departure board. As the narrow metal announcement slats rotate, changing over, we see listed as destinations the inscriptions 'Borderland', 'Second Wing', 'Intensive Care', 'Earth' and 'Elsewhere' as we hear:

Last call. Your attention, please. Last call.

And the prior announcement repeats through:

On station information booth where a Young Woman, train timetable in hand, is asking for information. She is clad in hospital gown, a robe and slippers. Behind the window, dispensing information, is a winged, white-robed Being, an angel.

And now the camera discloses in a stunning full shot that we are with Kinderman inside a titanic building whose smooth stone walls vault up to a ceiling of breathtaking height and contains a vast concourse, a seemingly infinite expanse filled with row upon row of hospital beds and teeming multitudes of people dressed in pajamas, hospital robes or gowns. More odd beings are walking around, more winged men, but these dressed as doctors. They move among the beds and the etheral columns of sunlight shafting through the high, round, stained-glass windows, and seem to be ministering and consoling, sometimes dispensing medication. These 'Doctor-Angels' are larger than life, their faces mythic with strength and searing goodness, Galahads painted by Michelangelo. Here and there we detect a hospital cart. The atmosphere is of peace.

On a String Trio resembling the one in the film The Green Man, *three ditsy-looking, grinning, bewigged old maids. They acknowledge us, smiling, as we go by them.*

On two Dwarfs as they struggle to carry a vastly oversized replica of the pendulum clock in Kinderman's kitchen. Its mechanism is working, producing the ticking sound we have been hearing – and will continue to hear – through the remainder of the sequence.

On hospital drug cart.

On luggage stacked forlornly, awaiting a departure. Tied old leather bags. Frayed travel stickers. A bright red volleyball bounces and dribbles through frame.

Close on hands holding hypodermic syringe up to the light, aspirating it.

Zoom to bed. On the bed, sitting up in a daze, his open eyes empty and stunned as he stares into memories of horror, is the murdered priest, Father Kanavan. His neck is circled with dark stitches, as if his head has been sewn back on with some leathery material. Sitting on the edge of the bed is a 'Doctor-Angel', who holds the priest's hand in a gesture of comfort and consolation. Behind the bed, another drug cart.

High full shot on the scene: the beds, the patients. Infinite extension.

Full front moving shot on Kinderman. He ambles at an easy pace, a sightseer, his expression pleasant, mildly curious. He is passing by the two Boys and a Girl – aged in the neighborhood of nine to twelve – who have been arguing over the game. They are at camera right. One of the Boys holds the bright red volleyball, arguing over some rules infraction with the other Boy, while the Girl sits on floor, face in her propped hands, disconsolately staring at Kinderman as he passes.

FIRST ARGUING BOY

No, Eddie, that *isn't* the rule!

SECOND ARGUING BOY

It *is*!

Close on Girl looking at Kinderman passing.

Close on Kinderman as he turns from the Girl to something off-screen at camera left as:

OLD MAN IN DREAM

(*off-screen*)

But I'm not dead!

Front moving shot: Kinderman's POV (*subjective camera*)*. To the right we see another 'Doctor-Angel'* (*Second Angel*) *at the bedside of an Old Man* (*Old Man in Dream*)*. The Old Man is protesting to the Angel, who is checking a hypodermic syringe for air bubbles.*

OLD MAN IN DREAM

I don't belong here! Can't you see? It's a mix-up.

Turning to camera (and Kinderman), the Old Man implores us:

Hey, tell him! Would you tell him, please? Tell him I'm alive!

SECOND ANGEL

This will help you to sleep.

Giving up on Kinderman, the Old Man sinks back on the bed with a despairing groan.

OLD MAN IN DREAM

Oh, for *God's* sake!

Close on Kinderman – front tracking. As he turns his gaze from camera left to camera right on hearing:

FIRST DREAM WOMAN'S VOICE

Earth, come in, please!

Moving shot: on Radio group (subjective camera). At camera left, we see a group huddled intently over a table on which stands a reel-to-reel tape-recorder hooked up to a powerful amplifier and pre-amp, and a noise-reduction unit. The group comprises a Woman (First Dream Woman) who is talking into a microphone that is plugged into the amplifier; a Man and a Child standing by her; and a Blind Man seated at side. All are wearing stereo headsets connected to the amplifier.

FIRST DREAM WOMAN

Can you hear us? We are attempting to communicate. Come in, please.

DREAM BLIND MAN

(*grumpily*)

The living are deaf.

The camera swings gently right as from there, back-pedalling before us as we continue to approach, a Second Dream Woman steps into our path, and speaks directly to us.

SECOND DREAM WOMAN

We come here first.

Hearing the growing loud ticking of the pendulum clock, she steps out of frame to the right and out of the way of the Dwarfs, who are coming at us from straight ahead, still precariously carrying the clock, and passing us, right. During this:

SECOND RADIO MAN
(*off-screen*)
I want to talk to my wife.

FIRST DREAM WOMAN
(*off-screen*)
Well, then, wait your turn!

And as we pass, a Young Man (Young Dream Man), aged around fifteen, stands sadly at the left.

YOUNG DREAM MAN
Tell my mom I'm okay.

And from the opposite perspective we hear the voice of Thomas Kintry:

KINTRY
(*off-screen*)
Lieutenant!

The camera swings right to pick up the young black boy introduced in the opening dream sequence – Thomas Kintry.

He carries a single red rose and wears a T-shirt emblazoned with 'Police Boys' Club' across its chest. He has the same vivid stitch marks circling his neck as did Kanavan and there are holes in his wrists and his feet: we see one of them clearly as he raises his hand in greeting. Yet his smile is wide and beaming as:

Hi, Lieutenant! How you doin'?

KINDERMAN
I'm so sorry you were murdered, Thomas. I miss you.

Kintry has seen something off-screen right, which has caused him to let go of Kinderman's hand and slip away and out of frame to the left, the smile gone from his face.

KINTRY

(*his eyes still on the off-screen something*)

Miss you, too.

As the camera slowly closes on him, Kinderman stares after Kintry, then looks to the right, checking to see what made Kintry leave him. Abruptly he stops. Though his expression remains pleasant, he looks mildly curious and surprised.

Close on hands laying out tarot cards. We are pulling back to disclose a huge and magnificent Black Angel (The Angel of Death) and Dyer sitting on edge of cot. The Angel is laying out the tarot cards which Dyer is studying. The Angel pauses, a card in hand and ready to lay down, as he looks up past Dyer, and at the off-screen Kinderman. Dyer turns to follow his gaze. On his face there is a slightly sweet-sad expression, mysterious but not unhappy, the shadow of a smile. His neck, like Kanavan's, is encircled by large and raw-looking stitches. On the cut, we have softly introduced the clarinet solo from Tommy Dorsey's 'Song of India', to which we then add a very muted sound of a ringing telephone; the ticking of the pendulum clock, speeded up.

On Tommy Dorsey double – a few Band Members/Angels. We jump to another part of the song, a loud full-band section. The band consists of Angels. The pendulum sound is loud, rapid fire.

On pendulum clock. The arm swinging at a furious pace. The telephone ringing sound has been growing.

On Angel's hand laying out tarot cards. Very speeded up, frantic.

INT. DYER'S ROOM IN HOSPITAL. NIGHT

We are close on Dyer. His eyes are wide open but dead as his head and torso are being alternatively lifted and powerfully slammed down on to the bed. The shriek of accompanying bursts of terrifying score, and then cut to the relative quiet of:

EXT. KINDERMAN'S HOME. DAWN

As we enter the shot, we hear a telephone rattling in its cradle as it is lifted off, and then quickly:

KINDERMAN
(*off-screen*)

Kinderman.

Four or five beats before, in a numb, low voice:

What are you telling me?

INT. HOSPITAL. ELEVATOR DOORS. EARLY MORNING

We are shooting at the elevator doors as they open, revealing a stunned Kinderman who simply stands, staring dully ahead. We hear the muffled sobbing of Nurse Keating from off-screen.

INT. HOSPITAL. HALL IN NEUROLOGY WING. EARLY MORNING

We are shooting down a long angle. In the medium distance, on the right, is the charge desk, and almost directly across from it is Dyer's room. Outside the door, uniformed policemen; a hushed hubbub among nurses and interns behind the desk; and from an indeterminate source, a muffled sobbing. One nurse guides a curious, befuddled patient back to his room as she soothes him. As Kinderman appears, all conversation ceases and only the sobbing is heard. Kinderman goes to door of Dyer's room, stops. A policeman opens the door for him. He stares into the room.

INT. DYER'S ROOM IN HOSPITAL. EARLY MORNING

We are shooting from the doorway. Ahead of us, on the bed, a white sheet covers Dyer's body, flattening at the point where his head should be. But it is not bloodstained. To the right of the bed, a few feet in front of a window, a bedside table on which are arrayed, in neat precision, a multitude of specimen jars that are filled with a reddish fluid. The bed has been pulled away from the wall, where Ryan is placing a plastic sheet over a legend scrawled above the bed in letters of blood, making a cast of it, so that we cannot make it out. A police photographer is photographing the bed, the strobe flashing, and as a hospital pathologist (Dr Bruno) stares down from the right side, Stedman is leaning over, drawing back the sheet. Pouring through the windows, an unearthly light that suffuses the room.

STEDMAN

I've just – [never]

RYAN
(*sotto*)

Alan!

Stedman looks up at Ryan, becomes aware of Kinderman's presence at the door, staring toward camera. As Stedman straightens, Bruno follows his gaze. Now we begin to move slowly toward the bed (subjective camera) from Kinderman's POV, and as we do, Ryan steps away to the side and Stedman and Bruno gravely move toward the door and out of frame. The camera halts. We still hear the sobbing, though more faintly.

On Kinderman, who is standing at the foot of the bed. Stedman, Bruno and the photographer settle themselves, wordless. Kinderman stares tragically.

Close on Stedman and Bruno watching Kinderman.

On photographer quietly and efficiently loading fresh film into camera.

Close on Ryan observing; reacting, lowering head; he is moved.

Wide side angle as Kinderman walks slowly around to the bedside. He is in shock. For a few beats he stands motionless. Then he reaches under the sheet covering Dyer, draws the left hand up to his view, and examines the palm. He nods slightly, replaces the hand, deliberately moves around to the other side of the bed and lifts Dyer's right hand. Kinderman stares, motionless – the index finger is missing. After two or three beats, he gently replaces the hand. Now, again, he pauses, staring down, head bowed. He moves to the head of the bed and again stands motionless for a time. Then at last he reaches out to grasp the top of the bed sheet covering Dyer. In the shot is the photographer, who pats the chest areas of his coat for a cigarette pack, finds it in a lower pocket, pops one into his mouth one-handed: utterly blasé.

On Kinderman. A barely audible sigh of heartbreak escapes him as he briefly gathers himself, then whips off the sheet. Though we cannot see what he sees, we see the photographer going numb at the sight of it. Kinderman looks up at something off-screen on the wall behind the bed. His expression is of wounded disappointment, despair, the emptying out of all hope. His eyes are glistening.

POV: Crucifix over bed.

Back to scene. Kinderman looks back down at head of bed. He tenderly replaces the sheet, and as we gradually widen the angle, we follow Kinderman to the window where he stands with his back to us and mourns.

Close on Ryan as he looks away from the head of the bed to off-screen Kinderman. He registers a surprising compassion. We hear the door open and close.

Full shot of the scene. Enter Dr Freedman, the agitated hospital administrator. A dynamic and formidable younger man, he is reminiscent of Rick Patino, coach of the NY Knicks.

FREEDMAN

Look, I'm Dr Freedman. I'm the chairman of –

KINDERMAN

(*quietly; not turning*)

Get out of here, please.

FREEDMAN

Oh, you're in charge? Well, then, I'd like to have a quiet [little word] –

KINDERMAN

(*a shout*)

Get out!

Freedman's face reddens with rage as the policeman (*Casparelli*) *takes his arm and gently but forcibly removes him from the room.*

CASPARELLI

Come on, sir.

FREEDMAN

Arrogant son of a –!

The door closes, cutting him off. Kinderman pinches his eyes with fingers, composes himself. Camera strobes keep flashing. Kinderman lowers his head for a time, absorbing the shock and grief. When at last he looks up:

KINDERMAN
(*with a deep breath*)

So.

He looks at the specimen jars on the meal tray to his right. He frowns.

On Kinderman from the other side of the tray, with the jars in the foreground of the shot. Kinderman moves toward the tray. On the cross:

What are these?

Wide angle of the room. Now the technician with the camera stops shooting, lowers the camera, turns and looks at the hospital pathologist. The man working at casting the writing on the wall also pauses in his work, his head at an angle suggesting he is listening attentively. A protracted silence as Kinderman stoops over the jars, examining them, but not touching. Outside, the sun is darkened and we hear a low, distant rumble of thunder.

Close on wall: crucifix over Dyer's bed. As the sunlight goes, a shadow slips up and over the crucifix.

On window as light rain spatters against it.

On Kinderman examining the jars. Except for the patter of the rain, the room is hushed. At last Kinderman notices the silence, stops his activity. He inclines his head to the side, turning it only slightly as he asks:

Well, what are they? What's in them?

A beat or two. Then:

BRUNO

Father Dyer's entire blood supply.

Perhaps Kinderman blinks; but he does not move a fraction or change expression. Then very slowly he turns to face Bruno. After a beat or two:

KINDERMAN

What?

No response.

High angle: the scene. Everyone is immobile, frozen in tableau; and except for the muffled, faint sobbing from off-screen, there is a deathly silence. A few beats. Then:

All of his blood?

No reaction or response, and after a few stunned, incredulous beats, Kinderman turns around to look down at the jars.

On the jars and Kinderman. We are shooting from behind the jars as the detective leans down closer to them.

STEDMAN

And not a drop of it spilled. All neat. There's not even a smudge or a smear on the jars.

Kinderman stares at the jars, unable to assimilate the stupendous, incredible horror. A few beats. Then, dazed, Kinderman turns to face Stedman, his back to us.

There's only the writing in his blood.

KINDERMAN

(*dazed*)

Writing?

Stedman nods toward something off-screen.

STEDMAN

On the wall.

Kinderman turns, staring at a spot on wall above Dyer's body, off-screen, where the plastic has been taped to take a cast of some writing there. Kinderman moves out of frame, walking deliberately toward the spot.

Close on wall: writing area. Kinderman slowly moves into the shot, stares, then abruptly rips the sheet of plastic off the wall.

Insert: writing on the wall. Scrawled in blood in a labored, uneven lettering:

IT'S A WONDERFULL LIFE

The flash of a strobe bounces off it.

INT. NEURO HALLWAY. DAY

Shooting long toward the charge desk again, from the start we are zooming steadily toward them as Kinderman emerges rapidly from Dyer's room, all business, and Atkins, leaning over side of charge desk, makes notes. A Police Sergeant at charge desk sees Kinderman, heads for him quickly.

POLICE SERGEANT

Lieutenant.

KINDERMAN

Get a squad of men to make sure all the hospital doors are locked. Make a patterned search.

(*grabbing Sergeant's arm as latter starts away*)

No one in, no one out except for emergency cases.

(*sending him off*)

No one!

POLICE SERGEANT

Right, sir.

KINDERMAN

(*to Atkins*)

And now when was the body discovered?

ATKINS

At six.

KINDERMAN

And by whom?

As Atkins gestures with his head toward the off-screen glass-enclosed office behind the charge desk:

ATKINS

Nurse Allerton.

Kinderman looks at:

Angle on glass booth/office. We are pushing in at Allerton, who is seated by the desk inside the office. She has an aura of inscrutability and a warm yet deadly competence. She has both hands folded in her lap, composed, as she stares downward, but on our move she is lifting her gaze to meet ours as we arrive close.

INT. NEURO CHARGE DESK GLASS-ENCLOSED OFFICE. DAY

We are close at Allerton's hands folded serenely in her lap as:

KINDERMAN
(*off-screen*)
You saw him at five a.m.

NURSE ALLERTON
(*off-screen*)
Yes, that's right.

KINDERMAN
(*off-screen*)
He was awake?

His gaze flicks down to the off-screen hands as:

ALLERTON
(*off-screen*)
He was awake. I'd come to give him medication.

KINDERMAN
And how long did that take you?

ALLERTON
About a minute.

KINDERMAN
Maybe more?

ALLERTON
Not much more.

KINDERMAN
And after that?

ALLERTON
I went to two other rooms.

KINDERMAN
Patient rooms?

ALLERTON
Patients' rooms. 403 and 408.

KINDERMAN

And what for?

ALLERTON

Routine checking.

KINDERMAN

And that took you how long?

ALLERTON

Couple of minutes.

KINDERMAN

For each room?

ALLERTON

No, both rooms.

KINDERMAN

And what then?

ALLERTON

I came back to the desk.

KINDERMAN

And you were here until you went to see Father Dyer again at six o'clock, is that right?

ALLERTON

Yes, that's right.

KINDERMAN

Inside here or were you out at the desk?

ALLERTON

Mostly here. I was writing up reports.

KINDERMAN

So that if someone had entered Father Dyer's room between the time that you left and the time you returned, you might well not have seen them.

ALLERTON

That's right.

KINDERMAN

Did you see anybody else go in the room?

ALLERTON

No, I didn't.

KINDERMAN

Or *leaving* the room?

ALLERTON

No, I didn't.

Kinderman is working himself up as:

KINDERMAN

Did you see anybody out in the hallway?

As Kinderman's flicking glance follows hers, she looks down at her hands, shrugs. Suddenly shouting in her face:

Did you see anybody in the hallway?

ALLERTON

(*with a swift look up at Kinderman*)

Mrs Clelia.

KINDERMAN

You saw a Mrs Clelia walking around?

ALLERTON

No, not exactly.

KINDERMAN

'Not *exactly*'?

ALLERTON

I found her completely unconscious in the hall around the corner.

KINDERMAN

When was that?

ALLERTON

Just before I gave the Father his last medication.

KINDERMAN

The five or six?

ALLERTON

The six.

KINDERMAN

Mrs Clelia's a patient?

ALLERTON

Yes, she is.

KINDERMAN

In Neurology?

ALLERTON

Neuro-psychiatric.

INT. 'OPEN WARD' OF PSYCHIATRIC. DAY ROOM. DAY

The room is very large and holds a ping-pong table, TV, book and magazine racks, art therapy canvases, and sofas and chairs where vacant-eyed dreamers sit catatonically or ceaselessly, silently, moving their lips. A group is gathered around the TV, its volume quite low. The patients are mostly elderly, have kindly, sweet Norman Rockwell faces, and are dressed in hospital gowns and robes. An orderly and three nurses work the ward. Some patients shuffle around aimlessly, their slippers making a distinctive sound. We establish the ward through a series of isolated scenes.

Full on TV screen: The Wizard of Oz. *It's the scene where Dorothy pours out her heart to Toto, the lead-in just before 'Over the Rainbow'.*

A circling, close-up pan of patients' faces as they watch the scene, rapt, almost wistful longing in their faces.

A zoom to a nurse dispensing medication to a patient.

A side-angle zoom to a nurse standing across from a bed where a male patient stares at her, as she holds a cardigan open, encouraging him softly to get up and slip into it.

A zoom to a woman patient staring out of the window. About sixty, she has a strong and scarred face. Her lips moving silently, her stare is vacuous. We will see her again in the final sequence as a character called Nurse 'X'.

A zoom to a nurse at the charge desk. She is filling in charts. We will see her again also in the final sequence (as the nude and bludgeoned nurse).

A zoom to full figure of a male patient shuffling along in slippers. His lips are moving as he mumbles to himself incoherently.

Medium rear tracking shot at entry doors: Kinderman and Temple. They take a step or two inside and then halt. Temple is a young Virginian who seemingly radiates robust mental health, a contrast to Kinderman's gloomy air of foreboding.

TEMPLE

No, this is the Open Ward. They're all harmless.

KINDERMAN

Yes.

TEMPLE

Some more serious problems here too, though, of course. Some catatonics. Some with Alzheimer's . . . autism.

Loose front tracking: Kinderman and Temple.

You can see, though, that mostly they're just old and very senile.

KINDERMAN

Then they move about freely?

TEMPLE

(*amused*)

Sure.

A toothless Old Man has entered frame, accosting Temple.

OLD MAN

I want cereal this morning. And figs. Don't forget the damned figs.

As they leave him behind, another patient accosts Kinderman, the Elderly Woman in Black. Her voice is that of the killer in the confessional box!

ELDERLY WOMAN

Are you my son?

Kinderman halts and removes his hat, speaks with gentility and courtliness:

KINDERMAN

I would be proud to believe so.

ELDERLY WOMAN

You're not my son.

She stands behind as they keep walking. Temple points off-screen.

TEMPLE

There's your girl.

High full shot: the day room. Kinderman and Temple are standing still, staring at an exceptionally frail-looking octogenarian (Mrs Clelia) who sits catatonically on the edge of a chair. In her face there is a transparent, helpless innocence. After a moment Kinderman walks up to her while Temple stands back, watching.

On Mrs Clelia. She is humming an airless tune, but as Kinderman's shadow falls across her she stops humming and looks up serenely and expectantly. Kinderman squats down close to her.

KINDERMAN

(*removing his hat*)

Mrs Clelia, my name is William Kinderman.

MRS CLELIA

Yes.

KINDERMAN

Would you help me, please?

MRS CLELIA

What about my radio?

KINDERMAN

Ma'am?

MRS CLELIA

My radio. Aren't you going to fix it?

(*grumbling; away*)

Nothing ever gets fixed around here. Just a whole bunch of pies and anchovies. Go away. I don't ever talk to strangers.

KINDERMAN

I'm the radio repairman, Mrs Clelia.

MRS CLELIA

Well, then, fix it.

KINDERMAN

What's wrong with it?

MRS CLELIA

Dead people talking.

(*she holds out her hands*)

It's right here. Do you see it?

KINDERMAN

Yes, I see it.

MRS CLELIA

I just knew you weren't really a radio repairman.

Kinderman looks quizzical.

(*compassionately*)

That's a telephone I'm holding.

Kinderman stares. She puts a maternal hand to his cheek. Her tone is comforting and consoling, and her expression is pitying as:

That's all right. Lots of people wouldn't know the difference either. It's all right. You have a very kind face. You'll do well.

Close on Kinderman turning to look at Temple.

Full on window: torrential rain.

INT. HALL OF PSYCHIATRIC WARD. DAY

Front tracking shot: Kinderman and Temple.

TEMPLE

You caught her on a talkative day.

KINDERMAN

You're being funny?

TEMPLE

No, she's quasi-catatonic. In and out.

Kinderman has stopped, looking ahead.

KINDERMAN

What's this?

INT. HALL OUTSIDE DISTURBED WARD. DAY

POV: The Disturbed Ward. Just ahead, the corridor has widened into a large square space. In the center is a circular glass booth, a control station. A nurse (Nurse Awad) looks up from some reading material and smiles. To the left is a formidable-looking heavy metal sliding door with a one-way glass panel in the center.

On Temple and Kinderman.

TEMPLE

The 'Disturbed' Ward.

Kinderman looks sideways at Temple, eyebrows arched. Temple reads his thoughts, shakes his head. Two Policemen brush briskly past them. The search team has arrived.

Sure, Neurology's just around the corner, but –

Kinderman puts a hand on his arm to stop him as he turns toward the Policemen who've gone by:

KINDERMAN

(*at Policemen*)

Look everywhere! Look in the closets! In the cracks in the walls!

(*back to Temple*)

I'm sorry. You were saying?

TEMPLE

(*bemused*)

Listen, no one could get out of there, Lieutenant. It's impossible.

KINDERMAN

Certainly. But open it, please.

Temple nods at the Nurse as he goes toward the door, Kinderman following. The metal door slides open revealing still another metal door. Another press of a button in the control booth and the second door starts to slide open.

INT. DISTURBED WARD. DAY

Shooting at inner metal door as it slides fully open, disclosing Kinderman and Temple standing there. Kinderman looks around, walks in, and Temple follows. The doors slide shut behind them, Kinderman turning to look at the sound when first door slides into closed position. Off-screen, muffled, we hear disjointed ravings and mutterings of the inmates. Temple has moved to a four-button panel beside door, indicating it to Kinderman.

TEMPLE

To get out, you punch a four-digit combination. That sends a signal out to the control booth. The inner door opens. The control booth operator visually checks through the one-way glass, and if it's staff, she lets them out. And there's a new combination every day.

KINDERMAN

I want to take a look around.

INT. ISOLATION CORRIDOR OF DISTURBED WARD. DAY

Kinderman and Temple are ambling toward us, Kinderman staring through each observation panel into the padded rooms. Muffled utterings, oaths and ravings. From somewhere, we hear a high-pitched Male Voice quietly calling out:

VOICE

Kinderman.

Kinderman stops short, turns half round to the cell he just peered into.

Reverse angle: Kinderman and Temple. Observation window of the cell Kinderman just passed is in the foreground of shot. Kinderman comes slowly back to it, frowning oddly. He stares into the cell.

Kinderman's POV: Padded cell. Light seeps through two high windows. A single bare light bulb hanging by wire from the ceiling. Against the left wall, a cot. Sitting on it, head slumped to his chest so that we cannot see his face, is a dark-haired man in a straitjacket. Long leather restraints affixed to his legs and to eyebolts in the floor. In the room, a cart bearing equipment for the checking of vital signs, a wash basin, a commode, and another fold-down at the right side of the room opposite the man in the straitjacket. He is Patient 'X'.

We hear brisk footsteps approaching.

ATKINS

(*off-screen*)

Lieutenant?

Kinderman, Atkins and Temple in the hall.

(*approaching Kinderman*)

Dr Freedman's really ticked. He wants to see you.

INT. PATIENT 'X''S CELL. DAY

We are close on the observation port, through which we see, but cannot hear, Kinderman and Atkins conversing further. Kinderman nods and quickly follows Atkins, disappearing from our view. Then, from here within the cell, we hear hushed voices. One stutters.

PATIENT 'X''S VOICE

Don't be frightened. It's all right, Tom. I'm here.

TOM'S VOICE

It's so d-d-d-dark!

PATIENT 'X''S VOICE

It's all right. I'm always with you, Tom. I'll always be with you.

TOM'S VOICE

D-don't k-kill anymore.

PATIENT 'X''S VOICE

It's all right, Tom.

TOM'S VOICE

N-n-n-no!

PATIENT 'X''S VOICE

It's all right. Not many more.

TOM'S VOICE

It's wr-wrong! It's no good! It's b-b – !

PATIENT 'X''S VOICE

Shhh!

The voices cut off just as the face of Dr Temple appears at the porthole, staring in at the off-screen Patient 'X' with foreboding and mystification.

Reverse angle. In the darkness, Patient 'X', his head still sagged to his chest. He is alone in the cell.

INT. NEURO CHARGE DESK AREA. DAY

Through the glass we see – but do not hear – Freedman continuing his harangue at Kinderman, whose head is lowered as he repeatedly nods, sometimes answers. Temple is out of the way, downcast, arms folded. Atkins talks on the telephone. We hear a door creaking as we see, reflected in the glass, two attendants wheeling Dyer's body out of his room on a gurney. Kinderman slowly looks up, stares numbly through the glass. Grief.

On attendants wheeling out a gurney with Dyer's body.

INT. NEURO CHARGE DESK OFFICE. DAY

FREEDMAN
(*simultaneously*)
Look, I fully appreciate your trying to prevent further tragedy and horror. But think of the state of our patients' minds when you've got these policemen here prowling the halls with their guns and their uniforms and SWAT teams, maybe. I mean, how can we – What? What was that he just said? He said fingerprints? Not on your life, goddammit! No, sir! No way, José! We've got patients with coronary problems, with cancer. Think I want a hundred lawyers running up and down the halls?

ATKINS
(*simultaneously*)
No no no! Send every schlepper and tech that we've got. Understand me? Everyone! Now! On the double! The Lieutenant wants fingerprints taken, all the hospital staff and some patients. Yeah, that's right, get 'em over here, Joey. Get 'em over here now. On the double. Listen, Joey, get it done or it's your ass. Understand me? Do it. Just do it . . . No, he's standing right here. You want to talk to him, Joey? No, I thought not.

Atkins hangs up, watches Freedman.

FREEDMAN
Ever hear of malpractice suits?

KINDERMAN
(*quietly*)
Have you heard of the Gemini Killer?

FREEDMAN
Have I *what*?

KINDERMAN

I said –

FREEDMAN

Yes, of *course* I've heard of him. So what?

TEMPLE

(*shadowed*)

He's dead.

KINDERMAN

That's right. He died in the electric chair.

TEMPLE

And so why are we –

He stops as Kinderman holds up a hand for silence.

KINDERMAN

Please. Just a moment. I'll explain. Yes, the Gemini Killer is dead, we all know that. But remember all those stories in the press and on TV about the Gemini's strange MO? I'll remind you. Supposedly – *supposedly* – the victim's left-hand middle finger was always found severed, always found missing. In addition, on the victim's back, we were told, the killer would carve out a sign of the zodiac, the Gemini symbol, the 'Twins'.

FREEDMAN

(*impatiently dismissing*)

That was fifteen years ago!

TEMPLE

Go ahead, Lieutenant.

FREEDMAN

Temple, why are you en [couraging] –

KINDERMAN

(*shouting*)

Will you shut your mouth!

Freedman is stunned into silence. After a pause, still pinning him with his stare:

(*quietly*)

The Gemini MO that you've heard about is false. The missing finger was not on the victim's left hand, it was on the *right*. And it was the *index* finger . . .

(*holding up finger*)

. . . *this* one! And the sign of the Gemini was carved not on the back, but on the victim's left-hand palm! Only San Francisco Homicide knew that, no one else. The misleading information was fed out to the press to help them weed out the crackpots coming every day and saying *they* were the 'Gemini Killer'. 'How'd you kill them?'

(*holds up left-hand middle finger*)

'This finger I cut off,' says the loony, 'and on their backs I put my mark.' 'Next case.' But in this case, gentlemen – in *this* – three decapitations – three victims with . . .

(*holds up right-hand index finger*)

. . . *this* finger severed, the correct one! And the sign of the Gemini . . .

(*displays left palm*)

. . . here. *Here*! And one more thing. The Gemini wrote letters to the *Chronicle* boasting of his murders. And always he doubled his final 'l's. Whatever the word. Two 'l's. As with 'wonderfull'.

Reaction shot of Temple. He looks stunned.

On Kinderman.

Yes. And the victims' names: always starting with a 'k', like his father, Karl, the famous evangelist that he hated and wanted to shame, that he wanted to kill and keep killing and killing.

FREEDMAN

(*awed murmur*)

But the priest. Father Dyer. Joseph Dyer.

KINDERMAN

Father Dyer's middle name was Kevin.

INT. PATIENT 'X''S CELL. NIGHT

The only illumination is from the light in the hall. We can dimly make out Patient 'X' sitting up on his cot, a straitjacketed figure in the darkness.

PATIENT 'X'
(*whisper*)

Kevin.

EXT. GEORGETOWN HOSPITAL. NIGHT

We are shooting slightly up from a low angle, the scene distorted by a very wide-angle lens. The street is nearly deserted and, still slick from the rain, reflects the gleaming moonlight. A breeze blows a styrofoam cup across the street.

INT. HOSPITAL PATHOLOGY LAB. NIGHT

A windowless basement area. Cadavers, the usual dissection tables, freezer lockers. Kinderman and Bruno. The latter is tall and very powerfully built; light reflects spookily from his rimless eyeglass lenses, further shielding whatever thoughts may lie behind this utterly stoical, expressionless face. The lighting is dim. As we come in, Kinderman is picking up a knife from a table on which is spread many other instruments of dissection.

BRUNO

Even that could do it.

KINDERMAN

Would it take a lot of strength?

BRUNO

No, not at all. Very little.

As Kinderman places the knife back on the table, we track with him and Bruno as they slowly move along it.

KINDERMAN

I'm surprised.

BRUNO

Even less with a wire or a coat hanger.

KINDERMAN

Really.

Kinderman has stopped, staring at the most wickedly terrifying instrument imaginable, something resembling large garden shears. Bruno has followed his stare, picked up the shears.

BRUNO

And even a child could manage it with this.

Kinderman takes the shears from him gingerly, regarding them with awe. He opens them part-way, but with great difficulty.

KINDERMAN

It takes strength just to open them.

BRUNO

(*taking the shears*)

Oh?

Bruno opens and closes the shears quite easily, though we hear the scrape of tight metal rubbing.

A little stiff. Needs adjustment.

KINDERMAN

What's this?

BRUNO

What?

KINDERMAN

This. This label.

BRUNO

Just a shipping tag.

KINDERMAN

It's new?

BRUNO

Just came in.

KINDERMAN

A replacement?

Bruno nods.

Where's the old one? Missing?

Extreme close-up on Bruno as he stares.

EXT. DAHLGREN CHAPEL. NIGHT (LIGHT RAIN)

Low angle up shot at Dahlgren Chapel. Wide-angle lens. Nightmarish distortion. Is there a mocking voice in the electronic moan that we hear?

EXT. HEALY BUILDING. NIGHT (LIGHT RAIN)

Angle on Healy Building from behind Dahlgren. An eerie, whistling wind gusts lightly. From ground-floor hallway and a second-floor office complex of the Healy Building, light glows. Wrapped in the wind sound is another: an eerie, lilting voice – Patient 'X''s – moaning 'Kinnnnndermannnn.' Simultaneously, all the lights along the ground-floor hallway begin to flicker.

INT. EMPTY GROUND-FLOOR HALL OF HEALY BUILDING. LONG SHOT. NIGHT (LIGHT RAIN)

An eerie, pneumatic, frightening sound. The hall lights continue to flicker, and then they go out. And now we hear the same female giggle that we heard in Holy Trinity Church.

INT. LANDING NEAR GEORGETOWN UNIVERSITY PRESIDENT'S OFFICE. NIGHT (LIGHT RAIN)

We are focused on a mural opposite office entry. From somewhere a muted sound of typing.

KINDERMAN
(*off-screen*)
Two priests and a crucified boy, Father Healy. There is clearly some religious connection. But what is it?

INT. UNIVERSITY PRESIDENT'S OFFICE. NIGHT (LIGHT RAIN)

The university President and Kinderman. The eerie, whistling wind blows outside and occasionally rattles a windowpane. Scotch bottle on desk. The President swirls a drink around in the glass he is holding.

KINDERMAN

I don't know what I'm looking for, Father; I'm groping. But, besides being priests, what might Kanavan and Dyer have in common? What connective little link might be between them?

As the off-screen typing sound stops, the President looks down into his sadness, shakes his head.

PRESIDENT

I don't know.

Kinderman acknowledges the reply with a slight nod, and then he too stares down reflectively. He sighs. And the pendulum clock in the office abruptly stops. As they notice the sudden silence, the two men look up, find the clock with their eyes. After a moment, the President looks out window. Murmuring:

It could be that exorcism.

Kinderman looks over at him questioningly. The President turns to meet his gaze.

That exorcism over on Prospect Street that Damien Karras did. The one that killed him.

From off-screen we hear that same suppressed, demonic, young female giggle. Both men turn their gaze to the sound.

POV shot: Door. It is ajar.

INT. UNIVERSITY PRESIDENT'S RECEPTION ROOM. NIGHT (LIGHT RAIN)

Shot through a crack in door. We see Kinderman and the President staring toward us. Kinderman rises, slowly and quietly walks to us, carefully pushes the door fully open, glancing back and forth warily, then steps into the reception room. As we hear a subtle creaking sound, as of a surreptitious footfall on an old wooden staircase, Kinderman turns and stares toward it.

INT. FOYER. NIGHT (LIGHT RAIN)

Shot at Kinderman from foyer as he stares toward us. He walks to us, looks right. We track front close as he walks to right, then stops as lights flicker.

High full shot: the scene. Kinderman moves warily to stare down a long corridor to left. Lights are out there, too. Eerie, gusting breeze, light spatter of rain on windows.

Close on Kinderman.

Kinderman's POV: Hallway. The lights are flickering, then go out. Again, the creaking sound from hallway to left off-screen.

Rear shot: close on Kinderman as he turns toward us and the sound. We track front with him as he moves toward stairs, warily flicking his glance to left and right. He stops.

High full shot: the scene. Kinderman is at the railing of steps to the floor below, the grand reception area. He leans over slowly, hands on the rail.

Down shot from staircase: below Kinderman. Hidden from his view and in the background of the shot is a frightening figure dimly discernible in the darkness. Back pressed against a wall, gaze angled toward Kinderman, it is an androgynous figure, hair long and unkempt, curly strings, and dressed in a priest's clericals, Roman collar and all. At its side a hand grips the handle of wickedly long, gleaming medical dissection shears. Is it 'Nurse X'? Mrs Clelia? Dr Temple? Kinderman looks up at us, then retreats out of frame.

Up shot from landing below railing: Kinderman walks into shot, leans over, scanning area below. The lights flicker, dim down eerily.

Rear close angle: Kinderman. We hear a muffled, quick padding of feet, very light. Almost in slow motion, Kinderman starts to turn to the sound. Then, simultaneously, a terrifying shriek of score assaults us, and a black-clad, gloved figure swiftly appears from the left side of frame and a little back of us, a gloved hand bolting to the nape of Kinderman's neck. The camera rushes back from him as he jerks around with a start, emitting a brief, loud, involuntary cry, only to find himself faced by a Secretary wearing a black sweater, black coat, jeans, bizarre black felt hat and Reeboks. In rapid succession:

SECRETARY

Oh, excuse me.

PRESIDENT
(*off-screen*)

Alice?

She holds out a folder.

SECRETARY

The speech!

(*hurriedly, she presses the folder on Kinderman*)

Would you give this to Father, please, Lieutenant?

And as she hurriedly leaves:

Gotta run. What's the matter with these lights?

PRESIDENT
(*off-screen*)

Good night, Alice?

We hear the outer door close. Lights come up full. Kinderman is still standing frozen, a statue, as his heart pounds and he absorbs the shock he's just had. Then, after he can catch his breath, composed, he looks toward the off-screen office and exits frame.

INT. UNIVERSITY PRESIDENT'S OFFICE. NIGHT (LIGHT RAIN)

The President, drained by events, buries his brow in a propped hand, shakes head slightly as he whispers:

PRESIDENT

Joe.

Kinderman enters. As the President unscrews the cap from a Scotch bottle for a badly needed additional finger or so, Kinderman puts some papers on the President's desk:

KINDERMAN

Your speech, Father.

PRESIDENT

Thanks.

KINDERMAN
(*sitting*)

That's all right.

PRESIDENT

Need a drink?

Kinderman demurs with a headshake, then looks up at the clock.

I do.

KINDERMAN

You believe in possession, Father?

PRESIDENT

Who cares? I've got enough to do worrying about kids who need scholarships.

KINDERMAN

Well, you mentioned that exorcism.

PRESIDENT

As a connection.

KINDERMAN

To the people who were murdered, you mean?

PRESIDENT

That's right. Joe and Damien Karras were close.

KINDERMAN

Yes, I know.

PRESIDENT

And Joe was also a friend of the MacNeils. He used to visit them a lot.

KINDERMAN

And Father Kanavan?

PRESIDENT

Kanavan had *my* job back then. He gave Damien permission to investigate the case.

KINDERMAN

But that leaves us with the Kintry boy, Father.

PRESIDENT

Does it? Damien had given our School of Linguistics a tape that he wanted them to analyze for him: the voice of the

MacNeil kid, supposedly possessed. He wanted to know if the sounds on the tape were a language or just a lot of gibberish. He was looking for proof the MacNeil kid was speaking in a language that she couldn't have known.

KINDERMAN

And was she?

PRESIDENT

No, the tape was really English in reverse. But the expert who initially figured that out . . .

KINDERMAN

(finishing it)

Was Kintry's mother.

EXT. BOTTOM OF 'EXORCIST STEPS'. NIGHT

We are angled up, shooting from close to the bottom. The macabre priest figure (Nurse 'X'), shears in hand and at side, walks quickly into shot, stands briefly staring down from top landing, then moves quickly out of frame in direction of hospital.

INT. CRIME LAB COMPUTER ROOM. DAY

Establishing shot. We are assailed by the loud whirring of the computers.

Close on two computers, side by side, they suddenly halt. They have found a match: two identical sets of fingerprints.

Close on Kinderman and Ryan from behind computers.

KINDERMAN

That's impossible!

INT. DYER'S ROOM IN HOSPITAL. DAY

Angle on jars on the bedside table. They are now empty. We hear slow, deliberate footsteps approaching off-screen.

Close on Mrs Clelia. She is sitting on edge of bed. She turns to the off-screen sound as the footsteps halt.

Full on Kinderman standing just past doorway.

Full side angle on the room. Temple leans against a wall, measuring the dramatic change in Kinderman as the detective removes his hat, silently stares at Mrs Clelia, whose hands are folded serenely in her lap as she turns her gaze away from Kinderman and casts her gaze downward and inward. A beat or two. Then Kinderman slowly advances to the bed, sits beside Mrs Clelia. His voice is almost gone.

KINDERMAN

Mrs Clelia?

No reaction. Temple stares down at his shoes.

Do you remember coming in here when the priest died, Mrs Clelia?

Now she turns to stare emptily at the detective, but makes no other move, no sound.

Do you remember?

MRS CLELIA

You're the radio man.

Temple, surprised, looks up.

KINDERMAN

Yes, that's right. Do you remember coming in here?

A silence as she simply stares vacantly. Kinderman acts defeated, then makes another foray. He points to the specimen jars, now empty.

Do you remember coming in here and touching those jars?

At first, no reaction. Then she turns her head slowly to stare at the jars.

Why did you touch them, Mrs Clelia?

Another silence. She does not move or speak.

Why were you in here? Did somebody *bring* you in here?

Another silence.

Was there anyone else in the room? Who was in here?

She turns her head back to Kinderman and points to the jars.

MRS CLELIA

That radio isn't mine. Mine is newer.

Kinderman looks mutely at the jars, and then at Temple.

INT. TEMPLE'S OFFICE. DAY (RAIN)

It is untidy. The desk is cluttered with reports, correspondence, ashtrays piled high with butts, stacks of books, and charms meant to ward off the 'evil eye'. The walls are covered with pin-up photos, framed skull X-rays, posed head shots of Temple himself, and a lettered, framed sign that reads: 'A psychotic is someone more neurotic than his doctor.' There is also an enlarged tarot card – the 'Hanged Man' – and an astrological chart. All around the room are two- to three-foot high stacks of the Washington Post. *As we come up on the scene, Temple, a cigarette in hand, is pacing, his lips moving as he studies a paper in his other hand. We get the impression he is memorizing whatever is written there.*

TEMPLE

(*a murmur*)

That man in the isolation tomb. You know, the one you looked in on?

Kinderman enters the office, and at the sound of the door opening, Temple crumples the paper and puts his hand down to his side furtively and swiftly.

KINDERMAN

You had something to tell me.

TEMPLE

(*moving to his own chair behind the desk*)

Please sit down.

Temple stuffs the paper in his hand into an open desk drawer. As he sits, Kinderman's glance takes in the newspapers.

KINDERMAN

There's a paper drive?

TEMPLE

I haven't had a chance yet to read them. I just keep them till I do.

(*stabbing out a cigarette more times than necessary*)
I hate to miss the science articles; they're good.

Kinderman makes no comment, his expressionless gaze fixed on Temple, who now rapidly reaches for another cigarette.

That man in the isolation tank. You know, the one you looked in on?

KINDERMAN

Yes?

TEMPLE

(*hesitant and strained*)
The police brought him in here fifteen years ago. They'd picked him up wandering the 'C&O' Canal down around Key Bridge. Total amnesia. No ID. They brought him to us here and his condition grew worse. He ended up a catatonic, completely withdrawn, without even any intermittent states of excitement, no going in and out of it at all. It was total. But recently . . .

He pauses, biting his lip, staring down. Kinderman waits.

Well, about six weeks ago he slowly began to come out of it. Every day he got better. Just a little. But better. And then all of a sudden he got violent; really bad news. We've been giving him electroshock therapy, and as of two weeks ago, he's been in isolation. The thing is, Lieutenant . . .

KINDERMAN

Yes?

TEMPLE

He says he's the 'Gemini Killer'.

INT. ISOLATION CORRIDOR OF DISTURBED WARD/CELL 11. DAY

Temple is unlocking the door to the padded cell. The door is pulled open and Kinderman looks in.

Kinderman's POV: Cell 11. Patient 'X'. His head is sagging to his chest so that his face is obscured.

INT. CELL 11. DAY

Reverse angle: Kinderman standing in hallway. He slowly starts toward us, halts, looking down.

Down shot: Kinderman's POV: Patient 'X'. Slowly, 'X' starts to raise his head, but before we see his face, we go to:

Close slightly up angle: Kinderman watching. Then suddenly his eyes widen in shock. He takes a step backward.

INT. CORRIDOR OF DISTURBED WARD. DAY

Kinderman bolts out into the hall, reaches out, and slams the door shut behind him. He covers his face with a trembling hand.

Temple stares at him, puzzled.

KINDERMAN

(*hand over face; shaking voice*)

I want a file on that man! Get it *now*!

INT. OPEN WARD. CHARGE DESK BOOTH. DAY

Through a glass wall we see activity in the patients' ward beyond. Agitated, Kinderman is whipping through the pages of a patient's file, turning each page with a loud, snapping sound. Then he tosses it roughly into a filing basket.

KINDERMAN

(*controlled edge to his voice*)

This file is thin, Dr Temple. It is thinner than a bakhlava leaf. No age. No description of what he was wearing. Were you here when this man was brought in?

TEMPLE

No, I wasn't.

KINDERMAN

Who was?

TEMPLE

Nurse Allerton, I think.

(*leaving*)

I'll go and get her, Lieutenant.

KINDERMAN

Yes, get her.

Kinderman watches Temple close the door behind him and move to Nurse Allerton, who is talking to Mrs Clelia in the ward.

Kinderman picks up the file again distractedly, desultorily scanning and turning a page or two as Temple and Allerton seem to converse conspiratorially, then come and enter Temple's office. As Allerton enters and sits:

ALLERTON

You want to know about the man in Cell Eleven.

KINDERMAN

Stretch your memory. What was he wearing when they brought him in? Can you recall?

ALLERTON

God, that's such a long time ago, Lieutenant.

KINDERMAN

Was he dressed like a priest?

She frowns in puzzlement at him.

ALLERTON

Like a priest?

KINDERMAN

Were there signs of any injuries? Blood? Lacerations?

ALLERTON

(*indicating file*)

That would be in the file.

Kinderman, clearly no longer himself, shouts harshly, picking up the file and slamming it down for emphasis.

KINDERMAN

It is *not* in the file!

(*to Temple*)

It is *not*!

INT. ISOLATION ROOM (CELL 11). DAY

Shooting from door: the door is pulled open by Allerton and Kinderman stands framed beyond the doorway, hands in coat pockets. He stares for a moment. Then he slowly walks forward into a close shot, staring down.

Reverse angle, close down shot, as the straitjacketed Patient 'X' slowly lifts his face up to camera.

PATIENT 'X'

It's a wonderful life!

The man is Damien Karras!

INT. NEUROLOGY WARD. HALLWAY. DAY

We track with Kinderman and Atkins as they walk briskly. Atkins tries to make notes as:

KINDERMAN

Two men in plainclothes on every ward. Rotate them. Twenty-four hours a day. And two in the Disturbed Ward; one *inside* close to the entry door, and one *outside* the door. Ask the Jesuits at Georgetown for dental records on a Father Damien Karras. And see if he ever had a saliva test taken. That would give us a positive identification.

ATKINS

What for?

Kinderman halts him.

KINDERMAN

Father Karras was a Jesuit psychiatrist at Georgetown University. The man was a saint. My friend. I loved him. Fifteen years ago he jumped or was pushed to his death down that long flight of steps next door to the Car Barn. Atkins, I saw it. I watched him die.

(*a beat*)

He appears to be the man in Cell Eleven.

INT. UNIVERSITY PRESIDENT'S OFFICE. DAY

Bathed in light from the window, the President stares out as we hear the sound of gravediggers in the final stages of unearthing a coffin from off-screen.

EXT. GEORGETOWN UNIVERSITY. JESUIT CEMETERY. DAY

Low wide shot at gravestones. They are row on row. We hear a low eerie wind and the sound of gravediggers, earth being shoveled and thrown.

At a nearby road: police ambulance and pathology attendants. The sound of the digging, deliberate, inexorable.

On Kinderman and Atkins. The angle is slightly low. The men are staring down at the off-screen grave being excavated. An occasional shovel of dirt flies through the frame and the wind has their coat-bottoms flapping.

KINDERMAN

Do you know what the physicists are saying now, Atkins? They are saying there are no such things as things; that matter is really a kind of illusion, and electrons can travel from place to place without having to move through the space in between and can at times even travel backwards in time. In such a world perhaps there shouldn't be a thing like surprise.

The digging sounds cease, the shovels are tossed aside. And now we hear hasps prying open the lid of a coffin. It slowly creaks fully open, the camera pulls back slowly and downward toward the grave, stops. Silence. Then:

It isn't him.

The wind picks up sudden energy and the coat-bottoms flap and billow vigorously amid swirling sand.

INT. PATIENT 'X''S CELL. DAY

A series of shots of cell detail: a slowly dripping faucet; a drain in the center of the cobbled floor; light shafting down through the high windows; an EEG machine; 'X''s restraints; an extreme close-up of 'X''s eyes.

Full low angle from door – wide-angle lens – distorted: Kinderman sits facing 'X'. The latter is in shadow, leaned back against padded wall. The faucet drips. Then:

KINDERMAN

Who are you?

Patient 'X' continues to stare. A long silence. The dripping. Then:

Who *are* you?

And now, in a voice that is a blend of electronics added to the voice of the actor:

PATIENT 'X'

No one.

(*a long beat; then*)

Many.

A protracted silence as the men continue to stare at one another, motionless. The dripping.

KINDERMAN

Are you Damien Karras?

PATIENT 'X'

Ah, you haven't any medical records for him, have you? No tedious fingerprints?

KINDERMAN

Are you Karras?

PATIENT 'X'

I'm the Gemini Killer, James Venamun!

KINDERMAN

The Gemini is dead.

PATIENT 'X'

No, not quite. Not quite. I'm at the station.

KINDERMAN

I don't know what –

'X' cuts him off as, in the voice of the Train Station Announcer in Kinderman's dream:

PATIENT 'X'/STATION ANNOUNCER

Your attention please! Your attention! The twelve-eighteen to Elsewhere now departing from track eleven.

Close on Kinderman reacting, stunned at 'X'.

Full shot from door.

PATIENT 'X'

Which is the dream world, Lieutenant? There – or here?

KINDERMAN

Why do you call me 'Lieutenant'?

PATIENT 'X'

Don't play games with me, fool! Remember Karen? Little ribbons in her hair? Yellow ribbons? I killed her. After all, it was inevitable, wasn't it? 'A divinity shapes our ends' and all of that. I picked her up in Richmond, and then I dropped her off at the city dump. At least some of her; some of her I kept: I'm a saver. Pretty dress she was wearing. Little peasant blouse. Pink and white ruffles. I still hear from her occasionally – screaming. I think the dead should shut up unless there's something to say.

A silence except for another drip of the faucet. Then:

I also killed the black boy by the river. And the priests. Oh, yes, their names began with 'K', that little modicum at least I was able to insist upon. But they were off my beaten track. You understand? I kill at random. That's the thrill of it. No motive. That's the fun. But the black boy and the priests were – different. I was – obliged to settle a score on behalf of – well – a friend.

KINDERMAN

What friend?

PATIENT 'X'

A friend over here. The other side. One needs friends. There is suffering over here. They can be cruel.

KINDERMAN

Who is 'they'?

PATIENT 'X'

Never mind. I cannot tell you. It's forbidden.

After a silence, Patient 'X' abruptly emits the lowing of a steer, resonant, loud, authentic and shattering.

I do that rather well, don't you think? Well, why not? After all, I've been taught by the Master.

KINDERMAN

Who is that?

PATIENT 'X'

The One. There is only One. By the way, do you know that you are talking to an artist? I sometimes do special things to my victims. Things that are creative. But, of course, it takes knowledge and a pride in your work. Did you know, for example, that decapitated heads can continue to see for about – oh, perhaps twenty seconds. So when I have one that's gawking, I hold it up so that it can see its body. That's an extra I throw in for no added charge. I must admit it makes me chuckle every time. But why should *I* have all the fun? I like to share. But, of course, I got no credit for that in the media. They only want to print all the bad things about me. Is that fair?

KINDERMAN
(*with a sudden loud sharpness*)

Damien!

PATIENT 'X'

Please don't shout. There are sick people here. Observe the rules or I shall have you ejected. Incidentally, who's this Damien you insist that I am?

KINDERMAN

Don't you know?

PATIENT 'X'

I know nothing. Except I must go on killing Daddy. I must shame and disgrace him over and over. Are they calling these 'Gemini' killings in the papers, Lieutenant? It's important. You must get them to do that.

KINDERMAN

The Gemini is dead.

PATIENT 'X'

No, I'm not! I'm alive! I go on! I breathe! Now see to it that it's known or I will punish you!

KINDERMAN

Punish me?

PATIENT 'X'

Yes. Do you dance?

KINDERMAN

What do you mean?

PATIENT 'X'

Never mind.

KINDERMAN

What do you –?

The question is interrupted as 'X' puts back his head and, with flawless pitch and in the voice of a choirboy, begins to sing the 'Gloria' from the Mass.

PATIENT 'X'

'Gloria, laus et honor. Tibi sit Rex Christe redemptor. Cui pue rele decus. Prompsit, hosannah –'

He breaks it off, eliding immediately into:

I like plays – the good ones – Shakespeare. I like *Titus Andronicus* the best. It's sweet.

He slowly leans back against the wall, eyes fixed on Kinderman.

Life is fun. It's a *wonderful* life, in fact. For some. Too bad about poor Father Dyer.

Kinderman stares. Silence. The dripping. Then:

You know I killed him?

A silence. Then, as the camera starts a slow move into Patient 'X':

An interesting problem. But it worked. First a bit of the old succinylcholine to permit one to work without annoying distractions; then a three-foot catheter threaded directly into the inferior vena cava – or, in fact, the superior vena cava – it's a matter of taste, don't you think? Then the tube moves through the vein from the crease of the arm and into the vein that leads into the heart.

Kinderman's eyes widen with growing certainty that this is the truth and his body leans slowly forward toward Patient 'X'. Meantime:

Then you hold up the legs and squeeze the blood manually into the tube from the arms and legs. A little shaking and pounding at the end for the dregs. It isn't perfect, there's a little blood left, I'm afraid, but regardless, the overall effect is astonishing, and isn't that really what counts in the end?

After the camera has achieved a close shot of Patient 'X', it pans over to Kinderman, who is terrifying in his stillness and stiffness of expression.

Yes, of course – good show biz, Lieutenant – the effect. And then off comes the head without spilling a single drop of blood. I call that showmanship, Lieutenant. But then of course no one notices. Pearls before sw –

Kinderman has risen, moved to 'X', and now backhands him across the face. Blood trickles down from 'X''s nose. Then he slowly lifts his head. A crooked grin. Kinderman trembles, still angry, but remorseful. 'X' is growing somnolent again as:

A few boos from the gallery, I see. That's all right. I understand. I've been dull. Well, I shall liven things up for you a bit, Lieutenant. The Master is throwing me a scrap from his table; a little reward for faithful service. Something fun. Something random. Something – *my* way.

'X''s head has sagged, his words grown slurry and barely audible. And now he emits a sardonic and weak little chuckle. Then Kinderman leans his head down close to 'X''s mouth to catch the faint words that now come:

Good night, moon. Good night – Amy . . . telling her beads . . . her beads . . . her –

His head drops all the way. Kinderman shakes him by the shoulder, looks up, alarmed, when he gets no response.

INT. HALL OF DISTURBED WARD. OUTSIDE CELL II. DAY

We are shooting down the hall, where two policemen are posted. Beside the door to the cell, in foreground of shot, is an emergency equipment cart. Atkins rounds a corner and is steadily approaching as Allerton hastily unlocks the cell door, rushes into the cell, disappearing from our view.

KINDERMAN

He passed out.

ALLERTON

Again?

Kinderman has emerged, and beckons the policemen to him.

KINDERMAN

On every shift – pass it on! – one of you never leaves this post! Have you got that? One of you never leaves!

Allerton has appeared at the door. Grabbing the cart and pulling it into cell:

ALLERTON

I think he's hemorrhaging!

Kinderman takes Atkins by the arm, and we track front with them as he draws Atkins forward and away from the policemen.

KINDERMAN

Atkins!

ATKINS

What is it?

KINDERMAN

The man in that cell: he knows the details of the murder of a girl named Karen that happened many years ago.

ATKINS

Yes.

KINDERMAN

It was a Gemini killing that never appeared in the press.

From inside the cell, an outraged shout:

ALLERTON

His goddamn nose is broken!

INT. TEMPLE'S OFFICE IN DISTURBED WARD. DAY

Kinderman sits at desk while Allerton bandages his hand.

KINDERMAN

When I told you that the man in Cell Eleven fell unconscious, you said something.

ALLERTON

Really?

KINDERMAN

Yes, I think you said, 'Again.'

ALLERTON

Might have done.

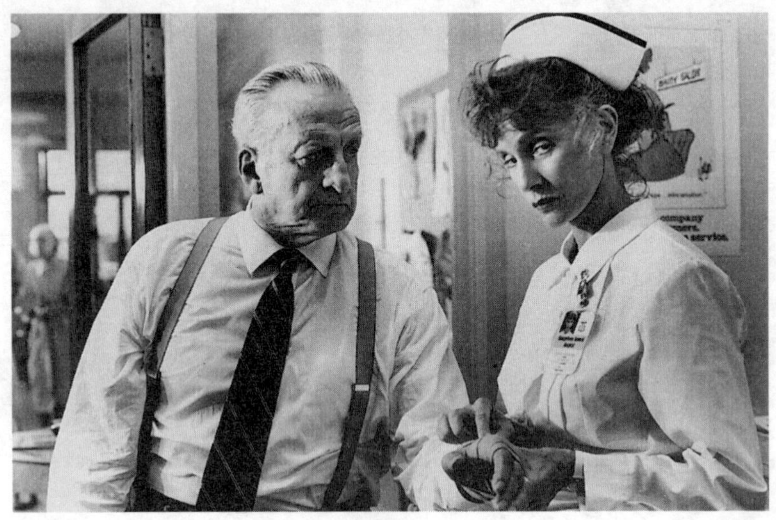

KINDERMAN

You mean it's happened before, this –

He suddenly winces as she touches the hand.

ALLERTON

You want to hit people, that's what happens.

KINDERMAN

How often has he fallen unconscious before? Many times?

ALLERTON

No, not really. It's just been this week. I think the first time was Sunday.

KINDERMAN

And again?

ALLERTON

The next day. If you want exact times –

KINDERMAN

It's on your chart?

ALLERTON

Yes, that's right.

KINDERMAN

Any other times?

ALLERTON

Early this morning. Just before we found . . .

She hesitates. He quickly leaps in.

KINDERMAN

Yes. That's all right.

ALLERTON

(*softly*)

I'm really sorry.

KINDERMAN

When this happens, does it seem like normal sleep?

ALLERTON

Nothing's normal about that man.

KINDERMAN

Does – ?

ALLERTON

His autonomic system slows down to almost nothing: heartbeat, temperature, breathing. But his brainwave activity's exactly the opposite. It accelerates.

KINDERMAN

(*softly pondering*)

'Accelerates.'

ALLERTON

There. Keep that on until the weekend.

Kinderman glances at the bandaged hand, flexes it absently.

KINDERMAN

You're most kind.

ALLERTON

I'm a bitch.

KINDERMAN

Have you ever told the man in Cell Eleven what happened to Father Dyer?

ALLERTON

No, of course not.

KINDERMAN

Might someone else have told him?

ALLERTON

Why would they?

KINDERMAN

(*eyeing her levelly*)

I don't know.

EXT. GEORGETOWN UNIVERSITY CAMPUS. DUSK

KINDERMAN

(*off-screen*)

He was buried the next morning. Closed coffin, the usual. All that I remember.

INT. RIGGS LIBRARY ON GEORGETOWN CAMPUS. DUSK

Kinderman and the university President are seated at a small round table in an alcove.

KINDERMAN

But who was the last person ever to see him? Would you know?

PRESIDENT

Brother Fain.

KINDERMAN

Beg your pardon?

PRESIDENT

Brother Fain. At least I think it was. Wait a second. Hold it.

(*looks up, now certain*)

Yeah, that's right. That's who it was. Brother Fain. He was left to dress the body and seal up the coffin. Then no one ever saw him again. Sad case. He'd always griped about the Order not treating him well. He had family in Kentucky and kept asking for assignment someplace near them. Never got it. Toward the end he –

KINDERMAN

Toward the end?

PRESIDENT

He was elderly; eighty, eighty-one. He always said that when he died he'd make sure he died at home. We always figured he just split because he sensed it was coming. He'd already had a couple of pretty bad coronaries.

Kinderman begins to pale, reacts strangely. The President notices.

What's the matter?

KINDERMAN

Brother Fain – he had two heart attacks precisely?

PRESIDENT

Yeah, two. What about it?

No response. Kinderman is still reacting, thinking.

Is –?

KINDERMAN

The man we found in Damien's coffin. You remember, he was dressed like a priest?

The President silently nods.

His vital organs were remarkably preserved.

PRESIDENT

Is that so?

KINDERMAN

We did an autopsy, Father, and discovered – Well, he was elderly, perhaps in his eighties, and we made out the scarring of three major heart attacks – two before, plus the one that killed him.

PRESIDENT

Yes?

KINDERMAN

We have every indication that he died of fright.

EXT. KINDERMAN'S HOME. NIGHT

Only the kitchen light is on. Kinderman sits at the kitchen table, reading. We hear the steady tick-tock of a pendulum clock in the kitchen.

INT. KINDERMAN'S KITCHEN. NIGHT

Full on pendulum clock. The ominous, steady sound. The clock shows it to be 3.10.

On coffee percolator on stove. Steam wisping up from the spout. During the above we hear:

KINDERMAN'S VOICE

'In the twentieth century, at least in the western world . . .'

Kinderman sits at the kitchen table sipping at a mug of tea while he reads from a copy of a book called Possession, *by Traugott Oesterreich. He wears thick reading glasses, and is huddled against the cold in his overcoat, which he wears over long flannel underwear.*

KINDERMAN

(*in a murmur*)

'. . . over seventy percent of all victims of possession insist they are the spirit of someone dead.'

He looks up thoughtfully.

Now we hear an ominous, low scuffing sound, rhythmic and approaching, a sound like the inmates' eerie walk heard in an earlier scene, and as Kinderman looks concerned and wary, we are pushing in to an extreme close-up of him, which we achieve just as the sound stops. Then, as Kinderman's eyes dart to the sound, we hear the sound of a refrigerator being opened.

On Julie. Dead on her feet, she stands in her nightgown and ballet slippers, one hand holding open the refrigerator door as her crusted eyes stare into the fridge vacantly. Suddenly her hand stabs into the fridge, removes half a sandwich, and she shuffles away as if in a trance, heading back to her room. We follow just long enough to tilt down for a low, close tracking shot of her ballet slippers.

On Kinderman. We hear the scuffing of the slippers again as he follows her with his eyes. She walks into the scene, kisses Kinderman on his forehead, leaves.

JULIE

'Night, Daddy.

KINDERMAN

Pleasant dreams, Julie, dearest.

JULIE

(*off-screen*)

It's so *late.*

KINDERMAN

(*softly to himself*)

Yes, it is. It's very late.

(*as his eyes find the text he was reading*)

Very late.

He angles his head to the side, staring at a folder on his desk.

INSERT:

Folder: slow zoom

In large, bold type on the cover:

PSYCHIATRIC PROFILE: GEMINI KILLER
MARCH 11, 1970
NAME: JAMES VENAMUN
FATHER'S NAME: KARL. EVANGELIST

Faint sounds sneak in – voices – gradually growing louder, along with an eerie wind.

VENAMUN'S VOICE

Some do not believe in the power they have witnessed.

Disapproving, inchoate murmurs and outcries from a mixed audience are heard. Then:

Do you believe in the power of the Lord?

Pious affirmative outcries.

Do you believe it, I said?

Kinderman's hand enters the frame, picking up the report as we hear:

AUDIENCE TOGETHER

We believe!

Slow zoom to pendulum clock. Its tocking grows increasingly louder as we hear:

VENAMUN'S VOICE

Say it louder!

VENAMUN AND AUDIENCE

We believe! We believe! We Believe!

And over the continued chant of the audience:

VENAMUN'S VOICE

Then my friends, you will be saved! You will be saved!

And with the wind and clock sounds at their loudest, we are suddenly in:

INT. AUDITORIUM. DAY

Silence. On stage the evangelist – Karl Venamun. We are shooting from behind him and from a low angle up into the spotlights that shine down on him from the auditorium balcony. Microphone in hand, he moves laterally, and we move with him as:

VENAMUN

The blood of Christ has guaranteed it!

MALE VOICE IN AUDIENCE

Praise Jesus!

On Woman in Wheelchair. Her eyes are brimming; her face, transfigured, radiant.

WOMAN IN WHEELCHAIR

(*muted*)

Praise him!

On TV camera in wings. The red light glows.

WOMAN IN AUDIENCE'S VOICE
(*effusive*)

Praise him!

VENAMUN
(*off-screen; muted*)

Praise him. And, remember that –

On photo backing above stage.

It is behind Venamun: a huge photo backing of the evangelist's logo: Michelangelo's depiction of God's index finger reaching out to touch Adam's.

(*off-screen, entering*)

– it isn't Karl Venamun who cures you!

High front shot: Venamun. We are shooting from the balcony, and the camera is already in motion, zooming to a close-up of Venamun, as:

Oh, no! It is the power of *Jesus* that cures you! Jesus! Jesus! Jesus!

The off-screen audience gradually takes up the chant – 'Jesus!' – along with Venamun and when we are close on him and the chant is deafening, we cut abruptly to:

EXT. BLUE RIDGE MOUNTAIN AREA. DAWN

The shock of the relative silence. The mountains are shrouded in mist, mysterious. The low crackle of bacon frying, a muted bird call.

INT. KITCHEN OF COUNTRY HOME. DAY

Tom and James Venamun are twins, aged twelve. Tom sits at kitchen table, doe-eyed and spacey, staring at cartoons on a miniature TV on the kitchen counter. Both boys are in pajamas. James turns the bacon, goes to the fridge, takes out a milk carton as the elder Venamun enters bleary-eyed, in pajamas, whiskey bottle in hand, utter meanness in his hooded eyes.

VENAMUN

What are you doing?

JAMES

Fixing Tommy his breakfast.

As James crosses his path with the milk, the father backhands his face, sending James flying across the room and to the floor near the doorway to the exterior.

VENAMUN

I can *see* that, you snotty little bastard! I said no food for him today! He dirtied his pants!

JAMES

(*holding his cheek*)

He can't help it!

The father is advancing on Tommy, who is so frightened he is shaking.

VENAMUN

And you! You were *told* not to eat! You were *told*!

On the last word, the father knocks everything on the breakfast table to the floor. As he roughly grabs Tommy by the arm, yanks him upright and hauls him toward the door:

You little ape, you're going down in the cellar with the rats!

An immediate outcry of terror from Tommy.

On Tommy.

TOMMY

No!

On James. He reaches up, grabs his father's wrist as the evangelist drags Tommy toward the door.

JAMES

Pa, don't! Please –!

Close on Venamun looking down at James, the terrified Tommy in his grip. We can hear the sickening thud as he kicks James brutally.

Close on James, eyes bulging in pain, gasping, his hands at his stomach. Tommy screaming, terrified.

VENAMUN
(*off-screen*)

Stay out of my way!

EXT. COUNTRY HOUSE. DAY

In the foreground of the scene – cellar doors. Venamun drags Tommy out and toward them. Tommy screams protestations as:

VENAMUN

You little ape! You'll learn obedience and cleanliness, damn you!

INT. COUNTRY HOUSE LIVING ROOM. NIGHT

The father is watching a tape delay of one of his services on TV, very drunk, speech slurry. James is tied to a straightbacked wooden chair, gagged, but faced toward the television screen. The front door is open. We can hear Tommy's muffled screams.

VENAMUN

Yeah, the rats'll keep 'im busy. Little bastard.

Extreme close-up on James, his eyes bulging with horror and alarm as:

TOMMY
(*off-screen; hysterical, terrified shrieks*)

Jim, help! Get me out of here!

EXT. COUNTRY HOUSE. AT CELLAR DOORS. NIGHT

The shrieking.

TOMMY
(*off-screen*)

Jim! Jiimmmm!

EXT. AT WINDOW OF COUNTRY HOUSE. DAY (RAIN)

Staring out at us is Karl Venamun.

INT. COUNTRY HOUSE. DAY (RAIN)

Neatly dressed and sober, the evangelist stands at the window, his hand holding the curtain pulled back slightly as he watches an ambulance team load a stretcher bearing Tom into the back of the ambulance. Hearing a door slowly creaking open, and sound of rain louder, he turns to look right.

VENAMUN

Keep your mouth shut.

Venamun's POV: Side angle of Tom

A hand still holding the door open, he is staring out at the ambulance. As we come up on him, the camera is already pushing in to him and he is turning to (us) his father. In his eyes, burning hatred; tears. The camera halts on the sound of the ambulance door clanging shut.

INT. D.C. AREA STATE MENTAL HOSPITAL. DAY

Beginning with a sun-drenched long shot of an outer corridor, there follows a montage of establishing shots. High ceilings, lots of sunlight shafting through tall windows and skylights. Through the montage, the sound of a daytime television program.

On Tom and James. They are now around nineteen or twenty years old. They are watching an off-screen TV. Tom sits in a wheelchair. Beside him, in a wooden chair, is James. They are holding hands. Tom – whose scar we recognize – has the expression of a man staring into oblivion.

INT. STATE HOSPITAL HALLWAY. NIGHT

Close on hands. We are shooting long. Down the hall a nurse (New Nurse) rounds a corner and comes slowly toward us, her head angled toward a voice emanating from the room nearest us in the foreground. Through the open door we hear James reading aloud from the beginning of a child's storybook – Good night moon. *Over a PA system, a recorded voice announces that visiting hours are over.*

INT. ROOM IN STATE HOSPITAL. NIGHT

Tom lies in bed, head propped up a little on a pillow. James sits in a chair beside him, reading from the storybook. We hear the muffled footsteps of the nurse approaching off-screen. The sound of her footsteps stops outside the door, James stops reading in mid-sentence and looks up toward the off-screen nurse.

INT. STATE HOSPITAL. CHARGE DESK. NIGHT

A mild bustle of activity. One nurse (Charge Nurse) is busy removing, annotating and then replacing location cards in a directory, while a New Nurse is engrossed in a stack of patient charts.

NEW NURSE

(*putting aside patient chart*)

Okay, that's 103, medication at nine. Say, what's the deal now on this one.

(*she picks up next chart*)

Venamun. No turning out his room light? What's that?

CHARGE NURSE

He's got a very weak heart and he's afraid of the dark.

NEW NURSE

(*incredulous*)

Are you –?

CHARGE NURSE

(*busy, waving her off*)

Doctor will explain the whole thing in the morning.

NEW NURSE

(*back to her charts*)

Didn't realize I'd been transferred to a nut house.

CHARGE NURSE

(*drily*)

You'll do fine.

NEW NURSE

It's about his brother . . .

CHARGE NURSE

Yeah, I know. He's come to visit every day now for years. He gets to stay after hours. It's all right.

NEW NURSE

So he said.

(*bending back to her work*)
God, if looks could kill.

INT. TOM'S ROOM IN STATE HOSPITAL. NIGHT

James reads end of Good Night Moon *and then wearily closes his eyes. His hand still grips Tom's. Tom's eyes are open, staring straight ahead. A tear rolls down from one eye as the camera is pushing in and:*

TOM

I l-l-love you, J-J-J-James.

It is the familiar stuttering once heard from Patient 'X''s cell!

Later. The New Nurse quickly walks by the open door to Tommy's room. Then she reappears, a hand on the doorframe, looking into the room with a sour grimace. James is gone. Tommy is asleep. The Nurse enters, shaking her head as she comes forward, moves past our view. We hear a metallic click as she turns off the light by the bed, and suddenly we are plunged into darkness. The Nurse exits, closing the door behind her. And now the blackness is total.

EXT. SECTION OF STATE MENTAL HOSPITAL. NIGHT

Silence. Then a shriek of terror, repeated and repeated.

INT. TOM'S ROOM IN STATE HOSPITAL. DAY

Shooting toward open door. Two attendants are lifting Tom's dead body, covered with sheet, on to a cart. Around the corner, swiftly, comes James; stops in the doorway; stares. Camera zooms to his face as it contorts into a terrifying rage. He raises his face, emits a blood-curdling, shattering cry of pain and fury that grows and grows in piercing volume as we cut abruptly into:

INT. KINDERMAN'S KITCHEN. NIGHT

On Kinderman, as he abruptly looks up from the text, as if he'd heard Venamun's cry. Then his gaze flicks to the pendulum clock.

Slow zoom to the pendulum clock as the arm moves inexorably back and forth, the sound growing larger than life, until finally we cut away to:

INT. CORRIDOR OF NEUROLOGY WARD. NIGHT

Dead silence. The same familiar angle we have been establishing all along: down the hall to the right, the charge desk; left and opposite the desk, Father Dyer's former room, now empty. A Police Officer ambles toward us and past frame: a Second Police Officer approaches the charge desk, leans across it to converse quietly with Nurse Keating, who is writing entries in charts on the desk. She is alone behind it.

A flirtatious, familiar conversation. Then the Second Officer wanders around the corner of charge desk and out of sight. We hear his soft steps fading down another corridor.

On Nurse Keating writing. We hear something: an odd, crackling sound. She looks up. Waits. We hear it again. She looks in the direction.

Angle from other side of charge desk: Nurse Keating staring at door to patient's room two to left of Dyer's room. Door is slightly ajar. The sound – twice.

Angle from end of hall: Nurse Keating stands staring for a time, motionless. Then slowly, reluctantly, she comes around from behind the charge desk. She stops in front of it, looks in each direction for a sign of a policeman. No one.

INT. PATIENT'S ROOM. AT DOOR. NIGHT

The sound. Louder. From somewhere in this room. Very slowly and apprehensively, Nurse Keating opens the door, enters a step, looks.

Keating's POV: Stillness. A patient sleeping on side, faced away from us. The patient's hair is long and dark.

On Keating entering very haltingly, scanning the room.

Subjective camera scanning from left to right, it then halts as we hear the sound again. Camera quickly shifts left to sound's source. A drinking glass on the bedside table. It contains melting, cracking ice.

Another angle as Keating silently approaches the glass.

Close angle at glass. The sound again: ice chips popping and cracking.

Angle on Keating, glass and bed behind her. She puts a hand to her heart and exhales a slight sigh of relief. And suddenly emits a startled, terrified yelp as the Patient rolls toward her in a lightning move, raising up and grabbing the bedrail.

PATIENT 'A'

God almighty, can't I get any sleep? What the hell do you want?

NURSE KEATING

I'm very sorry.

PATIENT 'A'

Bad enough you get me up at half past five to have breakfast!

On Nurse Keating backing out the door.

NURSE KEATING

Sir, I'm *sorry*!

INT. HALL IN NEUROLOGY WING. NIGHT

Nurse Keating backs into the hall, closing the door.

PATIENT 'A'

Yeah, you're sorry. You do it on purpose. What's your name, you? I'm going to report you.

NURSE KEATING

My name is Keating. Amy Keating. *Good night.*

Punctuating the line with a firm closing of the door, Keating starts back to the charge desk.

Long angle: hall. The same as before. As she crosses, we hear from inside the room:

PATIENT 'A'
(*off-screen*)

Angels of mercy, horseshit!

Reacting, Keating halts in mid-step for a beat or two as from various patient rooms comes a scattered and weak applause. The Police Officer who chatted with Keating earlier comes to her.

SECOND POLICE OFFICER

You okay?

NURSE KEATING

Yeah, I'm fine. I'm just jumpy, that's all.

SECOND POLICE OFFICER

Okay.

While she goes back to behind charge desk, he goes to end of hall opposite camera POV and posts himself in front of double doors, where there is a stool on which he sits and lights a cigarette. When Nurse Keating gets back to her papers, she looks over toward him and he waves reassuringly. She smiles and returns to her work.

Another sound. Different. Like an air compressor's sigh. Eerie. She looks up. Another sound – more like a hollow knocking cushioned by velvet. She has turned her head to its source: Father Dyer's empty room.

Close on Nurse Keating. Keating's POV: Dyer's room, the number above it.

The sighing sound. Long angle down the Neurology Corridor. Nurse Keating comes around the charge desk; hesitates to see that the Police Officer is still there, then moves slowly forward to the door. She does not see what we see in the background. A Third Police Officer has pushed open one of the double swing doors and silently beckons the Second Police Officer to come with him. The latter rises and both disappear behind the doors into the other wing. Meantime, Nurse Keating searches through her key hoop, finds the right one, unlocks the door to Dyer's old room. She pushes it open slowly and cautiously, and, before entering, reaches inside to the wall switch and turns on the lights in the room. Now she pushes the door fully open and looks around – then she enters with an assured manner, disappearing from our view. And now the Second Police Officer comes back through the doors, but walks briskly around the corner and out of sight down the hallway to the right, where we hear the sound of doors to another wing as he goes through them off-screen. At the door sound, Nurse Keating, brisk and calm, exits Dyer's old room, turns off the lights from outside, and starts back toward the charge desk.

Almost immediately, the door to Dyer's room flies open silently behind her and, with an accompanying shriek of the score, there swiftly emerges a figure hidden by the bedsheet draped over it, outstretched hands thrusting a pair of decapitating shears toward Keating at neck level.

The moment the figure appears, we swiftly zoom, but just before the shears overtake Keating, we go abruptly to the quiet of:

INT. NEUROLOGY WING HALLWAY. NIGHT

Close on headless statue of Christ. The sound of steady, deliberate footsteps reverberates.

INT. PATIENT'S ROOM IN NEUROLOGY WING. NIGHT

Close on Temple seated, hunched over in a chair, head buried in both propped hands. The footsteps approach.

Close on Atkins seated on a window ledge; he looks up toward the footsteps.

On Senile Old Man and Nurse Blaine. The Old Man is toothless, sits vacantly in a wheelchair. Seen leaning sideways against a wall behind him, red-eyed, face wet with tears, silently distraught, is Nurse Blaine. The footsteps are near. They stop.

SENILE OLD MAN

Is it dinner time? I like dinner.

On doorway: Kinderman is standing in the hall, looking into the room at the off-screen bed, removing his hat as we push to him.

Reverse angle: the room as we quickly zoom to the bed where a white and blood-soaked sheet lies atop a headless body.

SENILE OLD MAN
(*off-screen*)

I like dinner.

On Old Man. He looks up trustingly as Kinderman walks into shot, then stares into space and begins to make silent automatic movements. We push tighter as Kinderman crouches over, leans close to him, observing. Then Kinderman looks off-screen, first enquiringly to Temple, then Atkins.

ATKINS

He's a patient from the Open Ward in Psychiatric. They found him passed out in the hall near the charge desk.

TEMPLE

He's a semi-catatonic.

SENILE OLD MAN

I like dinner.

INT. CORRIDOR IN NEUROLOGY WING. NIGHT

In the foreground, Stedman leans back against a wall, tapping a notepad against his side as he stares down at the floor. Muted and routine hospital intercom announcements. Kinderman emerges from the patient's room, confronts Stedman. Stedman looks up at the detective's questioning eyes.

STEDMAN

Nurse Keating was slit down the middle. Cut open. All her vital organs were removed.

A silence as Kinderman struggles to absorb the deadly information. Then:

KINDERMAN

Yes?

STEDMAN

Then the killer stuffed the body with other materials and sewed her back up.

KINDERMAN

What other materials, Stedman?

STEDMAN

Light switches.

ALLERTON

(*off-screen; calling urgently*)

Lieutenant!

INT. TEMPLE'S OFFICE. NIGHT

On door as Kinderman slowly opens it and looks in. There is only a low desk-lamp light in the room.

Reverse angle. Temple is in his desk chair, his body angled back in a grotesque position, his left sleeve rolled up, his eyes wide and staring in death. His right arm is extended and resting on the desk, the open hand loosely holding an empty hypodermic syringe. On the arm, a tourniquet.

INT. DISTURBED WARD. ISOLATION CORRIDOR. EARLY MORNING

We are shooting down the empty hall. Kinderman is slowly approaching from the end of the corridor. Some of the light bulbs in the ceiling flicker and burn out. Kinderman halts and casts his gaze up toward the lights.

INT. PATIENT 'X''S CELL. EARLY MORNING

Close on slowly dripping faucet.

Close on leg restraints on Patient 'X'.

Close on light bulb dangling from ceiling as it begins to flicker.

Full side angle from door. 'X' is sitting on the cot. Kinderman is seated as before, on far side of room opposite 'X'. The light bulb continues to flicker, dims, flutters, puffs out. There is now light only from the hall (through the port) and the high windows.

PATIENT 'X'

Did you get my message? I left it with Keating. Nice girl.

(*a pause*)

Good heart.

KINDERMAN

(*softly*)

You killed her?

PATIENT 'X'

You must put it in the papers, Lieutenant. You must tell them these are Gemini killings. I will make it worth your while. Death will take a holiday. Just once. For one day. In the meantime, about this body of mine. Friend of yours?

(*chuckles*)

Well, there I was so awfully dead in that electric chair. I didn't like it. Would you? It's upsetting. There was still so much killing to do, and there I was, in the void, without a body. But then along came – well – my friend. You know – one of them – those 'others' over there – the cruel ones . . .

the Master. He thought my work should continue. But in this body. This body in particular, in fact. Let's call it revenge: a certain matter of an exorcism, I think, in which your friend Father Karras expelled certain parties from the body of a child. Certain parties were not pleased, to say the least – the very least. And so, my friend – the Master – he devised this pretty scheme as a way of getting back: of creating a stumbling block, a scandal, a horror to the eyes of all men who seek faith: using the brain of this saintly priest as the instrument of – well – you know – my work.

(*he rises, and with mounting, seething intensity*)

But the main thing is the torment of your friend Father Karras as he watches while I rip and mutilate the innocent, his friends, and again and again, on and on! He's inside with us! He'll never get away! His pain won't end!

(*abruptly calm and composed*)

Gracious me, was I raving? Please forgive me. I'm mad.

(*sits*)

Now where was I? Oh, yes. Yes, the Master. He was kind. You see, he brought me to our mutual acquaintance, Father Karras. Not too well at the time, I'm afraid. Passing on. In the 'dying mode', as we say. So as Karras was about to slip out of his body – is this true? – why, the Master was slipping me in. 'Ships that pass in the night' and all of that. Oh, some confusion by the bottom of the steps when the ambulance team pronounced Karras dead. Well, he *was* dead, technically speaking, of course. He was out. But I was in. A little traumatized, true; after all, his brain was jelly: lack of oxygen and all that sort of thing. But I managed. Yes, a maximum, superhuman effort that at last got me out of that cheap little coffin. Vow of poverty. Disgusting. Never mind. Then toward the end a bit of slapstick and comic relief when that old Brother Fain who was left to tend the body saw me climbing from the coffin. It's the smiles that keep us going, don't you think? The little giggles and bits of good cheer. But after that it was all blue Mondays for a while. Fifteen years. So much damage to Karras's brain cells. So many lost. It's not enough to be a spirit, you see. There's no magic. In this artificial box you call a world, we cannot touch except through bodies.

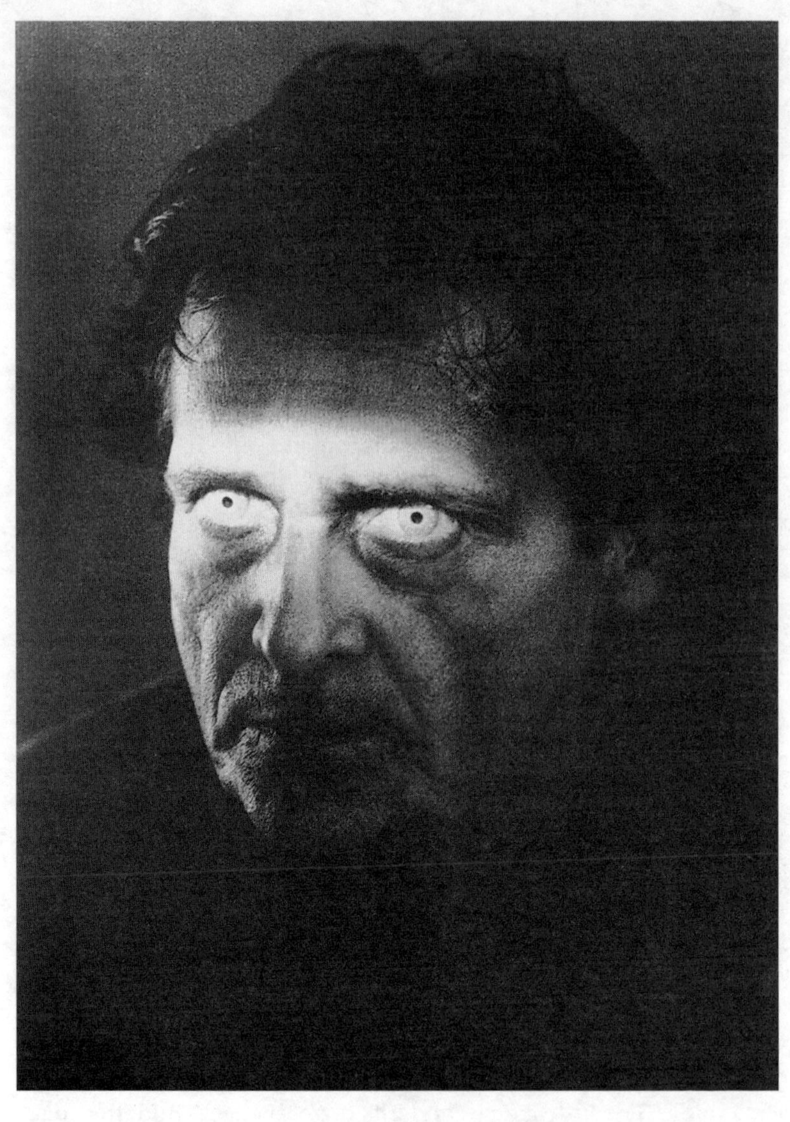

Understand? We must operate through neurologic systems – brains that function – and your friend's was nearly past resurrection. What a chore to regenerate his puny little brain cells!

(*going into a reverie, far away*)

It's taken fifteen years. So many years.

KINDERMAN

Who are you?

PATIENT 'X'

Just a traveling man – one who moves.

KINDERMAN

Are you Karras?

PATIENT 'X'

(*his eyes shift venomously to Kinderman*)

I'm the Gemini.

KINDERMAN

How can I believe that?

PATIENT 'X'

You are issuing a clear invitation to the dance.

KINDERMAN

What do you mean?

PATIENT 'X'

We shall see.

KINDERMAN

(*troubled*)

Please explain that.

PATIENT 'X'

We shall see! Incidentally, don't blame me for that idiot Temple. That was suicide. The man was a lunatic. A weakling. Still, he helped me. Are there services? I'd like to attend.

KINDERMAN

Temple helped you?

PATIENT 'X'

Of course. He brought you to me. I told him if he failed to convince you to come to me, he would suffer in unspeakable ways. Pain that cannot be imagined, I told him. Poor superstitious fool, he believed me. And you came! But he couldn't take the pressure, it would seem.

KINDERMAN

What pressure?

PATIENT 'X'

The pressure of inimitable me.

(*looking off*)

Some other tasks I said I had for him. Just things. You know. Little things.

KINDERMAN

Did Temple help you to get out of this cell?

'X' turns his dark gaze back to Kinderman. Just stares.

Does someone help you? Who helps you?

PATIENT 'X'

Just friends.

(*a long beat*)

Old friends. You know, Lieutenant, there are so many possibilities. I don't know. Do you think this might be true? I think possibly I really am your friend Father Karras. Maybe later I revived at – well – a terribly embarrassing moment and then wandered in the streets without knowing who I was. I still don't, for that matter. And needless to say, of course, I'm quite naturally, hopelessly mad. I have dreams – of a rose – and then of falling down a long flight of steps. Is that something that actually happened to Karras? If it did, then it surely must have damaged my brain. Did that happen, Lieutenant?

KINDERMAN

(*softly*)

Yes, that happened.

PATIENT 'X'

Other times I dream I'm the Gemini Killer. These dreams are

very nice. They feel so comfortable. I go butchering and slaughtering at will, but it's always in . . . Well. Never mind. In any case, I can't sort out the dreams from the truth. I'm quite deranged. You're very wise to be skeptical, Lieutenant. Still, in all, it's a fact that you're a homicide detective, so it's clear that there are people being murdered. I don't know. There are still so many other possibilities. Maybe the Gemini had an accomplice who is still at large and very active, Lieutenant; and perhaps I'm telepathic or have psychic powers that give me all my knowledge of the Gemini murders: the new ones; the old ones; the ones before time and space began and the fire and unquenchable rage were born. Tell the press that I'm the 'Gemini', Lieutenant. Final warning.

KINDERMAN

What was that?

PATIENT 'X'

Never mind.

KINDERMAN

What do you mean?

PATIENT 'X'

Never mind!

Silence. The dripping.

Father Dyer was silly; a silly person.

KINDERMAN

Who killed him?

PATIENT 'X'

I've told you.

KINDERMAN

Who – ?

Patient 'X' interrupts in a sudden shout that has the force of a thunderclap, a voice booming with an impossible volume and power:

PATIENT 'X'

How many times must I tell you it was I! I, the Gemini, fool! It was I!

During the few beats it takes Kinderman to recover from this astonishing outburst, we hear the sound of a nurse running toward us down the hall.

(*quietly*)

I can help.

KINDERMAN

Help what?

PATIENT 'X'

Your unbelief.

Another silence; then 'X' sags a little. A soft sigh of weariness.

I'm tired. So tired.

As 'X''s head droops, consciousness fading, Kinderman frowns, somehow disturbed.

Little – Jack Horner. Child's – play –

And he is gone. Kinderman's frown deepens. Quickly, he rises, exits frame.

INT. NEUROLOGY WARD CHARGE DESK. DAY

Close side tracking at the wheels of a wheelchair as it is pushed to charge desk by an Attendant. Coming up on the shot, we are pulling back and around to a front tracking on the patient in the chair, a three-year-old boy (Korner Boy). At the desk to receive him is Nurse Merrin. She looks at the boy, frowning and troubled, then at the Attendant as:

ATTENDANT

Here's a handsome little fellah for you, Nancy.

NURSE MERRIN

(*low and gritty*)

Are you kidding me?

ATTENDANT

Transfer up from Pediatrics.

NURSE MERRIN

Oh.

ATTENDANT

(leaning over to boy, cajoling)

Got to have an operation tomorrow, right?

He's handed Merrin a slip of paper.

NURSE MERRIN

What operation?

She quickly scans it, looks gravely up and meets Attendant's gaze: it's serious. She drops her gaze to Korner.

(tenderly)

Hello, handsome. What's your name?

On Kinderman as he comes to the counter, his mind and emotions in turmoil.

KORNER BOY

(off-screen)

My name is Charlie.

NURSE MERRIN

(off-screen)

Got a smile for me, Charlie? Come on and smile.

During this, bending his head into propped hands:

KINDERMAN

(a whisper)

Dearest God!

Close on Merrin.

NURSE MERRIN

Let's see the *biggest* happy face.

Close on Korner Boy smiling broadly, but with his mouth closed, teasing, shaking his head.

On Kinderman looking up and over at the boy, then at telephone on counter as:

I can't read this, Jim. The last name? Is it – ?

ATTENDANT
(*off-screen*)

Korner. K-o-r-n-e-r.

On Korner Boy as, happily, proudly:

KORNER BOY

Operation!

On Nurse Merrin. She's fighting tears.

NURSE MERRIN
(*writing*)

That's right. Going to make you lots better.

On Kinderman talking into a telephone.

KINDERMAN
(*consulting a slip of paper*)

May I speak to Father Healy, please? It's urgent.

NURSE MERRIN

Now, let's see where we can put you up today, my little man. Oh, here we go. 411. Let me double-check something.

KINDERMAN

Do you expect him back soon?

(*watching the boy*)

No, I'll try again later.

NURSE MERRIN

'Bye, sweetie.

ATTENDANT

Wave bye-bye.

KORNER BOY

Bye-bye.

KINDERMAN

All right, thank you.

NURSE MERRIN

(*waving*)

See you later, alligator.

Front angle on Kinderman. We are shooting from the POV of a bench opposite the charge desk. Kinderman comes to us, and we angle around as he sits. We come in close on him. He is thinking very hard. Then he looks up as he hears:

NURSE BLAINE

(*off-screen*)

Come on, sweetheart. Let's get back to your room.

Kinderman's POV: Nurse Blaine and an Old Female Patient. The nurse is guiding her. The Patient looks sweetly befuddled, wide-eyed and vulnerable.

Okay? Just take it easy.

The Patient turns to stare at Kinderman (off-screen).

Close on Kinderman. His brow furrows in deep thought. He remembers:

KINDERMAN'S VOICE

(*reverb*)

How do you get out of here?

PATIENT 'X''S VOICE

'Old friends' . . . 'Old friends' . . . 'I'm a traveling man. One who moves' . . . 'Old friends' . . . 'One who moves. One who moves. One who –'

It breaks as Kinderman lifts his head.

INT. OPEN WARD. DAY

On door. Kinderman enters, stops, scans the room, then begins to walk through it. We follow him as he carefully scrutinizes each and every one of the patients' faces, alertly searching for some anomaly. Some of them sit, semi-comatose, catatonic and making automatic movements and mouthing words without sound. Kinderman stops to observe an old

woman who is conversing with her radio. Then he turns his head, as if sensing some movement. Or sound. His brow furrows.

Long shot through glass booth window: Kinderman and the room. Above and unseen by Kinderman, is Mrs Clelia. She is upside down, her palms pressed to the ceiling, like an enormous insect. She scuttles rapidly about the ceiling in brief, silent, erratic bursts, making sudden stops, zigzagging, terrifying, as Kinderman slowly steps toward us, still seeking the source of his discomfiture.

Medium low angle on Kinderman. Above him, Clelia, her long hair flopping down, her face a demonic mask of insane rage.

Kinderman moves out of frame and we cut to:

INT. SUPPLY CLOSET IN OPEN WARD. DAY

The arm of a woman garbed in nurse's uniform slowly and silently pushes the door slightly ajar, and through the opening we see Kinderman. Clelia. Kinderman is looking around. Just as he turns to stare in our direction, the door is pulled shut.

INT. OPEN WARD. DAY

On Kinderman staring toward closet. He looks down. Something's bothering him. Then he looks up, scanning the room quickly, searching for something.

INT. NURSE'S BOOTH. DAY

We are shooting through the glass façade at Kinderman as he turns his gaze toward us. Thinks. Then he swiftly advances toward us. As he does, Clelia scuttles rapidly away from him.

INT. SUPPLY CLOSET. DAY

Again the door is pushed slightly ajar from within.

INT. NURSE'S BOOTH. DAY

Kinderman comes closer, and in the background a figure in nurse's uniform (Nurse 'X') crosses laterally from the supply closet alcove to the front doors of the room. She carries a white canvas shopping bag. She exits as Kinderman puts his face against glass, peers into the booth. His gaze flicks downward and suddenly he is alarmed. He rushes around to the door to the booth, enters.

KINDERMAN

Oh my God!

Kinderman's POV: Nurse – zoom. Sprawled on the floor, the almost nude body of the Open Ward/charge desk Nurse established in earlier scene. A small pool of blood around her head.

INT. HALLWAY NEAR 'HARMLESS' WARD. DAY

Medium close front tracking shot of Nurse 'X'. Cadaverous of visage, hollow-eyed, the late-middle-aged woman walks with inexorable rhythm. Background, the police guards in front of the 'harmless' ward conversing. As she rounds a corner into another hallway, she halts as we hear approaching conversation from behind camera.

Rear angle on confluence of corridors. Nurse 'X' slips into a darkened alcove and waits, staring sightlessly as Atkins and Dr Freedman appear and then stand in the confluence, continuing their conversation. The camera tilts down to the large shopping bag she is gripping. Poking out are the gleaming tops of the missing dissecting shears.

INT. ROOM IN HOSPITAL. DAY

The Korner Boy lies back on bed, Nurse Blaine fluffing his pillow.

NURSE BLAINE

Feeling sleepy yet?

Drowsy, the Korner Boy nods his head. TV is on. Cartoons.

Here, we'll leave on the picture but turn off the sound.

She does so, goes to door, turns off light, exits room.

Close down shot on Korner. He is sleeping. Flickering rays of TV cartoons running silently flick over him. Darkness: the blinds and curtains are drawn.

Full side angle so that the door to the room and all of the Korner Boy are visible in shot.

After three slow beats, the door flies open swiftly but soundlessly. A Nurse enters, closes door behind her. She is carrying a shopping bag.

Close down shot on Korner. Off-screen sound of shopping bag being set down on floor: rustling of paper as something is slipped out of the bag; the soft footsteps approaching us. Meantime, Korner stirs, turns over in bed, squinting at us.

Side angle of the room. Her back to us, the Nurse arrives at side of bed. She appears to be holding something in front of her, hidden. She starts to raise her arms and lean down toward the Korner Boy with:

NURSE

Look what I've got for you, dearie.

On the door to Korner's room as Kinderman, Atkins, two policemen burst into the room.

Side angle of the room. Outcries from Korner, the Nurse, the policemen as Kinderman grabs the Nurse in a stranglehold.

KINDERMAN

I've got her! Hit the light!

KORNER BOY

I want my – [mommy]!

KINDERMAN

Hit the light! The – [light]!

On Atkins as he hits light switch by the door and turns to camera.

On Kinderman and Nurse Merrin choking in his arm lock:

NURSE MERRIN

You're choking me to death!

She is gripping a teddy bear.

On Korner Boy and a Policeman.

The Policeman cradles Korner protectively in his arms as:

KORNER BOY

(*crying*)

I want Mommy.

On Atkins looking into the shopping bag, which is filled with toys and stuffed animals. As Atkins plucks out a robot:

NURSE MERRIN

(*off-screen*)

God almighty!

On Nurse Merrin kneading a sore neck as:

What the hell do you think you're doing?

On Kinderman staring at Merrin, perplexed.

(*off-screen*)

Are you crazy? What on earth – ?

On Kinderman as he shifts his gaze to Atkins.

(*off-screen*)

– is the *matter* with you?

On Atkins lifting a toy robot from the bag and holding it up for the off-screen Kinderman.

ATKINS

Just toys.

On bed and Korner Boy and Policeman. Merrin swoops into the scene, pushing Policeman aside and picking up Korner to comfort him.

NURSE MERRIN

Is that a crime? All right, sweetheart, don't be frightened.

On Kinderman.

KINDERMAN

(*to himself*)

Who is she after? She is after someone! *Who?*

On Merrin and Korner Boy.

NURSE MERRIN

Do you treat your own family like this?

Front tracking Kinderman with Atkins trailing as Kinderman speeds for the door.

KINDERMAN

Come on, Atkins! We may only have –

Abruptly he stops, registers a dawning and shocking realization.

On Merrin.

NURSE MERRIN

Aren't you leaving? *Please* leave!

Reverse angle on Kinderman. His back to us, he turns, staring at her, as:

(*off-screen*)

I cannot *wait* for you to leave!

Kinderman's POV: Merrin, with a quick zoom to an extreme close-up of Merrin's name tag. It reads: 'Julie Merrin'.

Close on Kinderman staring, wide-eyed. We push in gradually to an extreme close-up as we hear his thoughts:

PATIENT 'X'''S VOICE

Do you dance?

KINDERMAN'S VOICE

I don't know what you mean.

PATIENT 'X'''S VOICE

– that's a clear invitation to the dance – to the dance – to the –

The zoom abruptly halts as:

KINDERMAN

Julie!

EXT. HOSPITAL. DAY

Nurse 'X' walks out into the street, the shopping bag in hand.

INT. KINDERMAN'S KITCHEN. DAY

Close on telephone ringing. Mary's hand comes into frame, lifts off the receiver.

Full shot of the kitchen and Mary. She is answering the phone. Background, Julie is at table reading a magazine while Shirley stirs a pot on the stove, watching warily as:

MARY

(*into phone*)

Hello? Oh, Bill. Bill, honey, where –?

(*she listens*)

Um-hm.

(*she nods*)

Um-hm.

INT. NEUROLOGY CHARGE DESK. DAY

Kinderman, his manner urgent and fearful, is listening, a telephone at his ear. As the camera pushes in slowly, we can hear the busy signal, louder and louder, and as Kinderman takes the phone a little away from his ear, at the loudest. He looks up, alarmed, and we quickly cut to:

INT. KINDERMAN'S KITCHEN. DAY

Mary is still on phone.

MARY

Okay, sweetheart.

(*hangs up phone, moves to stove*)

That was Bill. There's a nurse coming over with a package.

EXT. GEORGETOWN STREET. DAY

A taxi tools along unhurriedly.

INT. TAXI BACK SEAT. DAY

Nurse 'X' sits expressionless, staring straight ahead. Beside her on the seat sits the canvas bag.

INT. KINDERMAN'S KITCHEN. DAY

Again, the phone rings. Both Julie and Shirley make as if to answer it, when:

MARY

No, don't answer it!

JULIE

What?

SHIRLEY

I shouldn't answer?

MARY

Bill wants to keep the line clear for a while. If he calls, he'll give a signal: two rings.

SHIRLEY

(*a mutter*)

Now it's signals.

EXT. HOSPITAL. DAY

Kinderman races out the doors, jumps into a waiting squad car.

INT. SQUAD CAR. DAY

On Kinderman and the police Driver. The Driver is a tall and very brawny stuntman.

KINDERMAN

Come on, move it! Move it! Hurry! Break laws!

EXT. SQUAD CAR. GEORGETOWN STREET. DAY

It lurches forward, burning rubber. Flashing lights come on, the siren wails.

INT. TAXI. DAY

Nurse 'X' 's face a blank mask of dread, she turns head lightly to look out window.

EXT. TAXI. GEORGETOWN STREET. DAY

Nurse 'X''s cab, moving along at a smooth and inexorable pace, turns a corner leading into a quiet and arboreal residential area.

INT. SQUAD CAR. DAY

Kinderman is frantic.

KINDERMAN

(*head bowed in finger-tips; murmurs*)

Oh, please, God! Please!

INT./EXT. SQUAD CAR. GEORGETOWN STREET. DAY

We are shooting through the windshield as the car screams around a corner precipitously, narrowly missing being sideswiped by an oncoming truck.

INT. TAXI. DAY

Still staring straight ahead, Nurse 'X' lifts a hand and rests it atop the canvas bag.

EXT. TREE-LINED RESIDENTIAL AREA. DAY

In a long angle, the taxi rounds a corner and approaches us, slowing down and pulling over to the curb in front of Kinderman's house, though we cannot see the latter.

INT. TAXI ON TREE-LINED STREET. DAY

The taxi slows to a smooth stop. Nurse 'X' turns head to stare out window toward off-screen house.

EXT. GEORGETOWN ROAD. SQUAD CAR. DAY

Screaming along.

EXT. TREE-LINED RESIDENTIAL AREA. DAY

Close-up woman's gloved hand ringing doorbell.

INT. KINDERMAN'S KITCHEN. DAY

Mary, Shirley and Julie reacting to ring of doorbell.

MARY

(*wiping hands on apron and moving to answer*)

It must be the nurse.

INT. SQUAD CAR. DAY

Kinderman and Driver.

INT./EXT. SQUAD CAR. STREET. DAY

Another hair-raising driving maneuver seen through the windshield. Screeching of tires and siren.

INT. PATIENT 'X''S CELL. DAY

We are close on the quiet scratchings of the EEG monitor on the emergency cart. The camera tilts up slowly to Allerton who lifts a section of the scrolling graph paper to examine it. Her narrowing eyes then shift to:

Patient 'X' unconscious on the cot, EEG sensors attached to his scalp, his eyelids fluttering rapidly. The scratching sounds.

EXT. SQUAD CAR. DAY

Close moving shot. We are tracking the flashing light, the siren atop the car.

INT. SQUAD CAR. DAY

KINDERMAN

Cut the siren! We're close!

Driver cuts off siren.

EXT. KINDERMAN'S STREET. DAY

With camera stationed in front of Kinderman's house, we see the squad car careen around a corner far down the street, head for us, stop. Kinderman and Driver leap out of car, guns drawn.

On Kinderman and Driver. We are shooting from the POV of the front door of the house as the Driver peels around to the side and Kinderman rushes toward us. Fishing for a key in his pockets, he suddenly halts, raising his gun, as we hear the turning of a door lock.

Close on front door knob turning and door starting to open.

On Kinderman leveling a gun. The creaking of the door opening. Then a look of surprise.

Reverse angle: front door and Julie. A copy of Vogue *in one hand, she stares at Kinderman, flicks her gaze down to the off-screen gun without interest, and then, picking up the magazine to her gaze, and in a bored, distracted voice:*

JULIE

Oh, hi, Dad.

And as she walks back toward kitchen and out of scene:

(*off-screen*)

Mother, Daddy's home.

Immediately, Mary is into the scene, blankly eyeing the gun.

MARY

What's this?

Now in beside Mary comes Shirley, her hands laden with napkins, silverware.

SHIRLEY

It's beginning. There's a Storm Trooper out in the back.

INT. ENTRY HALL OF KINDERMAN'S HOME. DAY

As the phone rings off-screen, Kinderman enters between them, sheathing his gun:

MARY

Billy, what is going on?

KINDERMAN

I am crazy. That's the whole explanation.

SHIRLEY

(*grudging praise as she exits into kitchen*)

Well, you're honest.

Kinderman starts walking to kitchen, and Mary and camera follow in a front tracking shot.

MARY

Bill Saroyan, meet the Kinderman family. Now, let's start from the beginning. What's this – ?

KINDERMAN

Everything's all right.

MARY

No, it *isn't* all right. What's this nurse thing?

KINDERMAN

(*halting*)

What nurse?

NURSE 'X'

(*off-screen*)

Hello, hello, hello.

He looks into kitchen.

INT. KINDERMAN'S KITCHEN. DAY

Julie is talking to a boyfriend on telephone. Shirley is setting the table. And seated at table is Nurse 'X', on her face a thin, inscrutable smile. We zoom to her as:

NURSE 'X'

So nice to see you.

On Kinderman drawing gun and settling quickly into crouch-firing position, aiming gun at 'X' as:

KINDERMAN

Julie, run! Get away!

MARY

(*aghast*)

Oh, my God!

On Nurse 'X'. Her expression is innocent, weary, befuddled.

NURSE 'X'

(*feeble, helpless*)

I'm so tired.

Shirley is setting the table, hesitates before setting a place in front of her.

SHIRLEY

Is she staying for dinner or what?

Full shot of the room as Driver comes quickly into the kitchen, gun drawn, and Kinderman stands dumbfounded, staring at Nurse 'X'. Kinderman holds an arm up, stopping him.

KINDERMAN

It's all right, Frank.

MARY

(*deeply disturbed*)

No, it *isn't* all right! Billy, *what is going on*?

Close on Julie.

JULIE

Look, I'm talking on the phone. Do you mind?

Front tracking shot of Kinderman and Driver. Kinderman is slowly advancing to table as:

DRIVER
(*befuddled*)

Lieutenant!

KINDERMAN
(*softly*)

Hold a bead on her, Frank.

Mary comes into the frame beside Kinderman as:

MARY

Bill, what kind of nurse is this? I open the door for the woman, she faints, she wakes up and says, 'When is it bedtime? I'm tired.'

KINDERMAN

It's all right.

Mary marches back toward cooking area with:

MARY

It's *all right*?

Kinderman has stopped; he crouches down slowly.

Kinderman and Nurse 'X' as his head comes into frame close to hers. His eyes examine her intently.

NURSE 'X'

Is it bedtime?

KINDERMAN
(*gentle compassion*)

Yes. Yes, it's almost bedtime, dear.

NURSE 'X'

I'm so tired.

KINDERMAN

Yes, I know, dear. I know.

On Julie.

JULIE

Okay, Stevie, I'll call you tomorrow.

MARY

Billy, tell me what is *happening* here!

On Kinderman and Nurse 'X' as Julie settles into a chair between them with her Vogue.

JULIE

Excuse me, Daddy.

Full shot from cooking area. Shirley is at a serving table or dresser to the left of table. Kinderman is straightening up, walking back toward us thoughtfully, shaking his head. Driver holsters his gun and goes to telephone, dials. Mary follows Kinderman.

MARY

Bill?

Kinderman is approaching, close to her; frowning in thought, he nods.

KINDERMAN

Yes, I'll explain it in a minute, dear. A minute. Just a minute.

He has now walked into a big close-up, stopped.

NURSE 'X'

(*off-screen*)

Catatonics are so easy to possess.

The voice is altered, deeper, husky – a voice like Colleen Dewhurst's.

On Kinderman as he turns head with awful surmise.

On Nurse 'X' as she bends toward the shopping bag at her side, reaches into it and extracts a twin to the terrifying-looking dissection shears seen in the hospital lab. On her face, a demonic, spiteful glee.

I've been waiting for you, Lieutenant. I wanted you to see this.

She has opened the shears, moving them toward Julie's neck. Julie is oblivious, absorbed in her magazine. We have narrowed the shot to the shears, and are traveling with them.

'X''s POV: Low angle front shot of Kinderman. He is tearing straight at us, right arm outstretched.

KINDERMAN
(*shouting*)

Julieeeeeee!

Close on Mary, screaming. Both hands to her cheeks, horrified.

Full shot on Julie and Shirley as Shirley reaches out to grab Julie by the hair.

Close on Julie and the shears' blades. Shirley's hand has Julie by the hair, yanking her out of reach just as the blades snap shut on the air where her neck was.

On Nurse 'X', Kinderman and Driver. A struggle. 'X' has enormous strength. She tosses off Kinderman and then tosses the Driver as if he were a Saltine cracker, sending him flying across room into wall.

Close on Shirley and Julie staring in terror. Shirley embraces Julie protectively.

JULIE

Oh, my God, Gramma!

On Nurse 'X', Kinderman and Driver. The two policemen again take hold of her. A fierce struggle. She hasn't her former strength. A transformation is taking place in her: first a sudden and surprising realization of something, like some knowledge at a distance. Then, her eyes wide and shining, the men hanging on to her, she cries out in a strange, hoarse voice that is a mix of her own and that of James Venamun:

NURSE 'X'

He's dead! The bastard is deaaaaaaaadddd!

On the long and unearthly, drawn-out cry, the camera tilts forward and down with Nurse 'X' as, filmed in slow motion, she falls backward to the floor with the men still hanging on to her. As they hit, we cut instantly to:

INT. CORRIDOR OF 'DISTURBED' WARD. DAY

The camera is positioned by the open door to Patient 'X''s cell. Far down the hall, his footsteps reverberant, Kinderman slowly comes toward us. As he reaches the cell, Nurse Allerton emerges, steps wordlessly past him, moving down the hall toward another cell. Kinderman stares after her, then looks into 'X''s cell. And slowly enters.

INT. PATIENT 'X''S CELL. DAY

Close front tracking shot on Kinderman as he moves toward the cot. He stops, looking down at:

Full shot: Patient 'X' on cot.

'X' lies on his back, apparently dead. On his face, a strangely benign and peaceful expression – more like the Jesuit Kinderman knew and loved. The restraints have been removed.

Close on Kinderman. The shot is loose enough so that we see the open door to the cell behind Kinderman. The detective looks suddenly sad; for a moment it is indeed his friend Father Karras who lies there. The detective shakes his head with a fond regret, then closes his eyes and bows his head with a sigh, his fingers pinching at the bridge of his nose.

Suddenly the door slams shut behind him.

Into the frame with lightning speed come 'X''s hands, shooting up to Kinderman's neck with a powerful, strangling grip!

Kinderman's hands weakly grasp at 'X''s, trying to pry them loose. A silent, voiceless struggle. Kinderman's eyes are bulging. He is being very surely and swiftly murdered.

Behind him the cell door opens. Allerton. She stands, observing Kinderman calmly. Then she closes the cell door behind her.

The door lock thuds shut.

Allerton calmly, casually and slowly advances toward Kinderman until she is standing beside him, hands in her coat pockets and making no move to help the detective. At last:

ALLERTON

Lieutenant?

Full side angle on the cell. On the cut, Kinderman freezes, ceasing his struggles as he opens his eyes. His hands are still to his own throat. But no one else's are. He looks down at 'X', still unmoving, dead, on the cot. It was all in Kinderman's mind.

Is there anything wrong?

Kinderman looks at Allerton, then back at 'X'. He lowers his hands.

KINDERMAN

No.

Kinderman continues to stare down at 'X'. Then he slowly turns, walks to the far wall, turns again, rests his weight against it. He is staring at 'X' as:

What time did he die?

Allerton picks a chart off a hook on the wall, reads a notation there, replaces the chart.

ALLERTON

Twelve minutes after ten.

Kinderman nods silently, still staring at 'X'. Allerton follows his gaze. The dim bulb in the ceiling sputters – then surges – for the first time – to full brightness. Kinderman and Allerton look up at it.

INT. 'HARMLESS' WARD. DAY

Normal activity. The light is brighter than usual: sunlight pouring through the windows. Kinderman appears at the entrance, looks in. His gaze singles out the patient who went to his apartment dressed as Nurse 'X'. She is sitting on the side of her bed. Nurse Blaine is morseling soup into her mouth.

NURSE BLAINE

There now, this will make you strong.

NURSE 'X'

It's good.

Blaine places another spoonful in her mouth, then turns her head to meet Kinderman's gaze as:

NURSE BLAINE

Yes, it's good. It's very good.

Close on Kinderman. A man lost – uncomprehending – awed – and still a little fearful.

EXT. GEORGETOWN UNIVERSITY QUAD. DAHLGREN CHAPEL. DUSK

Atkins is crossing the deserted quad, heading for the chapel.

INT. DAHLGREN CHAPEL. DUSK

Wide shot. A few votive candles burn in the mysterious dimness. Sitting alone in a pew, his expression numb, is Kinderman. He is staring up at the crucifix over the altar. He seems haunted by some knowledge he is carrying.

The sound of a creaking swinging door. Then Atkins enters, stands and observes the detective for a time; then he quietly walks down the aisle and sits beside him. Kinderman does not turn his head or in any way acknowledge him. A few beats as Atkins follows Kinderman's gaze to the crucifix, then turns back to him.

ATKINS

I tracked down the Gemini's father. He was working as a hotel clerk in Middleburg.

No response from Kinderman. A few beats. Then:

He's dead. A heart attack. He died this morning.

A few beats. Then, at last, Kinderman turns to look at him.

KINDERMAN

At what time did he die?

ATKINS

Twelve minutes after ten.

Long front shot on Kinderman and Atkins.

A few beats as they look at one another. Then Kinderman turns to gaze at our POV.

POV: Crucifix over altar.

INT. GEORGETOWN UNIVERSITY GYM. DAY

Basketball team practice. A scrimmage. Coach John Thompson shouting instructions.

THOMPSON

Patrick, where are you supposed to be? Where's your place?

EXT. UNIVERSITY JESUIT CEMETERY. EARLY MORNING

We are very slowly panning along a row of tombstones, and through them we catch fractured glimpses of the university President leading the burial service for the body of the man who looked like Karras. Kinderman is there, and a scattering of other Jesuits. The grave has been dug, beside it a mound of earth and before it the bier. The President reads from a copy of The Roman Ritual. *A low ground fog hugs the earth.*

PRESIDENT

'A dawning light from on high will visit us to shine upon those who are in darkness and entering the shadowland of death. God, by whose mercy the souls of the faithful have rest, may it please you to bless this grave and appoint your angel to watch over it. Release from all bondage of sin the soul of Damien Karras, who is buried here, through Jesus Christ, Our Lord.'

And the camera movement stops on:

OTHER JESUITS
(*in unison*)

'Amen.'

Shot from behind bier on funeral participants.

The university President sprinkles the coffin and grave with holy water.

PRESIDENT

'I am the resurrection and the life.'

Tight shot of other Jesuits. In their faces, perhaps a thought of their own mortality as:

'He who believes in Me will live even if he dies.'

Close on Kinderman.

'And no one that lives and believes in Me shall be dead for ever.'

The detective glances to side toward the President, as if seriously considering the possibility of this idea. And now the camera begins to pull back to a position behind the bier again as the President makes the sign of the cross over it.

'Lord grant him eternal rest.'

OTHER JESUITS

'And let perpetual light shine upon him.'

PRESIDENT

'May his soul and the souls of all the faithful departed through the mercy of God rest in peace.'

OTHER JESUITS

'Amen.'

Long shot from behind a row of gravestones.

PRESIDENT

'Death, be not proud; though some have called thee mighty and dreadful, thou art not so.'

Close on the bier.

'For those thou dost think'st thou dost overthrow, die not, poor Death, nor can'st thou kill me.'

Close low shot on the university President (crane). We see he is reciting from memory, staring down at the bier. On the cut, the camera is already moving, first swooping about to encompass the others, then slowly ascending to a very high shot from the vantage point of the campus White-Gravenor Building as:

'Soonest our best men with thee go, rest of their bones and soul's delivery. Thou'rt slave to fate, chance, kings and desperate men, and poppy or charms can make us sleep as well, and better than thy stroke. Why swell'st thou then? One short sleep passed, we wake eternally, and death shall be no more. Death, thou shalt die.'

The camera stops. All the funeral celebrants continue staring down at the bier for one or two beats, then all the Jesuits but the university President bless themselves and slowly disperse. Kinderman and the President keep staring down.

It must be quite a shock for you, Lieutenant.

Kinderman looks over at him, uncomprehending. The President looks up, sees his expression.

You've lost him twice.

Kinderman stares in silence. Then looks down at the coffin.

KINDERMAN

It wasn't him. It never was him.

The President looks back at the coffin. Kinderman wipes at the bottom of his nose with back of fingers; a slight sniffle.

KINDERMAN

What a mystery, Father. What a world. Do you really see the purpose of all this suffering?

PRESIDENT

(*nodding*)

'All of creation groans.' I know.

KINDERMAN

But why?

PRESIDENT

It could be that there's no other way to make a man. Without pain we'd be chess-playing panda bears, wouldn't we?

Kinderman looks down at the casket.

KINDERMAN

(*with a shrug*)

Maybe. I don't know.

PRESIDENT

I don't either. Who does? But they say that in surgery, even though you're under anesthesia, your unconscious is actually aware of everything. It hears the doctors and nurses talking about you. It feels the pain of the scalpel.

Kinderman is slowly reacting. These words were spoken to him verbatim by Dyer in the hospital.

But when you wake up from the anesthesia, it's as if it had never happened. So maybe when we all go back to God, that's how it will be with all the pain of the world.

The sound of a bell, then of students' laughter and chatter as they exit class. Kinderman's steady, probing gaze is on the President. Then:

Can I buy you a drink?

PRESIDENT

You know, I think I could use one.

And as they start to walk away from the graveside, their eyes on the ground:

KINDERMAN

Take the edge off, right?

PRESIDENT

Couldn't hurt'?

Kinderman looks up at the Jesuit, surprised and bemused.

KINDERMAN

'Couldn't hurt'?

The Jesuit turns to him with a warm little smile, then looks away again. Kinderman slips his arm around the old priest's shoulder and the camera hangs back and begins to rise as we watch the men slowly walk away. Another class bell rings and students cross their path with bright life as the detective glances up at the sky and we hear, from afar and almost lost in the laughter and the babble:

No clouds. Looks like it's going to be a nice day.

FADE OUT.

CAST AND CREDITS

The cast and crew of *Legion* (which was released as *The Exorcist III*) includes:

KINDERMAN	George C. Scott
FATHER DYER	Ed Flanders
PATIENT X/GEMINI KILLER	Brad Dourif
PATIENT X/FATHER DAMIEN KARRAS	Jason Miller
DR TEMPLE	Scott Wilson
NURSE ALLERTON	Nancy Fish
STEDMAN	George Dicenzo
RYAN	Don Gordon
UNIVERSITY PRESIDENT	Lee Richardson
SERGEANT ATKINS	Grand L. Bush
MRS CLELIA	Mary Jackson
NURSE X	Viveca Lindfors
DR FREEDMAN	Ken Lerner
NURSE KEATING	Tracey Thorne
SHIRLEY	Barbara Baxley
MARY KINDERMAN	Zohra Lampert
JULIE KINDERMAN	Sherrie Wills
FATHER KANAVAN	Harry Carey Jr
Casting	Sally Dennison Julie Selzer Lou DiGiamo
Set Decorator	Hugh Scaife
Production Designed by	Leslie Dillie
Film Editors	Todd Ramsay Peter Lee-Thompson
Music by	Barry DeVorzon
Director of Photography	Gerry Fisher
Executive Producers	James G. Robinson Joe Roth
Produced by	Carter Dehaven

Screenplay by	Willliam Peter Blatty (based on his novel)
Directed by	William Peter Blatty

A Morgan Creek Production